Solar Heating Systems for Houses
A DESIGN HANDBOOK FOR SOLAR COMBISYSTEMS

Solar Heating Systems for Houses
A DESIGN HANDBOOK FOR SOLAR COMBISYSTEMS

Editor: **WERNER WEISS**

INTERNATIONAL ENERGY AGENCY
Solar Heating & Cooling Programme

Published by James & James (Science Publishers) Ltd
8–12 Camden High Street, London, NW1 0JH, UK

ISBN 1 902916 46 8

Typeset by Saxon Graphics Ltd, Derby

Printed in the UK by The Cromwell Press

Cover photos courtesy of
SolarNor, Norway (top)
AEE INTEC, Austria (left, centre left and right)
Wagner & Co., Germany (centre right)

Contents

Preface

Since the beginning of the 1980s, the rate of growth in the use of solar collectors for domestic hot water preparation has shown that solar heating systems are both mature and technically reliable. However, for several years, solar thermal systems seemed to be restricted to this application.

When the first systems for combined domestic hot water preparation and space heating, called solar combisystems, appeared on the market, complex and individually designed systems were the rule.

The combination of thermally well insulated buildings and low-temperature heat supply systems offered a wealth of new possibilities for solar space heating systems with short-term storage. In addition, the growing environmental awareness and subsidies in some countries supported an increase in the market share of this system type in many European countries.

From 1990 onwards the industry offered new, simpler and cheaper system technologies, but basic scientific knowledge was lacking in certain areas and on some methods. The designs were mainly the result of field experience and had not been carefully optimized. A first international survey in 1997 revealed more than 20 different designs that did not simply reflect local climate and practical conditions. Collaborative work in analysing and optimizing combisystems was seen as a proactive action that could favour high-quality systems that would be appropriate for a more global market. However, there were no common definitions of terms or standard test procedures for this type of system. This meant that it was difficult to determine a meaningful performance rating, and even more difficult to compare the systems.

While a great effort was made in Task 14 of the Solar Heating and Cooling Programme (SHC) of the International Energy Agency (IEA) – *Advanced Active Solar Energy Systems* – to assess and compare the performance of different designs of domestic hot water systems, in 1997 there was no available method for finding the 'best' solution for a combisystem in a given situation.

International co-operation was therefore needed to analyse and review more designs and ideas than one country alone could cover. It was felt that an IEA activity was the best way to deal with solar combisystems in a scientific and co-ordinated manner. Since it was also considered that combisystems needed further development in terms of performance and standardization, the IEA SHC launched Task 26 'Solar Combisystems' in 1998.

From autumn 1998 to December 2002, 35 experts from nine European countries and the USA and from 16 solar industries worked together to further develop and optimize solar combisystems for detached one-family houses, groups of one-family houses and multi-family houses. Furthermore, standardized classification and evaluation processes and design tools were developed for these systems. Another major outcome of Task 26 has been proposals for the international standardization of combisystem test procedures.

The further development and optimization of system technologies and designs by the Task 26 participants has resulted in innovative systems with better performance–cost ratings. The architectural integration of the collector arrays and the durability and reliability of solar combisystems were also investigated. This will lead to greater confidence amongst the end-users of this technology.

Both the solar industry and builders were involved in all activities in order to accelerate the dissemination of results on as broad a scale as possible.

This design handbook for solar combisystems summarizes the results of Task 26 and is also a contribution to the dissemination of the collaborative work. We hope that it will contribute to the large-scale use of solar energy for hot water and space heating.

The work on Task 26 and on the design handbook proceeded at a very high level thanks to the excellent co-operation of all the experts involved, for which I am very grateful. In particular, my heartfelt gratitude is extended to Jean-Chistophe Hadorn, who originally initiated the task, and to Jean-Marc Suter, Huib Visser and Wolfgang Streicher, who acted as the leaders of the three subtasks:

- Subtask A: Solar combisystems survey and dissemination of task results
- Subtask B: Development of performance test methods and numerical models for combisystems and their components
- Subtask C: Optimization of combisystems for the market.

I also very much appreciate the co-operation of all of the authors of this book, the help of Dagmar Jaehnig and Michaela Meir who assisted me in compiling and editing it, and the contributions of William A. Beckman, Chris Bales, Jill Gertzén and Jean-Marc Suter in proofreading.

Werner Weiss

1 Solar combisystems and the global energy challenge

Werner Weiss

The increase of greenhouse gases in the atmosphere, and the global warming and climatic change associated with it, represent one of the greatest environmental threats of our time and, in the future, also one of the greatest social dangers. The anthropogenic reasons for this impending change in the climate can for the greater part be put down to the use of energy and the combustion of fossil primary sources of energy, and the emission of CO_2 associated with this.

To set the course towards a sustainable energy future it is necessary to look for solutions that are based on renewable energy.

1.1 TOWARDS A SUSTAINABLE ENERGY FUTURE

Today, the world's energy supply is based on the non-renewable sources of energy: oil, coal, natural gas and uranium, which together cover about 82% of the global primary energy requirements. The remaining 18% is divided into approximately two thirds biomass and one third hydropower.

According to many experts, the effective protection of the climate for future generations will demand at least a 50% reduction in the worldwide anthropogenic emission of greenhouse gases in the next 50 to 100 years. With due consideration of common population growth scenarios and with the assumption of a simultaneity criterion for CO_2 emissions from fossil fuels, an average per capita reduction in the yield in industrial countries of approximately 90% will be required. This means a reduction to one tenth of the current per capita yield of CO_2 (Figure 1.1).

A reduction of CO_2 emissions on the scale presented will, however, demand conversion to a sustainable supply of energy, which is based on the use of renewable energy with a high proportion of direct solar energy use.

There is no doubt that it would be possible to supply technologically advanced countries exclusively with renewable sources of energy in the next 50 to 100 years. For example, the overall solar energy incident on the earth's surface exceeds by more than 10,000 times the world's current primary energy requirement.

There are numerous studies based on socio-economic, technological and institutional–structural models of global and national energy supply scenarios, showing shares of renewable sources of energy of 50% up to almost 100% in the next 50 to 100 years.

A reliable, favourably priced and environmentally sensitive supply of energy is an important prerequisite for the development of modern societies and for upholding and further improving the standard and the quality of life.

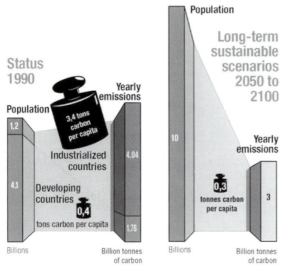

Figure 1.1. Per capita emissions of carbon into the atmosphere required to meet climate stabilization agreements with a doubling of the world population levels (Source: Lang et al. 1999)

Beginning with the Final Report *Our Common Future* of the World Commission on Environment and Development (Brundtland Committee), which was published in 1987, and the Conference of the United Nations for the Environment and Development (UNCED), which took place in 1992 in Rio de Janeiro, the term **sustainable development** became a central idea in the 1990s and the overriding goal of global environmental and development policy.

Essential elements for the implementation of the concept of sustainable development in the field of energy are the orientation towards energy services, the efficient use of energy and the greater use of renewable energy sources, especially the direct or indirect use of solar energy.

The 'Brundtland Report' (1987) and the discussion about sustainable development, as well as the climate and environment conferences held in Kyoto (1997) and Johannesburg (2002), have resulted in most countries having developed programmes and mechanisms to implement renewable energies as part of the existing energy system and to extend their use. New legal and institutional frameworks have had to be, and still have to be, developed to reach the goals set. As well as the environmental concerns, factors such as security of supply and socio-economic development play an important role in most national programmes.

The European Commission has laid down its goals with respect to future development in the field of renewable sources of energy in the White Paper *Energy for the Future : Renewable Sources of Energy* (European Commission, 1997). In the Commission's White Paper the following is mentioned as a strategic goal: '... to increase the market share of renewable sources of energy to 12% by the year 2010'. The yearly increase in the installed solar collector area in the Member States as given in the White Paper is estimated at 20%. Thus, solar heating systems in operation in the year 2010 would correspond to an overall installed collector area of 100 million m^2.

If the direct use of solar energy for heating purposes via solar collectors is to make a significant contribution to the energy supply in future, it is necessary that a variety of different types of systems are developed and established in the market, in addition to those supplying only domestic hot water. One very promising sector for solar thermal applications is space heating.

1.2 THE CONTRIBUTION OF SOLAR THERMAL ENERGY TO THE OVERALL HEAT DEMAND IN EUROPE

In 1998, energy consumption in the building sector totalled 16,077 PJ in European Union Member States, or around 40% of overall energy consumption in the European Union. Requirements for hot water and space heating amounted to 12,200 PJ, or 75%, of consumption in buildings. Of this, 9200 PJ was accounted for by residential buildings (Figures 1.2 and 1.3).

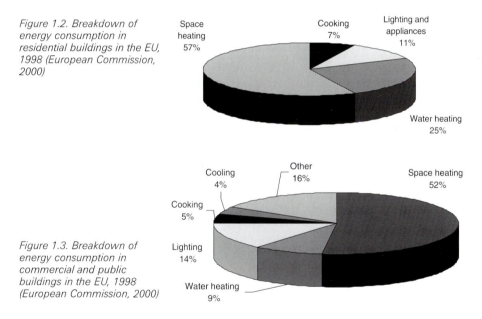

Figure 1.2. Breakdown of energy consumption in residential buildings in the EU, 1998 (European Commission, 2000)

Space heating 57%

Cooking 7%

Lighting and appliances 11%

Water heating 25%

Figure 1.3. Breakdown of energy consumption in commercial and public buildings in the EU, 1998 (European Commission, 2000)

Cooling 4%

Other 16%

Space heating 52%

Cooking 5%

Lighting 14%

Water heating 9%

Since the heat needed in the building sector is low-temperature heat, this shows the large potential for solar thermal systems to provide space heating as well as domestic hot water for the inhabitants of the building.

1.2.1 Collector area in operation in the year 2000 in Europe

Since the beginning of the 1990s the European solar market has undergone considerable development. As the figures from the IEA Solar Heating and Cooling Programme (Weiss and Faninger, 2002) and the German Solar Energy Association (Stryi-Hipp, 2001) confirm, sales of flat-plate collectors recorded a yearly average growth of 17% between 1994 and 2000. This meant that while 480,000 m² of collector area was installed across Europe during 1994, by 2000 the annual rate of installations was around 1.17 million m² of collector area, meaning that the rate had more than doubled within a period of six years.

The installed collector area in Europe was around 11.4 million m² at the end of 2000 (Table 1.1). Of this, 1.7 million m² was accounted for by unglazed collectors, which are used in the main to heat swimming pools, and 9.7 million m² by flat-plate and evacuated tube collectors used to prepare hot water and for space heating.

Table 1.1. Total collector area in operation in the year 2000 in EU countries (in m²)

| Country | Water collectors | | | Total |
	Unglazed	Glazed	Evacuated tube	
Austria	571,806	1,581,185	26,219	2,179,210
Belgium	21,875	19,400	1700	42,975
Denmark	15,563	243,169		258,732
Finland		10,200	100	10,300
France	84,500	470,000		554,500
Germany	615,000	2,399,000	392,000	3,406,000
Greece		2,815,000		2,815,000
Italy	20,000	300,000	20,000	340,000
The Netherlands	100,305	176,580		276,885
Norway	500	7000	100	7600
Portugal	1000	238,000	500	239,500
Spain		399,922		399,922
Sweden	30,000	175,045	3000	208,045
Switzerland	221,200	250,800	15,000	487,000
UK		149,000	2000	151,000
Total	1,681,749	9,234,301	460,619	11,376,669

If the installed flat-plate and evacuated tube collectors up to the end of 2000 are considered, then Greece and Austria are in the lead with 264 m² and 198 m² respectively per 1000 inhabitants. They are followed by Denmark with 46 m² per 1000 inhabitants, Switzerland with 37 m² per 1000 inhabitants and Germany with 34 m² per 1000 inhabitants (Figure 1.4).

The markets that underwent the greatest growth in the time period mentioned above included Spain, the Netherlands and Germany. In the main, this can be attributed to the fact that the dissemination of solar heating systems had been very low in these countries, compared with Greece and Austria. In addition to this, deliberate state programmes of financial incentives contributed to high growth rates.

As mentioned above, in the White Paper on renewable energy, the European Commission set the goal of installing 100 million m² of collector area in European Union Member States. To achieve this ambitious goal, a yearly rate of increase of 38% is required up to 2010, meaning that the present growth rate would have to be a little more than doubled. Such a rate of increase can, however, only be reached if the Member States and the Union support this with corresponding measures for speedy market introduction and for research and development.

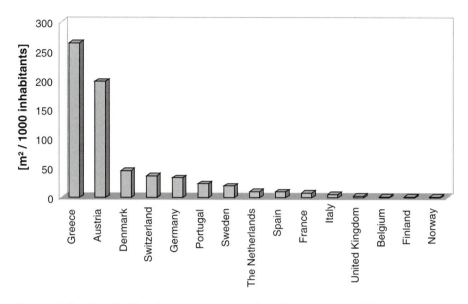

Figure 1.4. Total installed flat-plate and evacuated tube collector area per 1000 inhabitants in the year 2000

1.2.2 Current and medium-term energy supply from solar heating systems

Around 11.4 million m² of flat-plate and evacuated tube collectors were installed in Europe by the end of 2000. The calculated annual collector yield of all recorded systems in Europe is approx. 4600 GWh (17 PJ). This is annually saving the equivalent of 704 million litres of oil, thus avoiding the emission of 1.9 million tonnes of CO_2 into the atmosphere (Weiss and Faninger, 2002).

If it is assumed that the final energy consumption for hot water and space heating in the EU has not risen much since 1998, then around 0.14% of the overall requirements for hot water and space heating were covered by solar heating systems in 2000 across the EU. If the EC's goal for 100 million m² of collectors by 2010 is met, then the total area installed will generate 144 PJ of heat per annum. If this is compared with the overall hot water and space heating requirements – for residential, commercial and public buildings – in 1998, then 1.18% could be covered by solar energy (Table 1.2).

Table 1.2. Current and medium-term energy supply from thermal collectors in Europe

		Energy (PJ)	Solar share (%)
Europe	Requirements for hot water and space heating – EU (1998)	12,171	
	Solar heat 2000 – EU	17	0.14
	Solar heat 2010 – EU	144	1.18

Developments in the building sector (low-energy and passive-energy houses) show that it is possible to reduce the specific heating requirements of new buildings quickly. As studies illustrate, existing buildings have medium-term potential for a reduction of 20% in the energy required for heating (European Commission, 2000). If such a reduction in heating requirements can be achieved in the medium term (i.e. up to 2010), then solar energy could provide around 2% of the energy needed by residential buildings for hot water and space heating in Europe.

At this point it should also be remembered that, until now, solar heating applications have concentrated almost entirely on the supply of hot water to single-family homes, whether individually or in small groups. In countries such as Germany, Switzerland and Austria, there has been a marked trend towards solar space heating systems for some years, and in this respect significant increases are anticipated in the years to come.

Results from Austria show that the targets for Europe are realistic and they illustrate the medium-term potential in a country where the solar heating market is already widely developed compared with other European countries.

If both the contribution solar energy currently makes to the supply of heat in Austria and its potential up to 2010 are analysed (Table 1.3), it becomes clear that, in the medium term, solar collectors will be able to supply significant amounts of thermal energy to meet heat requirements.

Table 1.3. Current and medium-term energy supply from solar collectors in Austria

		Energy (PJ)	Solar share (%)
Austria	Requirements for hot water and space heating (1998)	303	
	Solar heat 2000	3.22	1.06
	Solar heat 2010	12.87	4.25

Figures for Austria in 2000 indicate that the solar contribution to hot water and space heating requirements is 3.22 PJ or 1.06%; this means Austria has already reached the amount which all Member States of the EU are striving for in the medium term. If it is assumed that the average growth rates in Austria up to 2010 will be below the European average at 20%, because the market is already highly developed, then the collector area can be quadrupled in the next ten years. This corresponds to an overall collector area installed in Austria of approximately 8 million m^2. Thus in 2010, around 4.25% of the country's overall hot water and space heating requirements can be covered by solar energy, provided that these requirements remain the same.

1.3 SOLAR COMBISYSTEMS – A PROMISING SOLUTION

The demand for solar heating systems for combined domestic hot water preparation and space heating, so called 'solar combisystems' is rapidly growing in several countries. In Sweden the share of the collector area installed for solar combisystems in 2001 was already significantly larger than the collector area installed for solar domestic hot water systems. In Austria, Switzerland, Denmark and Norway the collector area installed for solar combisystems and for solar domestic hot water systems was almost the same. In Germany, which installed 900,000 m² of collector area in 2001, the share of the collector area installed for combisystems was 25%.

Figure 1.5 shows that in some countries, such as Germany, Austria, Switzerland, Sweden and Denmark, solar combisystems already have a noteworthy share of the market. The primary energy sources of these solar combisystems are solar energy with auxiliary sources such as biomass, gas, oil and electricity, either directly or with a heat pump.

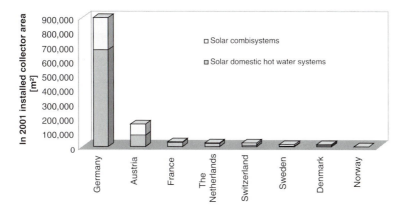

Figure 1.5. Share of collector area used for solar domestic hot water systems and for solar combisystems in selected countries

A realistic approach would be to assume that, in the next ten years, a minimum of 20% of the collector area installed annually at middle and northern latitudes will be used for solar combisystems. This means that around 120,000 solar combisystems with 1.9 million m² of collectors need to be installed per year in the countries of the European Union, if the goals set in the European Commission's White Paper are to be met (Figure 1.6). Increasing the installed collector area by a factor of 10

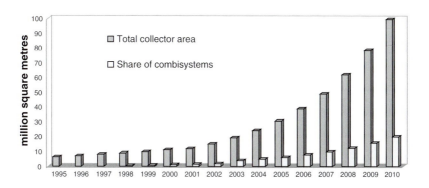

Figure 1.6. Objectives for the installed collector area and market share of solar combisystems up to 2010 in the member countries of the European Union

over 10 years is a major challenge, but this can be achieved if there is massive and continuous support, both political and financial, from the member countries.

Solar combisystems are more complex than solar domestic hot water systems, as there are more interactions with extra subsystems. The intrinsic complexity of implementing a solar combisystem working in conjunction with auxiliary heating has led to a large number of widely differing system designs. The most promising generic system designs are introduced in Chapter 4.

The solar contribution, which is the part of the heating demand met by solar energy, varies from 10% for some systems to up to 100% for others, depending on the size of the solar collector, the storage volume, the hot water consumption, the heat load of the building and the climate.

The different system concepts can partly be attributed to the different conditions prevailing in the individual countries. Thus, for example, the 'smallest systems' in terms of collector area and storage volume are located in those countries in which gas or electrical energy are primarily used as auxiliary energy. In the Netherlands, for example, a typical solar combisystem consists of 4–6 m² of solar collector and a 300 litre storage tank. The share of the heating demand met by solar energy is, therefore, correspondingly small.

Figure 1.7. A Dutch house with a solar combisystem (Source: ATAG, The Netherlands)

In countries such as Switzerland, Austria and Sweden, where solar combisystems are typically coupled with an oil or biomass boiler, larger systems with high fractional energy savings (the term is defined in the appendix) are encountered. A typical system for a single-family house in these countries consists of up to 15–30 m² of collector area and 1–3 m³ of storage tank volume (Figure 1.8). The share of the heating demand met by solar energy is between 20% and 60%. In some cases of extremely well insulated houses and low-flow mechanical ventilation, the solar contribution can even reach 100%.

Apart from collector types and storage tank details, the layout of the system, that is the connections between components, is one of the most differentiating items among the various system concepts analysed in Task 26. Based on the experience of Task experts, the requirements for the hydraulic layout of solar combisystems can be summarized as follows (Streicher, 2000):

Figure 1.8. Solar combisystem for a single-family house in Sweden (Source: K. Lorenz, SERC, Sweden)

- the delivery of solar energy to heat store(s) and heat consumers with as low a heat loss as possible
- the production and delivery of auxiliary heat to consumers with as low a heat loss as possible
- the distribution of all the heat needed to meet hot water and space heating demands
- the reservation of sufficient storage volume for auxiliary heating, with the minimum running time for the specific heater taken into account
- low investment costs
- low space demand
- easy and fail-safe installation
- reliable operation and low maintenance cost.

These conditions require simple systems in terms of connections, compared to the systems designed and constructed in the 1980s.

REFERENCES

European Commission, 1997, *Energy for the Future: Renewable Sources of Energy – White Paper for a Community Strategy and Action Plan*, COM. (97) 599 of 6.11.1997.

European Commission, 2000, *Green Paper – towards a European Strategy for the Security of Energy Supply*, Technical document, Brussels.

Lang R W, Jud T and Paula M, 1999, *Impulsprogramm Nachhaltig Wirtschaften*, Bundesministerium für Wissenschaft und Verkehr, Vienna.

Stryi-Hipp G, 2001, 'Der Europäische Solarthermiemarkt' *Proceedings, 11 Symposium Thermische Solarenergie, Staffelstein*, Ostbayerisches Technologie-Transfer-Institut e.V., Regensburg, Germany.

Weiss W and Faninger G, 2002, 'Collector Market in IEA-Member Countries 2000', *IEA, Solar Heating and Cooling Programme*, Gleisdorf, Austria, http://www.iea-shc.org

Streicher W, 2000, 'Solar combisystems – from small niche market to standardised application', *Proceedings Eurosun 2000 Conference, Copenhagen*, ISES-Europe, http://www.ises.org

World Commission on Environment and Development (UNCED), 1987, *Our Common Future*, Oxford University Press, Oxford.

2 The solar resource

Wolfgang Streicher

The Sun is the central energy producer of our solar system. It is a 1,390,000 km diameter sphere with nuclear fusion taking place continuously in its centre. A small fraction of the energy produced in the Sun hits the Earth and makes life possible on our planet. Solar radiation drives all natural cycles and processes such as rain, wind, photosynthesis, ocean currents and several others which are important for life. The world's energy need has been based from the very beginning on solar energy. All fossil fuels (oil, gas, coal) are converted solar energy.

The solar radiation is emitted by the Sun's corona at an effective blackbody temperature of approximately 5800 K with an **irradiance** (terms are defined in the Appendix) of 70,000–80,000 kW/m². Our planet receives only a very small portion of this energy. In spite of this, the incoming solar radiation energy in a year is some 1.5×10^{18} kWh; this is about 15,000 times the yearly energy need of the whole world in 2000 (10^{14} kWh/a; BPAmoco, 2002).

The duration of the sunshine as well as the solar irradiance is dependent on the time of the year, weather conditions and naturally also on the geographical location. The amount of yearly global radiation (on a horizontal surface) in the sunbelt regions may exceed 2200 kWh/m². In northern Europe, the maximum value is about 1100 kWh/m².

2.1 SOLAR RADIATION AND AMBIENT TEMPERATURE

The climate is one of the key factors influencing the energy yield of a solar combisystem. This interaction takes place on several levels:

- Solar collector:
  - The absorber temperature is dependent on the solar radiation on the solar collector.
  - Losses to the ambient are driven by the temperature difference between the collector absorber and the ambient.
- Heat demand of the building:
  - Heat losses to the ambient are driven by the temperature difference between the house and the ambient (air and ground).
  - Solar radiation through the windows can be seen as inner heat gains in the period of the year when space heating is effectively needed (heating season).
- Domestic hot water (DHW) demand
  - The cold water temperature from the mains varies over the year. This variation is mainly dependent on the average monthly ambient temperatures.

Climate varies from location to location and from year to year. Figures 2.1 and 2.2 show the world's yearly average global irradiation and the Earth's surface temperature. In Figure 2.3 the average values of solar irradiation and outdoor

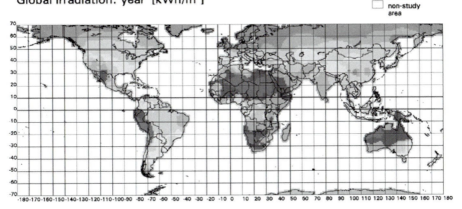

Figure 2.1. World map of yearly average global irradiation (on a horizontal surface) in kWh/m²a. (Source: METEOTEST, Berne, Switzerland, http://www.meteonorm.com). See also colour plate 1

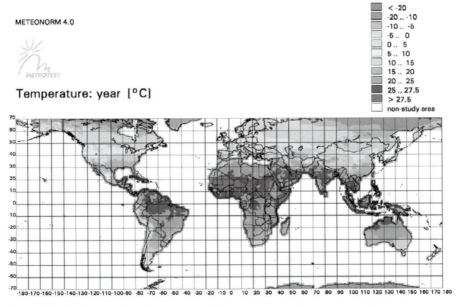

Figure 2.2. World map of yearly average ambient temperature in °C. (Source: METEOTEST, Berne, Switzerland, http://www.meteonorm.com). See also colour plate 2

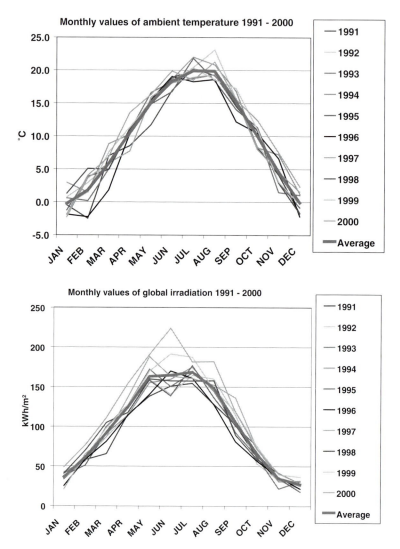

Figure 2.3. Ten-year monthly average ambient temperature and (horizontal) global irradiation for a central European location (ZAMG, 2001)

temperature for one location over 10 years are shown. Despite the obvious seasonal trend, a wide range of fluctuations between the months can be seen. In order to compare the performance of different combisystems under different climate conditions on the same basis, average data for each location are needed.

The orientation of the absorbers (window, collector) is also significant. Figure 2.4 shows the monthly **hemispherical irradiation** on differently orientated surfaces for a central European climate. It can be seen that horizontal surfaces and surfaces facing south with a tilt angle of 45° have much higher summer than winter

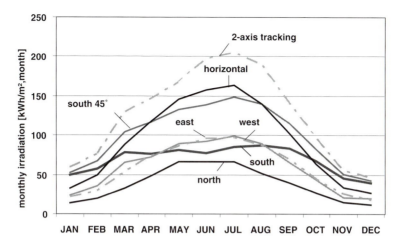

Figure 2.4. Hemispherical irradiation on surfaces of different orientations for a central European climate (Streicher, 2002)

irradiation. The winter incident radiation on the south-facing 45° tilted surface is much higher than that for the horizontal surface. Vertical surfaces facing south do have a nearly constant irradiation from March to September, and nearly as much irradiation in winter as surfaces facing south with a 45° tilt angle. Two-axis tracking mainly increases the solar yield in summer, while in winter the irradiance is similar to a 45° slope facing south.

In order to cover the geographical range for the main markets of solar combisystems, it was decided to choose a northern, a central and a southern European climate for all further investigations and simulations. Respectively, these were:

- Stockholm, Sweden
- Zurich, Switzerland
- Carpentras, France.

Table 2.1 shows the characteristics of the locations with respect to geographical data, design temperatures (for space heating) and yearly global irradiation (on a horizontal surface).

Table 2.1. Characteristics of the locations (Streicher et al.*, 2001)*

Location	Latitude ° North	Longitude ° East	Height above sea level m	Ambient design temperature for space heating °C	Yearly global irradiation kWh/m²a
Carpentras (F)	44.05	5.05	105	−6	1502
Zurich (CH)	47.37	8.543	413	−10	1088
Stockholm (S)	59.31	11.938	44	−17	981

Figure 2.5 shows the global solar irradiation and ambient temperature on a long-term average monthly basis for the chosen climates. The differences between the

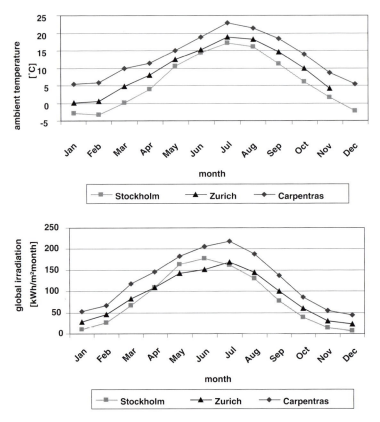

Figure 2.5. Monthly global irradiation (on a horizontal surface) and ambient temperature of the climates chosen in Task 26

three climates are obvious. In the heating season, Stockholm has the lowest irradiation coupled with the highest heat demand, due to the lowest ambient temperatures. The opposite is the case for Carpentras in France. Only a minor part of the solar irradiation is available during the heating period for all locations.

For simulations it is necessary to use hourly values of irradiance and ambient temperature (see Section 2.2). The hourly values of climate data for Task 26 (global and direct irradiance, ambient temperature, wind speed, relative humidity and dry-bulb temperature) were calculated with the Swiss climate data generator METEONORM (1999) using long-term monthly averages of global irradiation and ambient temperature. Figure 2.6 shows the daily fluctuations for a summer week in Zurich with cloudy weather at the beginning and sunny weather at the end.

The irradiance on the collector and on the windows has to be calculated separately and split into direct and diffuse (sky- and ground-reflected) radiation because of its different angles of incidence. This has been done in Task 26 using the TRNSYS (Klein *et al.*, 1998) radiation processor.

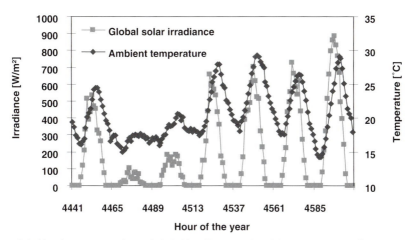

Figure 2.6. Hourly average values of global irradiance and ambient temperature for a summer week in Zurich, generated with METEONORM (1999)

2.2 AVAILABILITY OF CLIMATIC DATA

Climatic data for ambient temperature and global solar irradiance (on a horizontal surface) is available for a wide range of locations. In Figure 2.3 it was shown that both irradiation and temperature differ from place to place over a wide range on a monthly basis and less on a yearly basis. If different locations are to be compared, it is therefore necessary to use average climate data.

For simulating solar combisystems with one to three days of water storage, at least hourly climatic data is necessary to calculate correctly the behaviour of the storage. The same type of data is needed if the effect of the thermal active mass of the building (the storage of excess energy during the day for use at night to reduce the heat demand) is taken into consideration. One of the problems is to find hourly data that match long-term averages as well as standard fluctuations (sunny and cloudy weather situations in a realistic statistical distribution, where irradiance, temperature, humidity, wind speed etc. correspond with each other). Two methods are described in the literature.

2.2.1 Test Reference Years

Test Reference Years are generated by selecting time spans (typically one month) of measured climatic data from a number of measured years for one location in such a way that the long-term monthly averages of all climatic data for this location are matched. Using measured data ensures that the weather fluctuations of the region are correctly represented. Of course, the links between the time spans have to be smoothed. However, generating Test Reference Years (TRY) is very time consuming. Consequently, they are often very expensive (as for example the 12 available Test Reference Years for Germany). However, they are sometimes available free of charge, as for example the Typical Meteorological Years (TMY) for the USA for 234 sites (see http://rredc.nrel.gov/solar/old_data/nsrdb/tmy2/). In order to have data available for a whole country, it has to be divided into typical weather zones, for which Test Reference Years have to be developed.

2.2.2 Weather data generators

The second option is the use of weather data generators. These programs use long-term average monthly data of some key values (normally monthly average daily global irradiation and ambient temperature) and generate hourly data, using physical and statistical approaches. Well known are the weather data generators of the simulation tool TRNSYS (Klein *et al.*, 1998) and of the Swiss tool METEONOM (1999). The latter was used in Task 26. Long-term monthly average temperatures can be found at http://www.top-wetter.de/klimadiagramme/welt.htm. Worldwide irradiation data can be found at http://wrdc-mgo.nrel.gov/html/get_data-ap.html.

All of the combisystem simulations performed within Task 26 needed even smaller time steps (down to one minute) to model the behaviour of the systems correctly. Therefore the hourly values were linearly interpolated, ensuring that no irradiance occurs before or after sunset.

The simulations were set up in such a way that other locations can be easily included if hourly weather data are available in the proper format.

REFERENCES

BPAmoco, 2002, *BPAmoco Statistical Review of World Energy 2001*, BPAmoco, London.

METEONORM, 1999, Weather Data Generator. METEOTEST, Fabrikstrasse 14, CH-3012 Bern, Switzerland; www.meteonorm.com.

Streicher W, 2002, Lecture book *Sonnenenergienutzung*, Institute of Thermal Engineering, Graz University of Technology.

Klein, SA, Beckmann WA, Mitchell JW, Duffie JA, Duffie NA, Freeman TL, Mitchell JC, Braun JE, Evans BL, Kummer JP, Urban RE, Fiksel A, Thornton JW, Blair NJ, 1998, *TRNSYS, A Transient System Simulation Program – Version 14.2* (as used in project), Solar Energy Laboratory, University of Wisconsin, Madison, USA.

ZAMG, Zentralanstalt für Meteorologie and Geodynamik, Vienna, Austria, 2002.

INTERNET SITES FOR CLIMATE DATA

http://rredc.nrel.gov/solar/old_data/nsrdb/tmy2/: free TMY data sets for the USA.

http://www.top-wetter.de/klimadiagramme/welt.htm: long-term worldwide monthly average temperatures.

http://wrdc-mgo.nrel.gov/html/get_data-ap.html: worldwide irradiation data.

3 Heat demand of buildings

Wolfgang Streicher, Ulrike Jordan and Klaus Vajen

In this chapter, the building models used for annual system simulations in Task 26 are described and the requirements for the definition of the thermal quality of buildings are discussed. In order to fulfil the thermal requirements of a building, the room temperature, the indoor humidity and the air quality need to be adjusted by an active heating system within the building. Devices for active cooling have not been taken into account. Assumptions made concerning the effect of climate conditions during the year, as well as internal gains such as heat emitted by people, electrical appliances and lighting, are presented.

Finally, the load profiles for domestic hot water used for the annual system simulations are described. The profiles were generated with statistical methods in order to take into account fairly realistic conditions. The assumptions made concerning the probability distributions of draw-offs during the year and flow rates are shown.

3.1 THERMAL QUALITY OF BUILDINGS

The thermal quality of buildings can be viewed, on one hand, as the energy demand of the building and, on the other hand, as the indoor air quality, which is defined by temperature (air and surface of inner walls), humidity, air velocity and pollutants (CO_2, CO, NO_x, odours).

A major factor is the insulation level of the building envelope, which affects the thermal quality of a building in several ways:

- The space heating energy demand is directly related to the thermal quality of the envelope of the building.
- When the thermal quality of the building increases, the heat distribution system can be operated either with lower temperatures or with a smaller heating surface. This allows either integration of highly efficient heating devices that need low temperatures (e.g. condensing gas boiler, heat pump, solar combisystem) or a decreased investment cost for the heat distribution system.
- The indoor air quality of buildings is also related to the thermal quality of the envelope. The better insulated the building is, the smaller is the difference between the temperatures of the inner surface of the envelope (wall, ceiling, windows, floor) and the room air temperature. Figure 3.1 shows the recommended range of room air and surface temperatures that lead to

comfortable and still acceptable indoor temperature conditions. These values can also be used to determine the influence of the heat distribution system on indoor comfort (if wall or floor heating is used).

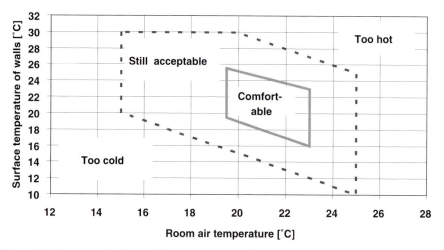

Figure 3.1. Recommended room air temperature as a function of wall temperature

Additional factors influencing the thermal quality of a building are the glazing area, the amount of thermally active mass, the ventilation rate and the indoor humidity level. Windows allow the use of daylight and permit solar energy to pass through and be absorbed inside the building (passive solar energy use). Passive solar gains reduce the space heating demand and connect the user inside the building to a certain extent with the ambient climate conditions. In order to avoid overheating in summer, the window area should mainly face south (see Figure 2.4). A second measure to avoid overheating and to damp the daily temperature swing within a building is the use of active thermal mass.

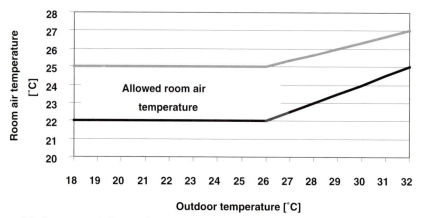

Figure 3.2. Recommended room air temperature for air conditioning in buildings (DIN 1946, part 2)

According to the German standard DIN 1946 the recommended room air temperature is 20°C in the case of space heating. For air conditioning, Figure 3.2 shows the recommended indoor air temperature range as a function of the outdoor ambient temperature according to the German standard VDI 2067: 22–25°C for ambient temperatures up to 27°C.

The indoor humidity should be kept within the ranges shown in Figure 3.3. This can be achieved either with air conditioning systems with humidification in winter and dehumidification in summer or with wall layers that can absorb and evaporate moisture in a manner analogous to energy in thermal active mass.

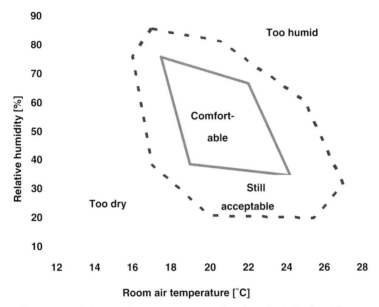

Figure 3.3. Recommended room air temperature as a function of relative humidity (Halozan, 1998)

The thermal insulation of buildings has increased significantly in the past 25 years. The specific space heating energy demand of buildings was about 200 kWh/m²a for Central Europe in the mid-1970s. New building codes in Germany, Austria and other European countries have reduced specific space heating energy demands below 70 kWh/m²a. Low-energy buildings with a space heating demand of less than 50 kWh/m²a can be built in Central Europe without increasing the investment costs compared to conventional buildings. Without air heat recovery of ventilation air the specific space heating energy demand can be decreased to about 30 kWh/m²a. So-called passive houses use fan-assisted balanced ventilation with air heat recovery. The resulting specific heat demand (without the electricity demand of the ventilation system) is below 15 kWh/m²a. Several thousand of these passive houses (as single- and multi-family houses or as office buildings) have been built in Europe so far. Of course, all of these buildings meet the indoor air quality criteria mentioned above.

The shape of such buildings can vary widely, because insulation can be put on all surfaces and in all kinds of shapes (see Figure 3.4). Most of these buildings have a compact form, in order to reduce the surface area exposed to the ambient, and have more window area facing south compared to the other directions to achieve high solar passive gains.

Figure 3.4. Examples of a low-energy multi-family terraced house (Source: Ökoplan, Rankweil, Austria) and a single-family house (Source: SOLVIS, Braunschweig, Germany) with solar combisystems

3.2 THE REFERENCE BUILDINGS OF TASK 26

Three single-family houses (SFH) with the same geometry but different building physics data were defined in such a way that the specific annual space heating demand for the Zurich climate amounts to 30, 60 and 100 kWh/m²a. Additionally, a multi-family house (MFH) with five apartments and a specific annual space heating demand for Zurich of 45 kWh/m²a was defined. Figures 3.5 and 3.6 show the principal design of these buildings. Table 3.1 shows the reference space heating load (according to the ambient design temperature of Table 2.1) and the layout characteristics of the radiator heat distribution system.

Table 3.2 shows heat transfer coefficients (U-values) of typical buildings from the past 30 years and the respective data for the reference buildings. SFH 100 represents

Table 3.1. Heat load for the buildings according to DIN 4701 and design temperatures for the heat distribution system

Space heating demand★	Heat load			$\Delta t_{\text{flow line/return line}}$ of heat distribution system	Design flow temperature of heat distribution system
	Stockholm	Zurich	Carpentras		
kWh/m²a	kW	kW	kW	K	°C
SFH 100	9.05	7.29	6.32	10 (5†)	60 (45†)
SFH 60	6.16	4.95	4.26	5	40
SFH 30	3.48	2.83	2.46	5	35
MFH 45‡	17.35	13.97	12.06	5	40

★ Gross area, Zurich conditions
† Recommended for the French solar heating floor system (generic System #3, Chapter 5)
‡ Multi-family house with flats of 100 m² gross area

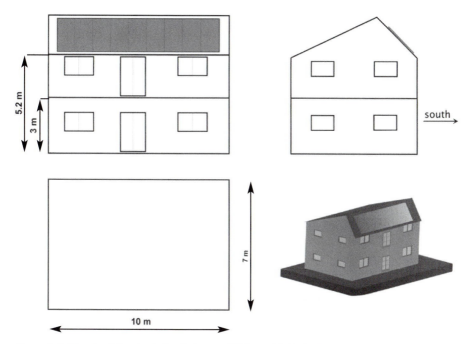

Figure 3.5: Sketch of the single-family house (SFH) used in Task 26

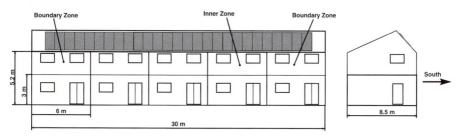

Figure 3.6: Sketch of the multi-family house (MFH) used in Task 26

a typical building that is about 10 years old, SFH 60 represents a building to the current standard and SFH 30 represents a highly insulated building.

Table 3.2. G- and U-values for historical buildings and the reference buildings in Task 26

U-values	Units	Historical			Task 26 reference buildings			
		1970	1980	2000	SFH 100	SFH 60	SFH 30	MFH 45
wall	W/m²K	1.50	0.80	0.50	0.51	0.34	0.14	0.37
roof	W/m²K	1.00	0.50	0.30	0.49	0.23	0.11	0.22
ground floor	W/m²K	1.00	0.60	0.40	0.55	0.20	0.12	0.23
window	W/m²K	5.00	3.00	1.40	2.80	1.40	0.40	1.40
G-values of window	–	0.90	0.75	0.50	0.76	0.49	0.41	0.49

Table 3.3 shows typical U-values of different European regions and, for comparison, for Mexico. These values were evaluated in Task 25 (Solar Assisted Air Conditioning of Buildings) and Task 27 (Performance, Durability and Sustainability of Advanced Windows and Solar Components for Building Envelopes) of the Implementing Agreement on Solar Heating and Cooling of the IEA. It can be concluded that the range of the buildings chosen in Task 26 covers the wide range of buildings presently built in Europe.

Table 3.3. G- and U-values common in different countries and chosen in IEA Solar Heating and Cooling Task 27 (Task 25, 2002)

U-values	Units	Freiburg Copenhagen	Perpignan	Madrid	Palermo	Athens	Merida	Task 27
external wall	W/m²K	0.35	0.32	0.59	1.26	0.60	0.70	0.38
roof	W/m²K	0.17	0.33	0.32	0.48	0.50	0.36	0.30
ground floor	W/m²K	0.35	0.42	0.36	0.85	1.50	1.50	0.26
floor	W/m²K	0.36	0.23	0.74	0.59	1.50	1.50	0.85
internal wall	W/m²K		0.29	1.57	1.25	1.50	1.50	0.42
window	W/m²K	1.10	1.40	3.90	4.13	3.70	5.32	1.56
frame	W/m²K	2.00	2.27	2.26	2.00	2.26	3.00	2.40
frame share of window	m²/m²	0.20	0.20	0.20	0.15	0.20	0.20	0.20
G-values of window	–	0.60	0.59	0.77	0.80	0.80	0.80	0.53

3.3 SPACE HEATING DEMAND

The space heating demand is dependent on the following factors:

- conduction/convection losses through the envelope
- ventilation losses to provide good indoor air quality (keep humidity, CO_2, CO, odours, etc. below specified values)
- infiltration due to incomplete tightness of the building
- passive solar gains through windows
- thermal gains from people inside the building, electricity demand of devices and artificial lighting
- the thermal mass (because of its ability to dampen daily indoor temperature fluctuations)
- user behaviour (in terms of indoor air temperature, which is often above 20°C, manual ventilation, and active shading in summer and winter).

Figure 3.7 shows the main energy flows between a building and the environment and within a building. If a room or group of rooms within a building acquires significantly different temperatures because of user behaviour or from passive solar gains, then this group has to be treated as a separate zone in the calculation of the energy demand. For Task 26, the SFH building was assumed to be a single zone. The MFH was first calculated as a two-zone model (one zone for the middle

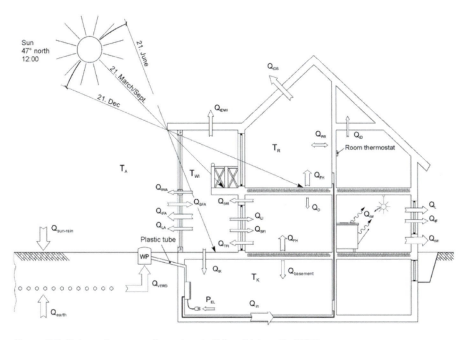

Figure 3.7. Schematic energy flows in a building (Heimrath, 1998)

apartments and one zone for the outer), but the differences turned out to be very small, so that finally the MFH was also assumed to be a single zone.

The space heating demand is strongly dependent on the user behaviour, especially for low-energy buildings. Figure 3.8 shows this dependency calculated for a low-energy building as a function of indoor air temperature and ventilation rate. Increasing the indoor temperature from 20–24°C doubles the space heating energy demand in this case, because the period where the space heating demand cannot be covered by the internal gains will be much longer. Also, the ventilation rate (Figure 3.8, right), which is user-dependent if no automatic ventilation system exists, has a high impact on the annual space heating demand. Even the presence of

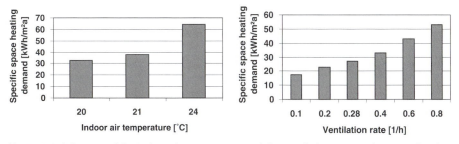

Figure 3.8. Influence of the indoor air temperature and the ventilation rate on the space heating demand of a low-energy building (Lari, 1999)

people in the building can have a significant impact on the space heating demand as shown in Figure 3.9. Consequently, user behaviour has to be clearly defined, when the space heating demand of buildings is to be calculated.

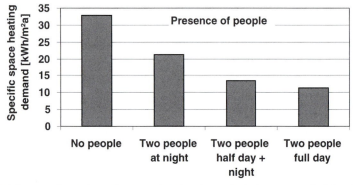

Figure 3.9. Influence of people on the space heating demand of a low-energy building (Lari, 1999)

The annual heat demand is normally calculated with standards that use either the annual heating degree days (i.e. the German VDI 2067) or monthly average climate values (i.e. EN832). Both methods take into account the above-mentioned items but are restricted to the building itself and provide only the annual (VDI 2067) or monthly (EN832) energy demand. To evaluate solar combisystems it is necessary to know at least the hourly values of the heat demand of the building because the heat storage volumes are normally sized for the heat demand of one to three days.

In Task 26 it was decided to simulate the building in parallel with the combisystem to model the dependencies between the two systems correctly. All calculations were performed with the simulation tool TRNSYS.

The following assumptions for the thermal requirements and the user behaviour were chosen for all buildings:

- *Room temperature:* The controls on the heating system were set in such a way that the room temperature is kept around $t_R = 20 \pm 0.5°C$ and never drops below 19.5°C during heating season. For buildings with a floor heating system that use the thermal mass of the floor as a heat storage, the room temperature was allowed to range between 19.5 and 24°C. Temperatures above 24°C were excluded from the analysis because solar combisystems for heating purposes and not the buildings (with their specific overheating characteristic) were to be compared.
- *Ventilation:* The air change rate of ventilation is assumed to be 0.4 h^{-1} based on the gross volume of the building. This rate is assumed in most European standards. No air heat recovery system was used.
- *Shading:* There was no internal or external shading device used, because only the heating period was analysed and shading is mainly used at times when overheating occurs and no space heating is needed.

- *Internal gains:* The user behaviour in terms of people present in the buildings was assumed to be the same for all buildings. The following internal thermal gains were taken into account:
  - According to ISO 7730:1994, internal thermal gains of 2.5 kWh/day were assumed, caused by one person at rest for 24 hours/day, and one person for 14.5 hours/day.
  - Constant thermal gains of 700 kJ/h, caused by lighting, electrical devices, etc. were taken into account for single-family houses and constant thermal gains of 550 kJ/h for multi-family houses

The hydraulic layout of the reference space heating system is shown in Figure 3.10. The space heating is simulated with radiators and thermostatic valves, which adjust the mass flow controlled with a PID controller (non-standard TRNSYS Types 162 and 120). Floor heating systems are simulated with transfer functions (non-standard TRNSYS Type 100). The design flow temperatures of the space heating systems are shown in Table 3.1.

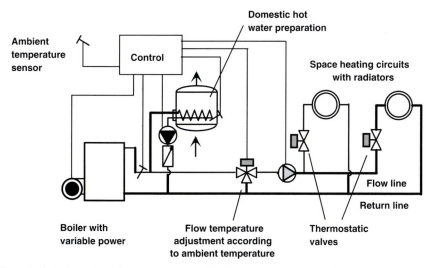

Figure 3.10. Schematic of the space heating distribution system of the reference buildings

Figure 3.11 shows the control characteristics of the radiator heating system for a time period of three weeks in spring. In the first and third weeks, there is space heating demand, while in the second week the room air temperature rises above 20.5°C because of passive gains and the finite thermal mass of the building, resulting in no additional heat demand. The outdoor temperature in the second week remains below 20°C for most of the day. Therefore the flow temperature to the radiators is kept above 20.5°C. The flow temperature to the heating system is directly dependent on the outdoor temperature. When the sun is shining during the day or when other internal gains occur, the room air temperature rises and the mass flow rate of the heating system is reduced by the thermostatic valves. These fluctuations of the mass flow rate can be clearly seen in Figure 3.11.

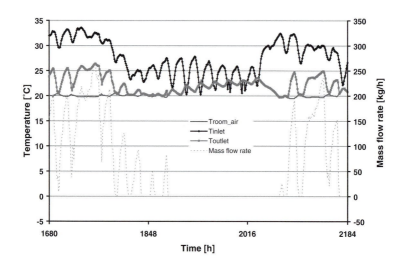

Figure 3.11. Heat demand, mass flow rate and temperatures of the reference heating system for a time period of three weeks in spring, with radiators and PID controller (thermostatic valve), using DIN 4701 heating load for the reference SFH 60 in Zurich as the design heating rate (Streicher, Heimrath, 2003)

Figure 3.12 shows the specific energy demand of the four reference buildings in the three climates. The expected high dependency of the space heating demand on the location, as a result of different ambient temperatures and lengths of the heating season, can be seen (see also Figure 2.5). This high dependency has to be taken into account when solar combisystems are optimized for different regions or when solar combisystems optimized for different regions are compared.

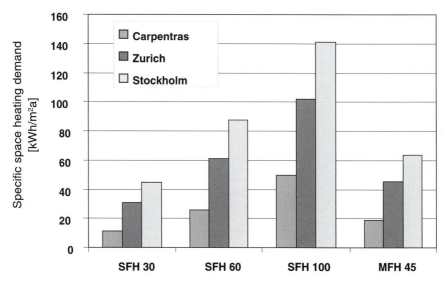

Figure 3.12. Specific space heating demand for the reference buildings

In Figure 3.13, the monthly sums of space heating and domestic hot water demand for the different buildings are plotted, as well as the solar energy incident on different collector areas facing south with a slope of 45° for the climates of Carpentras and Stockholm. The different annual characteristics of incident solar energy and heat demand of the building can be seen clearly. The annual solar fluctuation is much higher for Stockholm than for Carpentras. On a monthly average basis, a solar plant with a 10 m² collector area is sufficient to cover the total load of the SFH 30 building and 20 m² is sufficient for the SFH 100 for Carpentras. With the efficiency of the solar collector, and the real weather with its daily and hourly fluctuations in solar irradiance and ambient air temperature (which partly drives the space heating demand of the building), taken into consideration, 100% fractional savings are not possible, of course. For Stockholm in winter, even with the largest collector, the incident solar energy is much smaller than the heat demand.

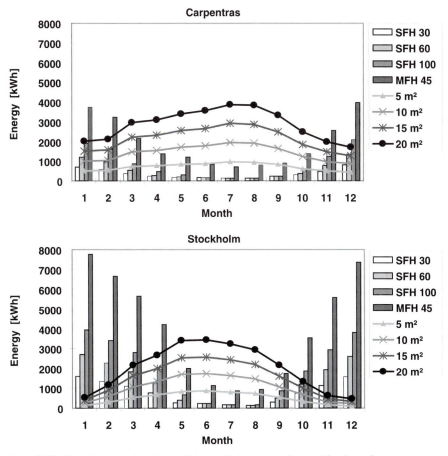

Figure 3.13. Monthly space heating and domestic hot water demand for the reference buildings and incident solar energy on different collector areas (facing south, slope of 45°) for Carpentras and Stockholm climates

3.4 HOT WATER CONSUMPTION

Several research projects in the past have shown that the domestic hot water (DHW) consumption of different households can vary broadly (e.g. Dittrich *et al.*, 1972; Loose, 1991; Dichter, 1999; Nipkow 1999). In VDI 2067, Part 4, values of DHW consumption between 15 and 120 litres per day per person, at a temperature of 45°C, are given. According to that, the demand for the Task 26 simulation studies has also been fixed at the specific value of 50 litres per day per person at a temperature of 45°C.

Different concepts are used for DHW preparation in the various combisystems analysed in Task 26. In some systems, separate DHW stores are used, while in others, instantaneous DHW heat exchangers are used. For the various designs, the thermal stratification in the storage tank and therefore the fractional energy savings of the system (the values of the target functions F_{sav}, $F_{sav,ext}$ and F_{si}; see Chapter 6) can be quite differently dependent on the number and duration of draw-offs. In addition, fluctuations in the DHW temperature at the beginning of a draw-off can occur. These temperature fluctuations have an additional effect on the F_{si} target function. The generated DHW draw-off profiles are presented in the following.

Each profile consists of a value of the DHW flow rate for every time step of the year. Profiles were generated for three different timescales. In order to take into account fairly realistic conditions, a **time step of 1 minute** was chosen. In order to carry out system simulations with time steps higher than 1 minute, profiles were generated on a **6 minute timescale**. The reference conditions concerning the distribution of the draw-offs were chosen similar to those of the 1 minute profiles. Finally, a third set of profiles with hourly mean values of the 6 minute profiles was produced. The third set of profiles is necessary in order to simulate large solar heating systems with a simulation time step higher than 6 minutes. Because the flow rates become very small when mean values are calculated, the flow rates of the profiles on an hourly scale may not be regarded as realistic for small and medium-sized solar heating systems.

The values of the flow rate and the time of occurrence of every incidence were selected by statistical means. The basic load in each set of DHW profiles is 100 litres/day at a temperature of 45°C. For higher demands, the profiles were generated with the demand doubled at each step (100, 200, 400, 800, 1600, 3200 litres/day), with different initial random values. In this way, it is possible to produce a load profile for multi-family houses (for demands that are a multiple of 100 litres/day) very easily by superposition.

In addition to the flow rates, a function representing the temperature of cold water from the mains during the year needs to be defined. The cold water temperature can be described as a sinusoidal function given by Equation 3.1:

$$T_{frwat} = T_{av} + \Delta T_{sh} \cdot \sin(360 \cdot \frac{\text{time}+(273.75-d_{off}) \cdot 24}{8760}) \tag{3.1}$$

with T_{frwat} the cold-water temperature in °C, T_{av} the yearly average cold water temperature in °C, ΔT_{sh} the average amplitude for seasonal variation in K, 'time' the hour of the year (a TRNSYS internal value) and d_{off} the time-shift parameter (day of the year with maximum temperature).

The amplitude of the seasonal variations ΔT_{sh} and the time offset d_{off} differ significantly for different locations. For the reference locations chosen for the simulation studies, the values for ΔT_{sh} and d_{off} are given in Table 3.4.

Table 3.4. Temperature shift of the cold water for the different climates (adapted from EN 12976–2:2000, 2000)

Location	T_{av} °C	ΔT_{sh} K	d_{off} d
Carpentras	13.5	4.5	19
Stockholm	8.5	6.4	80
Zurich	9.7	6.3	60

3.4.1 DHW load profiles on a 1 minute timescale

For the simulation studies, a mean load volume of 200 litres per day was chosen for a single-family house. As an example, a three-day sequence of the profile is shown in Figure 3.14.

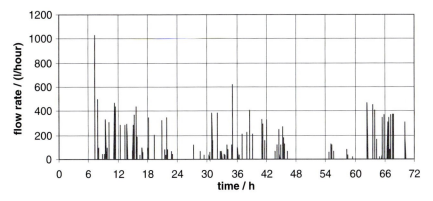

Figure 3.14. Load profile for 72 hours, 1–3 January (200 litres/day, 1 minute timescale) created according to the procedure described below

3.4.4.1 Basic assumptions
Four categories of loads are defined. Each category profile is generated separately and they are superposed afterwards. The actual values of the flow rates are spread around the mean value according to a Gaussian distribution, as described by Equation 3.2:

$$\text{prob}(\dot{V}) = \frac{1}{\sqrt{2\pi}\sigma} \exp \frac{-(\dot{V}-\dot{V}_{mean})^2}{2\sigma^2} \qquad (3.2)$$

The probability functions are shown in Figure 3.15.

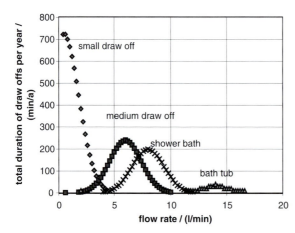

Figure 3.15. Total duration of draw-offs during a year as a function of flow rate. The duration of draw-offs was fixed. For example, 702 showers during the year were taken into account with a duration of 5 minutes each. The flow rates are distributed as a Gaussian function. Discretization of flow rates: 0.2 litres/minute

Four categories to describe the different types of loads are defined:

- Category A: short load (washing hands, etc.)
- Category B: medium load (dishwasher, etc.)
- Category C: bath
- Category D: shower.

Assumptions were made for each category for:

- the mean flow rate V
- the duration of one load
- the number of incidences (loads) per day, 'inc/day'
- the standard deviation of different flow rates, σ.

From these assumptions, the corresponding values for the following can be derived:

- the mean volume of each draw-off
- the total volume per day
- the water volume share of each category.

The values for a load profile, with a mean load of 200 litres/day, are listed in Table 3.5.

The maximum energy of one draw-off is:

14 litres/minute × 10 minutes × 1.16 Wh/(kgK) × 35 K = 5680 Wh.

The suggested maximum heat demand according to DIN 4708 is:

Q = 5820 Wh.

Table 3.5. Assumptions and derived quantities for the load profile with a minimum draw-off duration of 1 minute

	Category A: short load	Category B: medium load	Category C: bath	Category D: shower	Sum
$\dot{V}$ in (litres/minute)	1	6	14	8	
Duration (minutes)	1	1	10	5	
Number of incidences per day	28	12	0.143 (once a week)	2	
Standard deviation, σ	2	2	2	2	
Derived assumptions:					
Water volume per load (litres)	1	6	140	40	
Water volume per day (litres)	28	72	20	80	200
Average water volume share	0.14	0.36	0.10	0.40	1

The chosen reference conditions are based on a few research studies about DHW consumption patterns in Switzerland and Germany. In these investigations, measurements of the power of electrical DHW heating elements, measurements of temperatures or flow rates, and a representative phone research study were, for example, taken into account (e.g. Dittrich *et al.*, 1972; Loose, 1991; Nipkow, 1999; Real *et al.*, 1999, Dichter, 1999).

3.4.1.2 Probability function

With the assumptions described above, the number of draw-offs and the flow rate of each load are fixed. As a final step, the incidences need to be distributed throughout the year. A probability function describing variations of the load profile during the year (also taking into account European daylight saving time), the weekday and the day is defined for each category. The **cumulative frequency method** is used to distribute the incidences described by the probability function.

$$\text{prob(year)} = \text{prob(season)} \times \text{prob(weekday)} \times \text{prob(day)} \times \text{prob(holiday)}.$$

The following assumptions are made for the terms of the probability function:

- The course of probabilities during the **seasons** is described by a sinusoidal function with an amplitude of 10% of the average daily discharge volume (see Mack *et al.*, 1998).
- The assumptions for the **daily distribution** used, are shown in Figure 3.16.
- The probability function of different **weekdays** for taking a bath and the mean distribution for the total volume per day are shown in Figure 3.17. For Categories A, B and D, the probability distributions are identical for all days of the week, although not for Category C. This approach was taken based on the results of research studies (e.g. Dichter 1999).
- **Holidays**: a period of two weeks of no DHW consumption is taken into account between 1 June and 30 September for each load of 100 litres/day. The beginning of the holiday period is given by a random number. The initialization of the random number generator is set in such a way that the holidays for a single-family household with a load of 100 litres/day start on

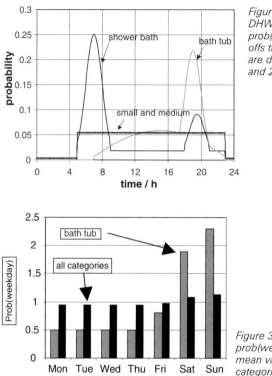

Figure 3.16. Probability distribution of the DHW load during the course of the day, prob(day). For short and medium draw-offs the probability distributions for a load are distributed uniformly between 5:00 and 23:00 h

Figure 3.17. Probability function prob(weekday) for Category 3 (bath) and the mean value of the weekly distribution of all categories

1 August. For a profile with a mean daily load of 200 litres/day (single-family house in Task 26) the DHW load is reduced by 100 litres/day in *two periods*. The duration of both periods is also two weeks, starting on 14 July and 8 August, respectively. In multi-family houses the number of reduced DHW load periods is given by the average daily load volume divided by 100 litres/day. Therefore, for the multi-family house modelled with an average load of 1000 litres/day, 10 periods are taken into account.

For the overall distribution of the energy necessary for the DHW supply during the year, Mack *et al.* (1998) found a variation of 25% in the form of a sinusoidal function. These variations were found to be due to variations of the cold water temperature by 5K (14% of the energy supply), due to the holidays (3.8% of the energy supply), and due to the consumption patterns during the different seasons of the year. These variations are taken into account by the functions prob(season) and prob(holidays).

Distributions of draw-off volume per day over the course of the year, with a mean daily draw-off volume of 200 litres/day, are shown in Figure 3.18 for a single-family house and in Figure 3.19 for a multi-family house. The sinusoidal function, used to calculate the probability during the course of the year with an amplitude of 20 litres/day (10%), is shown by a solid line.

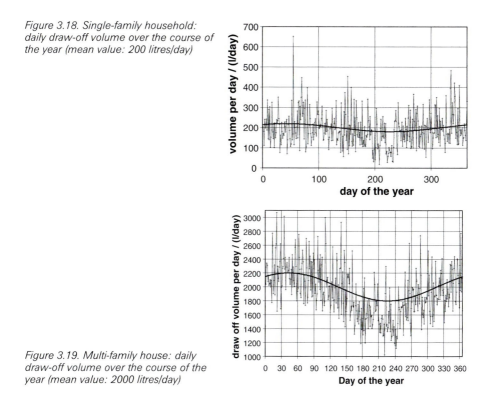

Figure 3.18. Single-family household: daily draw-off volume over the course of the year (mean value: 200 litres/day)

Figure 3.19. Multi-family house: daily draw-off volume over the course of the year (mean value: 2000 litres/day)

Investigations of the influence of the DHW profile showed that the profile details are important when combisystems are compared, especially if the duration and flow rate of a DHW draw-off have a major influence on the temperature stratification in the storage tank (Jordan and Vajen, 2000). Further investigations of the influence of the presented DHW profiles on a 1 minute scale have been carried out, for example by Frei *et al.* (2000) and Knudsen (2001).

3.4.2 DHW load profiles on a 6 minute timescale

For the 6 minute profiles only draw-offs with a minimum duration of 6 minutes are taken into account. This means that only one category of loads is defined for the 6 minute profiles, representing all types of draw-offs (small and medium draw-offs, shower and bath-tub filling). As an example, a sequence of the profile of one week is shown in Figure 3.20.

The assumptions made for the 200 litres/day profile are given in Table 3.6. The values of the flow rates are distributed around the mean value with a Gaussian distribution as shown in Figure 3.21. A probability function describing variations of the load profile during the year (also taking into account European daylight saving time), the weekday and the daily distribution is defined in the same way as for the 1 minute profile. In addition, the probability distribution (Figure 3.22) is based on

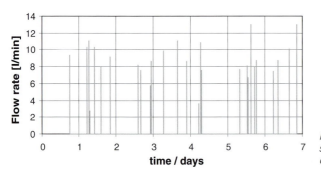

Figure 3.20. One-week sequence of a DHW profile on a 6 minute timescale

Table 3.6. Assumptions and derived quantities for the load profile (with draw-off durations of 6 minutes)

One category		
Total load volume	73,000.2★	litres/annum
=> mean load	≈200	litres/day
Mean flow rate	8	litres/minute
Minimum flow rate	1	litres/minute
Maximum flow rate (single draw-off)	15	litres/minutes
Maximum flow rate (superposition)	23.9	litres/minute
=> maximum energy demand of one draw-off	5,822†	Wh
Discretization of flow rates	0.1	litres/minute
Duration of each load	6	min
Standard deviation, σ	4	
Total number of draw-offs	1,521	per annum

★ Due to the discretization of flow rates of 0.1 l/min, only multiple values of 0.6 l are possible for the yearly volume.
† The maximum energy of one draw-off is 23.9 litres/minute × 1 kg/litre × 6 minutes × 1.16 Wh/(kgK) × 35 K = 5822 Wh (the suggested maximum heat demand according to DIN 4708 (1994) is Q = 5820 Wh, => V_{max} = 23.9 litres/minute).

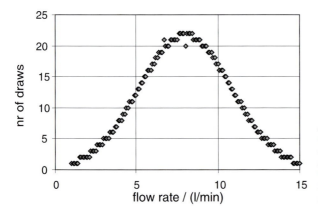

Figure 3.21. DHW profile on a 6 minute timescale: Number of draw-offs as a function of flow rate. The deviations from the Gaussian function are due to the discretization of the flow rate

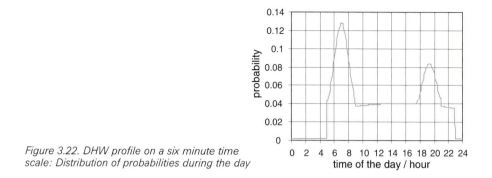

Figure 3.22. DHW profile on a six minute time scale: Distribution of probabilities during the day

the relations that were chosen for the 1 minute profile. The functions are multiplied by the volume share of each category defined for the one-minute profile. Variations of the probability of draw-offs per day at different weekdays are given in Table 3.7.

Table 3.7. Mean probability distribution of DHW loads among days of the week

Day	Probability
Monday to Thursday	0.9
Friday	1
Saturday, Sunday	1.2

3.4.3 DHW load profiles on an hourly timescale

The DHW load profiles on a timescale of one hour are produced by taking hourly mean values of the 6 minute profiles. This is done only for the purpose of simulating large solar heating systems with a time step of one hour. Because the flow rates become very small when mean values are calculated, they may not be regarded as realistic flow rates. However, the effect of 'smearing out' the DHW draw-offs becomes smaller for an increasing total load.

3.4.4 Final remarks

The influence of the DHW profile on the annual system performance of a solar combisystem depends on the system design. The thermal performance tends to be overestimated if simplified load profiles with either a fixed number of draw-offs every day or with relatively long draw-off durations are used. However, the differences in performance can be neglected for a large number of system designs. For example, combisystems with conventional internal-coil heat exchangers for domestic hot water preparation show only small differences in system performance when the 1 minute profile is applied as opposed to simplified profiles (Frei, 2000). On the other hand, significant differences of up to 3.5 percentage points of the fractional energy savings $f_{sav,ext}$ were found in system simulations of discharge units using a thermosiphon as the driving force, when simulation results with simplified and 1 minute draw-off profile were compared (Jordan, 2000). These heat exchangers can only be adequately modelled with transient heat exchanger models, and the thermal stratification in the tank depends significantly on the dynamics of the DHW profiles. In this case the 1 minute profiles should be applied. Consequently, no general recommendations can be given about which DHW profile to use. What can be recommended, however, is using profiles with small time steps, if the thermal stratification in the storage tank is largely influenced by the dynamics of the DHW profile, and if the main focus is on the design of charge and discharge units of the storage tank. Furthermore, the one-minute profiles should be applied for investigations of the size of the storage volume that is heated up by an auxiliary energy supply system and the power of such a system.

The draw-off profiles are available as ASCII files (see Appendix 1; or e-mail solar@uni-kassel.de).

REFERENCES

DIN 1946-2:1994, 1994, Raumlufttechnik: Gesundheitstechnische Anforderungen (VDI-Lüftungsregeln).

DIN 4701–1: 1983, 1983, Regeln für die Berechnung des Wärmebedarfs von Gebäuden

DIN 4708: 1994, 1994, *Zentrale Wassererwärmungsanlagen. (1) Begriffe und Berechnungsmethoden. (2) Regeln zur Ermittlung des Wärmebedarfs von Trinkwasser in Wohngebäuden. (3) Regeln zur Leistungsprüfung von Wassererwärmern in Wohngebäuden.*

Dichter E, 1999, *Dusch- und Badeverhalten. Bericht zu einer Repräsentativumfrage*, Eidgenössische Drucksachen- und Materialzentrale, Bern, Switzerland.

Dittrich A, Linneberger B and Wegener W, 1972, 'Theorien zur Bedarfsermittlung und Verfahren zur Leistungskennzeichnung von Brauchwasser-Erwärmern', in *HLH Heizung, Lüftung/Klima, Haustechnik*, Vol. 23 (2).

EN 832: 1998, *Thermal performance of Buildings, Calculation of Energy Use for Heating Residential Buildings.*

EN 12976–2: 2000, 2000, *Thermal solar systems and components – Factory made systems* Part 2: *Test methods.*

Frei U, Vogelsanger P and Homberger D, 2000, 'Domestic hot water systems: testing, development, trends', in *CD-ROM of the Third ISES Europe Solar Congress EuroSun 2000*, Copenhagen, Denmark.

Halozan H, 1998, Grundlagen der Gebäudetchnik, Lecture book, Institut für Wärmetchnik, Graz University of Technology.

Heimath R, 1998, Senstitivitätsanalyse eines Erdreichwärmepumpensystems, Diploma Thesis, Institut für Wärmetechnik, Graz Univeristy of Technology.

ISO 7730: 1994, 1994, *Moderate Thermal Environments. Determination of the PMV and PPD Indices and Specifications of the Conditions for Thermal Comfort.*

Jordan U and Vajen K, 2000, 'Influence of the DHW profile on the fractional energy savings – a case study of a solar combisystem', in *CD-ROM of the Third ISES Europe Solar Congress EuroSun 2000,* Copenhagen, Denmark.

Knudsen S, 2001, 'Consumers' influence on the thermal performance of small DHW systems – theoretical investigations', in *9th International Conference on Solar Energy in High Latitudes, NorthSun*, Leiden, The Netherlands.

Lari A, 1999, Wissenschaftliche Begleitung zur Sicherung der energetischen Optimierung für das Projekt Solarsiedlung Plabutsch, Dissertation am Institut für Städtebau und Umweltgestaltung und dem Institut für Wärmetchnik, Graz University of Technology.

Loose P, 1991, 'Der Tagesgang des Trink-Warmwasser-Bedarfes', in *HLH Heizung, Lüftung/Klima, Haustechnik*, Vol. 42(2).

Mack M, Schwenk C and Köhler S, 1998, 'Kollektoranlagen im Geschoßwohnungsbau – eine Zwischenbilanz', in *11. Internationales Sonnenforum, Tagungsband*, pp. 45–52, Köln, Germany.

Nipkow J, 1999, *Warmwasser-Zapfungsverhalten*. Schlussbericht, Industrielle Betriebe der Stadt Zurich, Zurich, Switzerland.

Real M, Nipkow J, Tanner L, Stadelmann B and Dinkel F, 1999, *Simulation Warmwassersysteme. Schlussbericht Forschungsprogramm Wasser*, Eidgenössische Drucksachen- und Materialzentrale, Bern, Switzerland.

Streicher W, Heimrath R, 2003, *Structure of Reference Buildings of Task 26*, A technical report of Subtask C, IEA–SHC Task 26, Solar Combisystems, http://www.iea-shc.org/task 26.

Task 25, 2002, Evaluation of typical building insulation data for several countries, internal paper.

VDI 2067, part 2, 1993 Berechnung der Kosten von Wärmeversorgungsanlagen, Raumheizung, Verein Deutscher Ingenieure.

4 Generic solar combisystems

Jean-Marc Suter and Thomas Letz

Despite their great variety, solar combisystems all have common features and similarities. The systems available on the market have been grouped according to these features, leading to a number of generic systems described in the final section of this chapter.

4.1 BASIC FEATURES OF SOLAR COMBISYSTEMS – A SHORT SUMMARY

In this section, the basic technical understanding required to make a meaningful intercomparison of the various solar combisystems presented in Sections 4.2 and 4.3 is recalled.

4.1.1 Comparison of combisystems with solar water heaters

Solar combisystems are similar to solar water heaters in the collection of solar energy and the transport of the heat produced to the storage device. The major difference is that the installed collector area of a combisystem, which provides two energy needs, is larger than in the case of a solar water heater, which supplies only one energy need (Table 4.1).

How much heat is needed in a year for space heating in comparison to domestic hot water depends on the building size, its thermal insulation, ventilation, passive solar use and internal heat loads, as well as on the number of its inhabitants. Figures indicate that the DHW heat demand usually amounts to 10–40% of the total heat demand for space heating and DHW.

In a combisystem there are at least two energy sources used to supply heat to the two heat consumers: the solar collectors deliver heat as long as solar power is available, and the auxiliary energy source (oil, gas, wood, electricity, etc.) supplements the missing solar power. As a general rule, collectors should be operated at the lowest possible temperature in order to achieve a good efficiency; at high temperatures they have significant heat losses. Other individual requirements arise from the auxiliary heat source selected.

The key challenge for the engineer creating a combisystem is how to combine the different requirements of heat suppliers and heat consumers into one single, cost-effective, durable and reliable heating system, achieving the most benefit from each installed square metre of collectors.

Table 4.1 Features of the two different heat loads: space heating and hot water

Space heating system	Domestic hot water (DHW) load
Large seasonal variation, due mainly to the variation in outside air temperature; no heat demand in summer (Figure 4.1)	All-year-round heat demand, with small seasonal variation (Figure 4.1)
Daily profile shows a continuous, moderate heat demand, with some periods of reduced or zero demand, e.g. at night or when the control unit gives priority to charging the hot-water store, or in most periods with solar irradiation through windows (passive solar gains). See Figure 4.2a	Daily profile shows a lot of short, high-power peaks, with extended periods without DHW consumption (Figure 4.2b). In multi-family houses: smoother daily profiles
Relatively low delivery temperature (typically 30–50°C, depending on heat emission system design and weather conditions); but relatively high return temperature (25–45°C, varying together with the delivery temperature); small temperature difference between hot and cold parts of the space heating loop	Low temperature of water entering the system (4–20°C, location and season dependent); high delivery temperature (45–60°C); large temperature difference between hot and cold water
Oxygen-free non-corrosive water in closed loop	Oxygen-rich corrosive water, run to waste after use

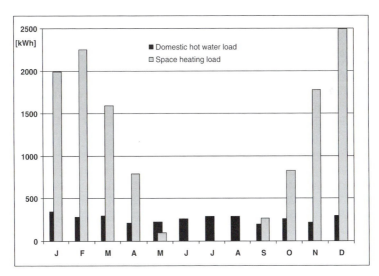

Figure 4.1. An example of seasonal variations of the (measured) heat demand for space heating and DHW in a well insulated building in France

4.1.2 Stratification in water storage devices

To supply the two heat consumers (domestic hot water and space heating), water should be simultaneously available at two different temperature levels. Operating two different storage tanks with a 'clever' control unit acting on valves and pumps can do this. However, it is also possible to use a single storage tank if care is taken to avoid mixing water of different temperatures. As hot water has a lower density than cold water, hot water is always located in the upper part of the storage tank;

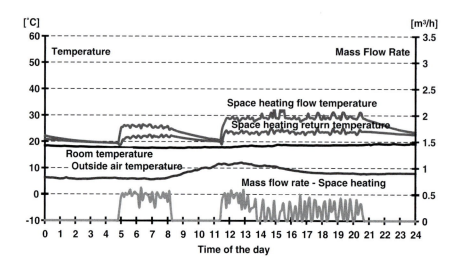

Domestic Hot Water Demand: Mass Flow Rate and Temperature

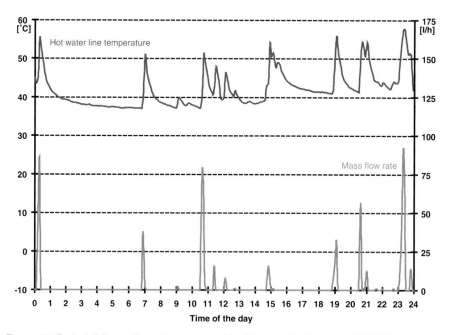

Figure 4.2. Typical daily profiles of heat demand for (a) space heating and (b) DHW in a single-family dwelling near Graz, Austria. The heat supply to space heating was interrupted twice on the day of the measurements (3 November): at night and in the morning hours. The second break is due to passive solar heating of the house through its large south-east-facing windows. Clouds ended this process at about 11:20. With regard to DHW shown in (b), draw-off peaks appear mainly before noon for cooking, in the evening and at night. Small DHW draw-offs for, for example, hand washing may not have been recorded. Note: after the water flow in a line is stopped, the water temperature decreases slowly towards the temperature of its surroundings

conversely, cold water is found at its bottom. This feature is called **vertical stratification** of the storage tank.

Stratification can be built up by adding heat (**charging**) at the top of the store or by removing heat (**discharging**) from the lower part of the store. Charging or discharging can be achieved either *directly* via inlets/outlets, where the water is either injected or removed to or from the store, or *indirectly* via a heat exchanger placed inside the store and surrounded by store water. Heat exchangers placed inside the store tend to create zones of uniform temperature above (in the case of charging) or below (in the case of discharging). For example, in the first case, heated water from an immersed heat exchanger rises and simultaneously mixes the water above the heat exchanger. Heat exchangers can therefore only create a limited amount of stratification and in some cases can destroy existing stratification (*mixing*). Direct charging and discharging can create good stratification, but only if the inlets are designed correctly and if the inlets and outlets are at heights that are well adapted to the total system design.

4.2 CLASSIFICATION OF SOLAR COMBISYSTEMS

It should now be clear that the main differences between the various generic combisystems are related to the *heat storage and heat management philosophy* chosen by the design engineer, which includes:

- the decision whether or not to store the heat produced by the auxiliary heater
- the number of storage tanks
- the design of the loop(s) in which the fluid will serve as heat storage medium
- the type of the heat exchangers used for transferring the heat from one medium to another
- the geometry of the fluid inlets into the storage tanks and the flow rates used, both having an impact on the mixing in the stores
- the geometry of mechanical inserts called **stratifiers**, aimed at enhancing stratification
- the control algorithms used
- the dimensions of all components.

Accordingly, the IEA Task 26 has identified two main features characterizing combisystems:

- The method used for *storing the heat produced for space heating by the solar collectors*; this heat storage may, or may not, be combined with DHW storage, and also with storage of the heat produced for space heating purposes by the auxiliary heater. Four *heat management categories related to stratification*, denoted respectively A, B, C, and D (see Table 4.2), describe this first feature. B and D may be combined.
- The management philosophy chosen for the *heat produced by the auxiliary heater*. Will this heat be stored? For how long? How does the controller make sure

that the auxiliary just supplies the heat that the solar collectors cannot deliver? Three *auxiliary heat management categories*, denoted respectively M, P, and S (see Table 4.2), describe this second feature.

The categories to which a particular combisystem belongs may be determined by analysing its hydraulic scheme, without doing any measurement on the system.

Table 4.2. Classification of solar combisystems

Feature 1: Heat storage categories	Feature 2: Auxiliary heat management categories
No controlled storage device for space heating	**Mixed mode:** The space heating loop is fed from a combined store charged by both solar collectors and the auxiliary heater
Heat management and stratification enhancement by means of multiple tanks ('distributed storage') and/or multiple inlet/outlet pipes and/or three- or four-way valves to control the flows through inlet/outlet pipes	**Parallel mode:** The space heating loop is fed *alternatively* by the auxiliary heater or by the solar collectors (or a storage unit for solar heat); or, there is no hydraulic connection between the solar-heat distribution and the auxiliary-heat emission
Heat management using natural convection in storage tanks and/or between them to maintain stratification to a certain extent – but without a built-in stratification device	**Serial mode:** The space heating loop may be fed by the auxiliary heater, or by both the solar collectors (or a storage unit for solar heat) and the auxiliary heater connected in series on the return line of the space heating loop★
Heat management using natural convection in storage tanks and built-in stratification devices ('stratifiers')for further stratification enhancement	**Combination of B and D:** Heat management by means of natural convection in storage tanks and built-in stratification devices as well as multiple tanks and/or multiple inlet/outlet pipes enhancement and/or three- or four-way valves to control the flows through inlet/outlet pipes

★ In periods when the solar collectors are able to cover by themselves the whole space heating demand, the water for space heating, after being heated up by solar energy flows through the turned-off auxiliary boiler. However, in some systems it is possible to bypass the auxiliary heating device by means of manually operated valves

The classification code of a solar combisystem includes one letter for Feature 1 and a second letter for Feature 2. In addition, there are *three optional features* indicated by lower-case symbols after the main code, if relevant for the generic system under consideration:

- *d* indicates that the solar combisystem is a *d*rainback system, i.e. a solar thermal system in which, as part of the normal working cycle, the heat transfer fluid is drained from the solar collectors into a storage device when the pump is turned off, and refills the collector when the pump is turned on again.
- *i* indicates that there is a *gas or oil burner i*ntegrated into and sold with the storage device. The *i* indicator always implies the mixed mode as the auxiliary heat management category (M as second main code letter).
- *l* indicates that the combisystem may be used with an auxiliary energy source like wood in the form of *l*ogs, which require a *l*ong running time for the auxiliary boiler at more or less fixed power. A long-running-time auxiliary

requires the capability to store the heat produced until the heat consumers need it. For some of the systems presented, hydraulic scheme and dimensioning have to be adapted accordingly. (There are other kinds of biomass fuels, e.g. wood chips or pellets, that do not require similar storage capacitance, because the corresponding boilers have nearly the same characteristics as gas- or oil-fired boilers; their thermal power may be modulated in a simple way, e.g. through intermittent operation.)

4.3 THE GENERIC SOLAR COMBISYSTEMS CONSIDERED

Table 4.3 gives an overview of the solar combisystems considered by Task 26. It mainly results from an initial review of the systems available on the market in the participating countries. The review was made in 1999 at the beginning of the project and published in 2000 (Suter *et al.*, 2000) as well as on the Task 26 website (www.iea-shc.org/task26/). In 2002 the review was repeated, and the changes encountered within the three-year period compiled. The system numbering defined in 1999 had to be partly updated. To prevent any confusion, each generic system number designates a unique system. Table 4.3 reflects the status from the final review 2002.

Table 4.3. The generic solar combisystems considered by Task 26

#	Generic system designation	Category code★	Country
1	Basic direct solar floor	AP	France
2	Heat exchanger between collector loop and space heating loop	AS	Denmark
3a	Advanced direct solar floor (status 2002)	AP	France
4	DHW tank as a space heating storage device	CS (*d*)	Denmark, the Netherlands
5	DHW tank as space heating storage device with drainback capability	CM *id*	The Netherlands
6	Heat storage in DHW tank and in collector drainback tank	CM *id*	The Netherlands
7	Space heating store with a single load-side heat exchanger for DHW	CM *i*	Finland
8	Space heating store with double load-side heat exchanger for DHW	CM *i*	Switzerland
9a	Small DHW tank in space heating tank	CM *l*	Switzerland, Austria
9b		CM *d(i)l*	Norway
10	Advanced small DHW tank in space heating tank	BS	Switzerland
11	Space heating store with DHW load-side heat exchanger(s) and external auxiliary boiler	CM (*i*)*l*	Finland, Sweden
12	Space heating store with DHW load-side heat exchanger(s) and external auxiliary boiler (advanced version)	BM *l*	Sweden
13	Two stores (series)	BM *l*	Austria
14	Two stores (parallel) (2 different versions)	BP or BM *l*	Austria
15	Two stratifiers in a space heating storage tank with an external load-side heat exchanger for DHW	DM *il*	Germany
16	Conical stratifier in space heating store with load-side heat exchanger for DHW	DS *d*	Germany
17	Tank open to the atmosphere with three heat exchangers	DS	Germany
18	Finned-tube load-side DHW heat exchanger in stratifier	B/DS *l*	Germany
19	Centralized heat production, distributed heat load, stratified storage	B/DM *l*	Austria
20	Large tank-in-tank for seasonal heat storage	BM (*l*)	Switzerland
21	Large stratified tank for seasonal heat storage, air heating system	BM/S (*l*)	Germany

★ Indications in parentheses refer to options

The order of the combisystems has been chosen so that the reader may easily follow, step by step, a short presentation of their similarities and differences in ascending numerical order. *This numbering is used throughout this Handbook*. For each combisystem, a single data sheet with technical details may be found in Section 4.4, presented in the same order as in the above table.

The first six generic combisystems have **no store with water from the space heating loop**. The storage fluid is either domestic hot water or water in the collector loop in the case of a drainback system. The heat storage can also be in the concrete of a floor heating system.

The simplest solar combisystem (#1) is the French **'Basic direct solar floor'**. The collector array is directly connected to the heating floor; the floor acts as both the store and the heat exchanger. A connection in the hydraulic loop provides for solar DHW heating, especially outside the heating season. The auxiliary heater for space heating is often a wood stove. The users are responsible for comfort control, as no connection is provided between the solar heating system and the stove. The room temperature may have large fluctuations, depending on the user's skill.

In the Danish system **'Heat exchanger between collector loop and space heating loop'** (#2) the heat distribution system for space heating – in this case either radiators or a heating floor – is also connected, via a heat exchanger, to the solar collector loop without any intermediate store. Here, there is only one stratified DHW store instead of the two as in the French system (#1). The objective of the heat exchanger, which is series-connected to the auxiliary boiler on the space heating return line, is to allow for normal water instead of an antifreeze solution to be used in the space heating loop.

Unlike the 'Basic Direct Solar Floor' the second French system **'Advanced direct solar floor'** (#3) integrates the auxiliary heating into the solar heating system. Accordingly, it is operated automatically, in the parallel mode. The first variant (#3) of the year 1999 had two DHW stores. By 2002, it had been replaced by a second variant considered here (#3a), with one single DHW store. The heat management philosophy is unchanged, the space heating store being the heating floor itself.

In the next system **'DHW tank as a space heating storage device'** (#4) – originally from Denmark but by 2002 no longer sold there, although now being sold in the Netherlands (see below) – the DHW tank is also used as a space-heating storage device. This DHW tank is the only storage tank in the system and is provided with three immersed heat exchangers, each with a dedicated function. If solar heat is available in the store for space heating, it is used to preheat the returning water from the heat distribution loop ahead of the auxiliary boiler (serial mode).

The Dutch system **'DHW tank as space heating storage device with drainback capability'** (#5) has a similar structure to System #4. The major differences are the drainback feature and the gas boiler integration into the storage tank. The collectors are drained as soon as the circulating pump stops. The drained water is retained in the mantle heat exchanger until the control unit turns on the pump again. By 2002, this system was no longer manufactured; it has been replaced by a drainback version of System #4.

The second Dutch system **'Heat storage in DHW tank and in collector drainback tank'** (#6) has many similarities to System #5. However, System #6 has two stores, whereas System #5 has only one store with a mantle heat exchanger. A special feature is the use of the collector drainback tank as a heat store. Accordingly, there is a heat transfer capability between this store and the DHW store, in the form of an immersed heat exchanger and a loop operated by gravity (thermosiphon; no pump in this loop). The heat is delivered to the space heating loop via a second immersed heat exchanger. Gas is the only possible auxiliary energy source for System #6, which has an integrated burner.

*This completes the short description of the combisystems using either DHW or the concrete of the floor for the storage of heat for space heating purpose. Systems #7–#21 all store heat for space heating in a medium other than in the domestic hot water, mostly the **water of the space heating loop itself**. This often includes the main body of water in the heat store.*

The Finnish system **'Space heating store with a single load-side heat exchanger for DHW'** (#7) has many similarities with Systems #4 and #5. However, the storage medium is now space heating water and the DHW is heated via a **load-side heat exchanger**. Such heat exchangers have to be large, as the heat power transferred through them when DHW is drawn off is very high. In addition, the temperature drop across the heat exchanger must be kept small; otherwise, the DHW consumer will be supplied with water colder than the desired (set-point) temperature. This system has either an oil or a gas burner integrated into the store.

The Swiss system **'Space heating store with double load-side heat exchanger for DHW'** (#8) has a double load-side heat exchanger to enhance stratification, and either an integrated oil or gas burner. The other features are similar to those of System #7. System #8 is also similar to the Scandinavian System #11, except that in System #11 the burner is mostly located outside the store.

The next system, **'Small DHW tank in space heating tank'** (#9), originates from Switzerland and is also found today in Austria. This system replaces the double load-side heat exchanger of System #8 by a small but tall stainless steel tank placed inside the space heating tank. The DHW contained in the small tank is heated by the surrounding space heating water; it is ready for DHW draw-off at high rates at the same temperature as in the store, although the draw-off volume is limited by the small tank capacity. The size of the small tank is optimized according to the user's minimum DHW temperature requirements, as well as their draw-off volume and profile. After a large draw-off the small tank needs 30–60 minutes to recover to the set-point temperature. The auxiliary boiler delivers its produced heat directly into the store. Long-running-time auxiliary boilers may be installed with System #9.

A second version of System #9 is found in Norway, which joined Task 26 after the publication of the original brochure. The Norwegian system mainly differs from the Swiss/Austrian version in two ways: (i) it is a drainback system with space heating water flowing also through the polymer flat-plate collectors, and (ii) the built-in DHW store only acts as a pre-heat device for DHW.

The third Swiss system **'Advanced small DHW tank in space heating tank'** (#10) has two features to enhance the stratification in the store. It combines (i) a load-side heat exchanger and a small tank for DHW and (ii) an additional immersed heat exchanger and a three-way valve in the collector loop, to heat the upper part of the store directly, whenever possible. The auxiliary heat management is in the serial mode. Long-running-time auxiliary boilers may also be installed with System #10.

The Scandinavian system **'Space heating store with DHW load-side heat exchanger(s) and external auxiliary boiler'** (#11) may be compared, on the one hand, with System #7, and on the other with System #8. A second load-side heat exchanger for DHW is common but not always provided, and provision is made for the coupling to either a conventional auxiliary boiler or a long-running-time auxiliary boiler. By 2002, there was also a variant with an integrated wood pellet burner. System #11 may also be compared to System #4, where the respective roles of DHW and space heating water in the storage devices have been interchanged and the auxiliary heat management is different.

The Swedish system **'Space heating store with DHW load-side heat exchanger(s) and external auxiliary boiler (advanced version)'** (#12) is an advanced version of System #11. A three-way valve is provided, together with a second immersed heat exchanger in the collector loop, and a four-way valve, with two outlets from the store, in the space-heating loop. In this way, stratification in the storage tank is enhanced.

*The next group of systems all have **two stores** and, accordingly, features such as valves, pumps, pipes, sensors and control facilities direct the heat to the one store or the other, depending on the relevant control temperatures in the system.*

In the Austrian system **'Two stores (series)'** (#13), both the solar heat and the auxiliary heat for DHW first pass through the space heating store before being transferred to the DHW store by a separate loop with a pump, heat exchanger and corresponding control. Solar-heated fluid is injected into the space heating store at two different heights via an external heat exchanger as a stratification-enhancing feature. Long-running-time auxiliary boilers may be installed with this system.

'Two stores (parallel)' (#14) is also an Austrian system, with two versions: one for an oil or gas auxiliary boiler, and the second for a long-running-time auxiliary boiler. 'Parallel' means that the solar heat as well as the heat produced by the auxiliary boiler may be directed either to the space heating store or to the DHW store, by means of valves and a controller. In the case of a gas or oil boiler as auxiliary, the auxiliary heat management is in the parallel mode.

*The following four systems from Germany all have **built-in stratifiers** in the storage tank, mostly vertically mounted along the tank axis, in addition to possible stratification-enhancing features like those described for the previous systems.*

The first system, called **'Two stratifiers in a space heating storage tank with an external load-side heat exchanger for DHW'** (#15) is fitted with an integrated gas burner. Other external auxiliary heaters may also be used. The solar heat exchanger is located in the lower part of a stratifier, the upper part of which is provided with several horizontal outlets for stratified charging of the storage tank. A second stratifier is provided for the return line of the space heating loop. The load-side DHW heat exchanger is external, with a variable-speed circulating pump on the primary side.

The next system '**Conical stratifier in space heating store with load-side heat exchanger for DHW**' (#16) is a German drainback system. The solar heat exchanger is conically shaped, and again located in the lower part of a stratifier. A horizontal plate minimizes water mixing between the upper DHW part and the lower space heating part of the tank. The load-side DHW heat exchanger is a long, spirally wound pipe, mounted near to the storage tank side wall. The auxiliary heat management is in the serial mode.

In System #17, '**Tank open to the atmosphere with three heat exchangers**', from Germany, the heat storage medium is water at atmospheric pressure in a so-called unpressurized or open store. Hence, heat exchangers are used for heat transfer from the solar collector loop, from and to the space heating/auxiliary heat source loop, and to DHW. Stratifiers are used both for the solar heat exchanger and for the load-side DHW heat exchanger. This load-side stratifier has a long 'tail' directing the tank water, after it has been cooled by DHW in the heat exchanger, to the tank bottom, hence minimizing its mixing with warmer water. The auxiliary heat management is in the serial mode.

The fourth German system '**Finned-tube load-side DHW heat exchanger in stratifier**' (#18) combines several features already encountered in other systems with one unique feature: a compact load-side DHW heat exchanger built from finned tubes, mounted in the upper part of a stratifier similar to that in System #17. This stratifier, however, has a valve to regulate the flow of water sinking to the bottom of the store, aiming to further improve stratification. The other features of this system are an external heat exchanger in the collector loop, with selective heat transport to the storage tank at two different heights, and the auxiliary heat management in the serial mode. By 2002, this system had disappeared from the market.

This completes the description of the combisystems designed principally for buildings housing up to two or three families (collector area less than 50 m²; however, some of the designs are also suitable for larger buildings).

The Austrian system, '**Centralized heat production, distributed heat load, stratified storage**' (#19), is designed for large buildings or building groups. The collector area may reach 800 m². A local heating network connects the individual houses or flats to the central storage tank (up to 60 m³). Originally (in 1999), DHW was prepared and stored in a decentralized way and the local heating network was periodically operated at a higher temperature, enabling the charging of all decentralized DHW stores. By 2002, the decentralized DHW stores had been abandoned. DHW is now continuously available directly from the local heating network by means of once-through heat exchanger units installed in the individual flats. The new network operating temperature is constant at about 60°C. All heat exchangers are external. The central store is fitted with stratifiers for the collector loop and the local network return line.

As an opportunity for further developments, Task 26 also considered the following two generic systems, but did not go into as many details as for the smaller systems (#1–#19).

System #20, '**Large tank-in-tank for seasonal heat storage**', from Switzerland is derived from System #9, a smaller system of similar configuration. It is sized in such a way that a large fraction of the yearly heat demand may be supplied by solar energy.

In the climatic conditions of central and northern Europe this implies that the excess heat produced in the summer months is stored for use in wintertime, so-called **seasonal storage** of solar heat. These systems are technically feasible, but less cost-effective than the small ones. However, they could become an important option in the medium term, when large contributions from solar energy will be required.

System #21, '**Large stratified tank for seasonal heat storage, air heating system**', also stores summer heat in a large stratified tank for later use in the winter. In this German system, space heating is air-based with a ventilation system. The system is, so far, a prototype installed in a well insulated office building with a cogeneration unit as the auxiliary heating device.

4.4 TECHNICAL DESCRIPTION OF THE GENERIC SYSTEMS

In this section, technical details are given about each generic solar combisystem.

4.4.1 General remarks

The *collector area and storage volume ranges* indicated at the top of each data sheet are simply typical figures. Different dimensions are also possible in practice.

The *cost figures* mentioned in the data sheets have to be interpreted cautiously. They are simply *typical costs* and may be subject to *large variations* in practice.

For each generic combisystem the *total cost without taxes* includes the following components and their installation:

- solar collectors mounted into the roof (integrated collectors)
- collector piping with insulation
- solar hydraulic equipment (storage tanks, pump, valves, controllers etc.)
- auxiliary boiler
- boiler piping with insulation
- antifreeze fluid
- space heating loop (heat distribution lines and heat emission devices) designed for heating rooms with a total floor area of 130 m².

The total cost of a *reference system in the same country of origin* is given for comparison. The *difference* between the cost of the solar combisystem and the cost of this reference system is believed to be more reliable for system intercomparison than the total cost itself, even within a single country. However, when comparing figures, the reader should remember that the *economic background of the manufacturer*, the *national market structure and price level* as well as the *level of comfort* offered by the systems under consideration are also reflected in the cost information.

The choice of the **reference system** depends on the generic system under consideration. The reference system has no solar collector, but has the same auxiliary energy source, the same heat distribution lines and heat emission devices, and a comparable DHW production unit as well as a similar controller. The heating services delivered to the inhabitants in the form of space heating and domestic hot water by the solar combisystem and its reference system are supposed to be equivalent.

In many cases the **auxiliary heating concept** indicated in a data sheet may be replaced by another one. For instance, a built-in electric heater or a heat exchanger with external auxiliary heater can replace an integrated gas burner. The specific heat transfer characteristics of the different devices should be taken into account.

For some generic system concepts, system units may be connected in **cascade** to match a larger space heating and DHW load.

4.4.2 The symbols used

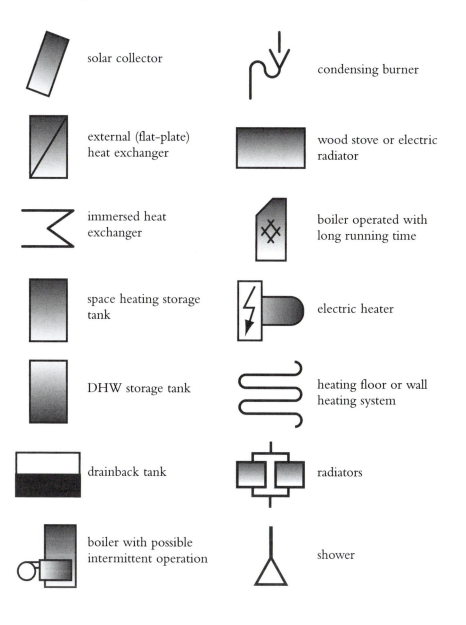

solar collector

condensing burner

external (flat-plate) heat exchanger

wood stove or electric radiator

immersed heat exchanger

boiler operated with long running time

space heating storage tank

electric heater

DHW storage tank

heating floor or wall heating system

drainback tank

radiators

boiler with possible intermittent operation

shower

Codes for pipes are:

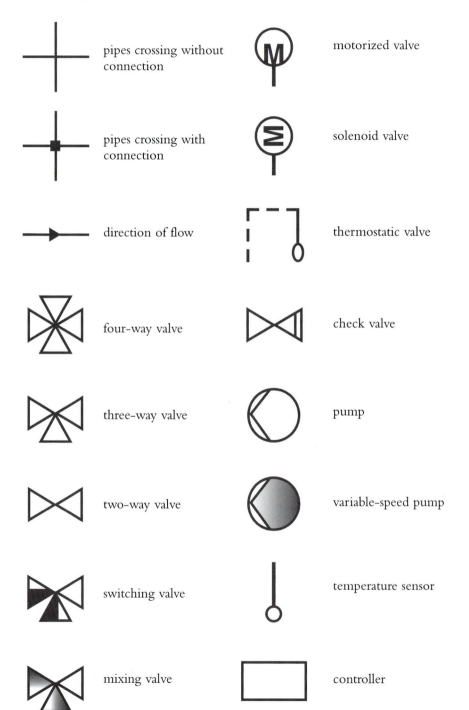

pipes crossing without connection

motorized valve

pipes crossing with connection

solenoid valve

direction of flow

thermostatic valve

four-way valve

check valve

three-way valve

pump

two-way valve

variable-speed pump

switching valve

temperature sensor

mixing valve

controller

Controlled loops are shown as follows:

S   solar collector loop

A   auxiliary heater loop

H1   space heating loop number 1

H2   space heating loop number 2

DHW   DHW-related loop

4.4.3 System #1: basic direct solar floor (France)

Main features

This combisystem features heated floors, which combine the functions of heat delivery and space heating storage. The heat-transfer fluid heated by collectors flows, without intermediate heat exchanger, in the concrete slabs. The typical slab thickness is increased by between 12 and 15 cm, so as to store the solar energy and shift its release to the evening. This system was developed at the end of the 1970s, to simplify former hydraulic schemes.

A diagram of the system is shown in Figure 4.3.

Heat management philosophy

Each of the two pumps is under the control of a differential controller. Priority is given to the load (DHW or space heating) with the lowest temperature level, so that the solar collector works with the highest efficiency. If the temperature at the outlet of the heating floor is higher than the set-point temperature, the pump of the space heating loop is turned off in order to prevent overheating in the house.

Specific aspects

All the components shown in the central box of the hydraulic scheme are factory-assembled in compact units, which makes the work of the installer in the house easier. Because of the solar floor, this system is well suited for new houses or for retrofits where the floors are being rebuilt. Figure 4.4 is an example of a heating floor built on the ground. For floors located above heated or unheated rooms, other types of construction are possible. Apart from the increased slab thickness, the only

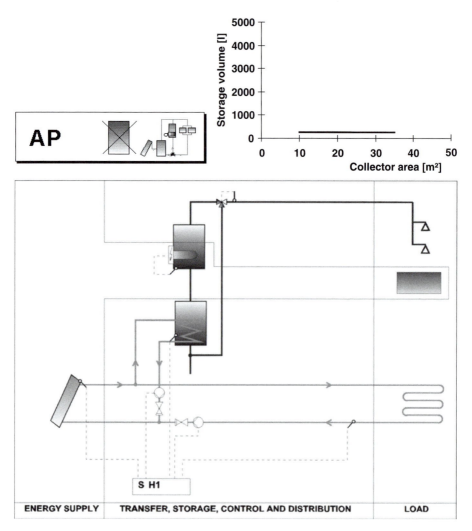

Figure 4.3. Hydraulic scheme System #1

difference between the typical heating floor and the solar floor is the location of the polyethylene pipes at the bottom of the slab.

Influence of the auxiliary energy source on system design and dimensioning
Auxiliary energy for space heating is delivered to the house with an independent system, such as a wood stove or electric radiators. The auxiliary electric heater for DHW may be integrated in the upper part of the solar DHW tank.

Cost (range)
A typical system with 15 m² of solar collectors, a 250 litre tank, components for the heating floor, pipes and installation, auxiliary energy provided by a wood stove and

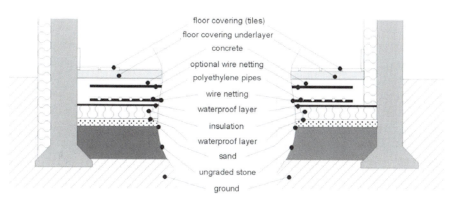

Figure 4.4. Cross-section of a heating floor

an electric tank for DHW, costs about €13,000. Self-installation is made easy through the high level of component integration, so the total cost can decrease to about €11,500. Costs for the reference system, including a wood stove and an electric tank for DHW only, are about €2000.

Market distribution
This system is marketed mainly in France, and was almost the only type installed between 1986 and 1992; solar heating systems with water storage disappeared in France 20 years ago. More than 300 units were sold prior to 2000, utilizing more than 4500 m² of solar collectors. The market for this system is expanding. Some 60 units were sold in 2001. Cost is stable.

4.4.4 System #2: heat exchanger between collector loop and space heating loop (Denmark)

Main features
This system is derived from a standard solar DHW system, but the collector area has been oversized in order to deliver energy to an existing space heating system. The connection between the solar collectors and the existing system is made through a heat exchanger included in the return pipe of the space heating loop. The store is dedicated for DHW preparation, with two immersed heat exchangers: the solar one in the bottom of the tank, and the auxiliary one at the top. A three-way valve directs the antifreeze fluid coming from the collector to either the DHW heat exchanger or to the space heating heat exchanger.

A diagram of the system is shown in Figure 4.5.

Heat management philosophy
The controller does not manage the auxiliary part of the system. As long as the temperature at the collector outlet is higher than either the return temperature from the space heating loop or the temperature at the bottom of the tank, the pump

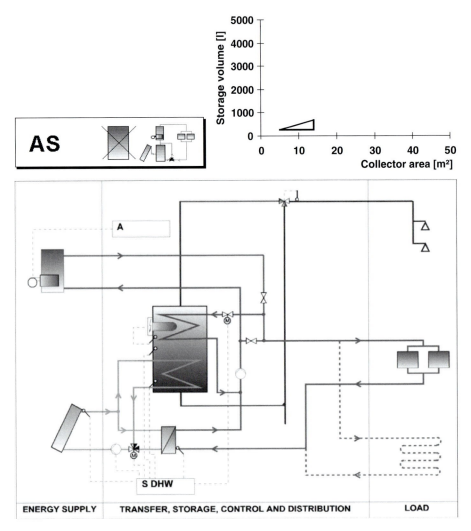

Figure 4.5. Hydraulic scheme System #2

of the collector loop operates. The three-way valve is managed so as to deliver solar energy to the space heating loop, i.e. when the temperature at the collector outlet is lower than the temperature at the bottom of the tank, or when the storage is warm enough (temperature at the top of the store higher than the set-point temperature). When the DHW temperature is too low, auxiliary heat is delivered to the tank through the two-way valve.

Specific aspects

Because of the lack of a store for space heating, the solar gain will be increased the more variations of indoor temperature the inhabitants tolerate. In this system, the building itself plays the role of space heating store. Therefore, the system will work better with a high-capacitance heat emission system, like heating floors. Solar-induced variations in the indoor temperature are only possible when the boiler is turned off (i.e. in summer). The system could be controlled so that it delivers heat to the space heating loop independently of any space heating needs if there is a risk of overheating in the system.

Influence of the auxiliary energy source on system design and dimensioning

This system can work with any auxiliary energy source (gas, fuel, wood, district heating). It could also be used with separated electric radiators. There are often two separate auxiliary heaters, alternately used: a gas or oil boiler for the space heating period and a store-integrated electric heater for the summertime.

Cost (range)

A typical system with 7 m² of solar collectors and a 280 litre store costs about €5200. This amount only includes the solar part (comprising collectors, storage device, controller and heat exchanger, installation), since the auxiliary part (comprising boiler, radiator circuit) already exists. Total cost for a complete heating system with solar is €13,800 and reference cost for a complete heating system without solar is €9300.

Market distribution

This system is the most common in Denmark. Prior to 2000, about 100,000 m² of solar collectors had been installed by 12 manufacturers and 400–800 installers all over Denmark.

4.4.5 System #3a: advanced direct solar floor (France)

Main features

This combisystem is an enhancement of the basic direct solar floor concept. The essential idea is to couple the heat emission device used for space heating to both the auxiliary heater and the solar collectors in such a way that inhabitants can benefit from the heating floor comfort throughout the heating season. A heat management philosophy is used to optimize the solar heat sharing between DHW production and space heating.

A diagram of the system is shown in Figure 4.6.

Heat management philosophy

The floor mixing valve is under the control of a heating curve derived from a predicted outside air temperature and the room temperature. When solar energy is delivered to the floor, the flow temperature in the floor is allowed to rise in such a way that the room temperature exceeds the auxiliary set-point room temperature by at most 4°C. But when auxiliary energy is delivered to the floor, the space heating loop pump is turned off as soon as the room temperature exceeds the

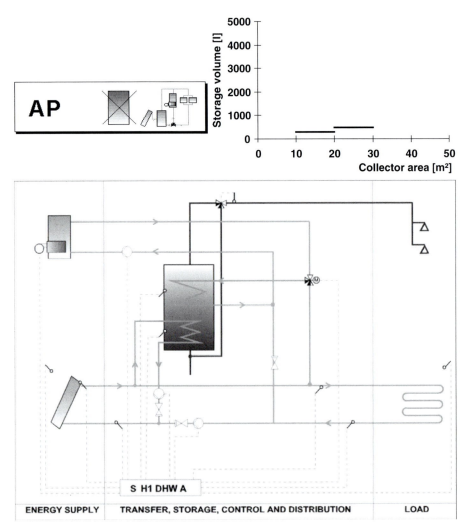

Figure 4.6. Hydraulic scheme System #3a

auxiliary set–point room temperature by 0.5°C. The auxiliary boiler is controlled by the solar controller in such a way that the heat losses are reduced when no auxiliary energy is needed.

In summer, the whole volume of the DHW tank is used for solar energy storage.

Specific aspects

The current variant (#3a) with one DHW tank has been developed from a previous one (#3) with two DHW stores, recorded at the beginning of Task 26. The reasons for this new development were a simplification of the hydraulic scheme and a cost optimization. The manufacturer is marketing the system as a whole, including the DHW store. This is a positive point for failure-free system operation.

All of the components shown in the transfer, storage, control and distribution region of the hydraulic scheme are factory-assembled in compact units, which makes the installation easier. Because of the heating floor, this system is well suited for new houses or for retrofits where the floors are being rebuilt.

Monitoring features are included in the controller, which can compute energy balances and send the information to a remote computer through a built-in modem. In this way, proper operation can be verified.

Influence of the auxiliary energy source on system design and dimensioning
A gas, oil or electrical boiler can easily be connected to the storage and control unit. It is also possible to use a wood boiler, but that requires an additional buffer tank.

Cost (range)
A typical system with 15 m² of solar collectors costs about €17,000, which can be roughly divided into two halves: (i) the auxiliary part (comprising boiler, heating floor piping, auxiliary DHW tank, control, etc.) corresponding to the reference system (€8500); and (ii) the solar-related additional investment (comprising solar collectors, solar DHW tank, control, etc.). The high level of component integration and the possibility of partial self-installation lead to reduced installation costs.

Market distribution
Like the basic direct solar floor, this system is only found in France, in an expanding market. Only one company manufactures this system. Between 1992 and 2000, more than 300 units were sold, with a total collector area exceeding 4500 m². In the period 1999–2002, more than 400 units were sold. Cost is stable.

4.4.6 System #4: DHW tank as a space heating storage device (Denmark and the Netherlands)

Main features
As is the case for System #2, this system can be added to an existing space heating system. Heat coming from the solar collector is delivered to a DHW tank, which acts also as a small buffer tank for space heating. The DHW store is equipped with three immersed heat exchangers: the solar one in the bottom of the tank, the auxiliary one at the top and an intermediate one connected to the return line of the space heating loop. A three-way switching valve directs the fluid from the space heating loop either to the intermediate heat exchanger or directly to the auxiliary boiler.

Originally from Denmark, by 2002, a Dutch variant of this system became available, with drainback capability. In the latter, the whole storage/auxiliary equipment is subdivided into two factory-assembled parts, to be connected at installation time. The first includes the auxiliary heater, a condensing gas burner. This part is mounted by the installer on the top of the second one, which includes the store and all other components.

A diagram of the system is shown in Figure 4.7.

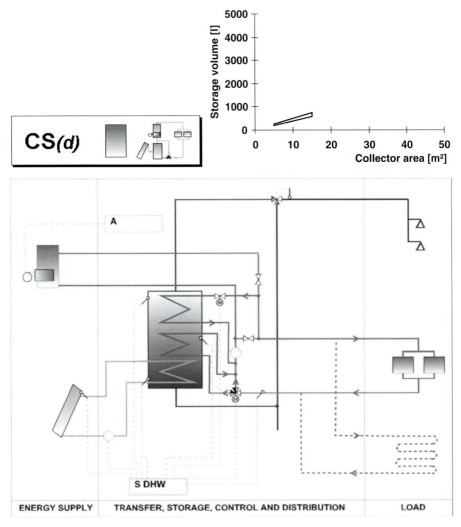

Figure 4.7. Hydraulic scheme System #4

Heat management philosophy

If the temperature at the collector outlet is higher than the temperature at the bottom of the tank, the pump of the collector loop is on. The three-way valve is controlled so as to deliver solar energy to the space heating loop, i.e. water flows through the intermediate heat exchanger only when the temperature in the middle of the tank is higher than the return temperature of the space heating loop. When the DHW temperature is too low, auxiliary heat is delivered to the tank through the two-way valve. The auxiliary part of the system is under control of a separate control unit.

Specific aspects

Solar heat used for space heating is stored in the domestic hot water tank.

Influence of the auxiliary energy source on system design and dimensioning
This system can work with any auxiliary energy source (gas, oil, wood or district heating). It could be also used with separated electric radiators.

Cost (range)
A typical system with 15 m² of solar collectors and an 800 litre storage unit costs about €7000. This amount only includes the solar part (comprising collectors, storage tank, controller and heat exchanger, installation), since the auxiliary part (comprising boiler, radiator circuit) already exists. Total cost for a complete heating system with solar is €15,600, and reference cost for a complete heating system without solar is €9300.

Market distribution
In 1999, this system was quite new in Denmark, but it is no longer marketed or sold very much. Only one company still markets this system, and total collector area in operation is 100 m². The system is marketed by the manufacturer and is available anywhere in Denmark from the nearest installer (400–800 potential installers).

The Dutch drainback variant is quite successful in the marketplace. Recent Dutch market figures are given together with those for System #6 in Section 4.4.8.

4.4.7 System #5: DHW tank as space heating storage device with drainback capability (the Netherlands)

Main features
This system is a compact unit for space heating and DHW, with an integrated gas burner. The 240 litre or 650 litre DHW tank is surrounded by a double-walled tank connected to the solar collector. This mantle tank simultaneously works as a heat exchanger and a drainback tank for the collector.

A diagram of the system is shown in Figure 4.8.

Heat management philosophy
The pump of the collector loop is under the control of a differential controller, which switches the collector loop pump on if the temperature of the collector absorber is well above the temperature in the mantle. If the temperature of the DHW in the auxiliary part is too low, the gas burner is switched on. In the case of radiators used as heat delivery devices, the burner is controlled using two sensors: the room's thermostat indicates that there is a heat demand and an outdoor sensor provides the information needed for turning the burner on.

Specific aspects
Overheating and freeze protection are provided by the drainback principle.

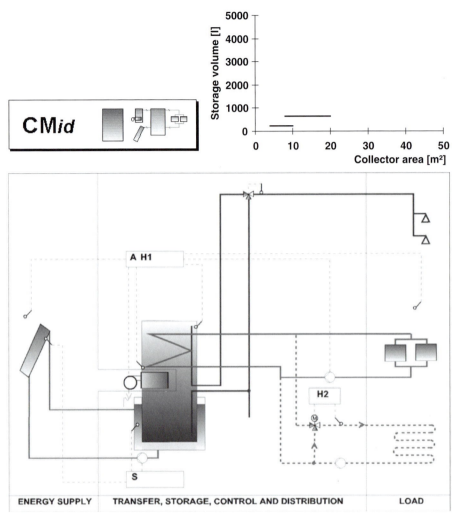

Figure 4.8. Hydraulic scheme System #5

Influence of the auxiliary energy source on system design and dimensioning

This system is designed with a gas burner integrated into the storage tank. However, the tank can also be provided with an electric element for auxiliary heating.

Cost (range)

A typical system with 4.2 m² of collector and a 240 litre storage tank with an integrated gas burner costs about €3500. Installation costs in a new building amount to approximately €750 for the collector and the heat store. With additional costs for the space heating distribution system (radiators) of about €2200, total cost is €6450. A similar reference system without solar heating costs about €3400 with the heat distribution system.

Market distribution
This system has been marketed in the Netherlands since 1994. In total, 4250 systems
had been installed prior to 2000. The total collector area in operation is about 15,000 m².
However, by 2002, System #5 was no longer manufactured. It has been replaced by
the drainback variant of System #4 described in Section 4.4.6. This new system with
two separate pre-assembled parts is easier to handle at installation time.

4.4.8 System #6: heat storage in DHW tank and in collector drainback tank (the Netherlands)

Main features
This system is a compact unit for space heating and DHW, with two superimposed
storage tanks and an integrated gas burner. The collectors are connected to a 100
litre solar storage tank, which also works as the drainback vessel. A DHW pre-
heating heat exchanger is located within this tank. DHW is then further heated in
the second tank containing the vertically integrated gas burner.
   A diagram of the system is shown in Figure 4.9.

Heat management philosophy
The pump of the collector loop is under the control of a differential controller. If
the temperature of the DHW in the auxiliary storage tank is too low, the gas burner
is switched on. When radiators are used as the heat emission devices, the burner is
controlled using two sensors: the room's thermostat indicates that there is a heat
demand, and an outdoor sensor provides the information needed for turning on the
burner.

Specific aspects
Overheating and freeze protection are provided by the drainback principle.

Influence of the auxiliary energy source on system design and dimensioning
This system is designed with a gas burner integrated into the storage tank. No other
auxiliary energy can be used.

Cost (range)
A typical system with 4.1 m² of collector and a 180 litre storage tank costs about
€3300. Installation costs in a new building amount to approximately €750 for the
collector and heat store with integrated burner. With additional costs for the space
heating distribution system (radiators) of about €2200, the total cost is €6250. A
similar reference system without solar heating costs about €3400 with the heat
distribution system.

Market distribution
This system was launched on the Dutch market in the autumn of 1999. The Dutch
market share for solar combisystems of types #4 and #6 together has increased in

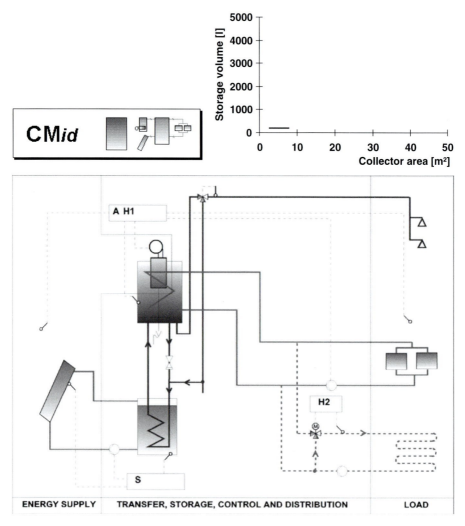

Figure 4.9. Hydraulic scheme System #6

recent years from about 5% of all solar heating systems sold to about 15%. This corresponds to 750 systems sold in 2000 and 950 in 2001.

4.4.9 System #7: space heating store with a single load-side heat exchanger for DHW (Finland)

Main features
This system has a storage volume of 300 litres and an integrated oil or gas burner. A solar collector area of 2–8 m² can be installed with this system.
  A diagram of the system is shown in Figure 4.10.

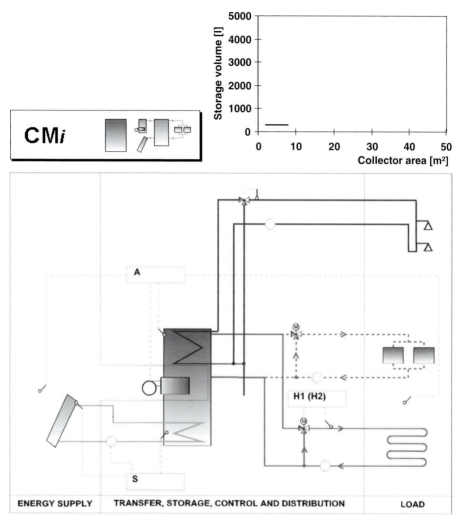

Figure 4.10. Hydraulic scheme System #7

Heat management philosophy

The pump of the solar loop is under the control of a differential controller that also provides storage-overheating protection. The burner has its own control, which is subject to the room and outside air temperatures.

Specific aspects

A large expansion vessel, dimensioned so that it is able to contain the fluid volume expelled from the collectors by the vapour produced in them when stagnation occurs, provides overheating protection.

Influence of the auxiliary energy source on system design and dimensioning
This system is always equipped with an integrated oil or gas burner. The solar collector area (one to three collectors, 2.5 m² each) is dimensioned in accordance with the heat demand and the customer's desires.

Cost (range)
A typical system with 7.5 m² of solar collectors and a 300 litre storage tank costs about €10,600, including a heating floor and the installation costs. A similar reference system without solar heating costs about €7600.

Market distribution
At the end of 1999, about 50 systems were in operation. The oil heating option is more common than the gas heating option.

4.4.10 System #8: space heating store with double load-side heat exchanger for DHW (Switzerland)

Main features
This system is a compact unit for space heating and DHW, with an integrated gas or oil burner. The storage tank is fitted out with two immersed horizontal finned-coil heat exchangers (one in the upper and one in the lower part) for DHW preparation, and a third one in the bottom for the collector loop.
   A diagram of the system is shown in Figure 4.11.

Heat management philosophy
The speed of the collector loop pump is varied in accordance with the temperature in the middle of the tank and the temperature difference between the collector outlet and the bottom of the storage tank. The storage tank set-point temperature, which controls the auxiliary burner, is automatically adjusted to the space heating needs.
   The controller is able to anticipate when solar heat is available from the collector and then switches off the burner. The controller, taking into account solar passive gains detected by a second room temperature sensor, manages space heating. In the case of heating floors, a storage tank discharge can be forced in order to store heat in the building structure. In such a case, the room temperature may deviate from its set-point value by as much as 5°C. The control strategy is designed to adjust the start time to improve thermal comfort.

Specific aspects
One single controller is in charge of the whole system (collector loop, DHW, space heating and auxiliary burner), with a display that indicates proper operation. Overheating is prevented by cooling the lower part of the storage tank after the sun has set by using the collector as a heat sink. There is no legionella risk because DHW does not stagnate in the storage tank.

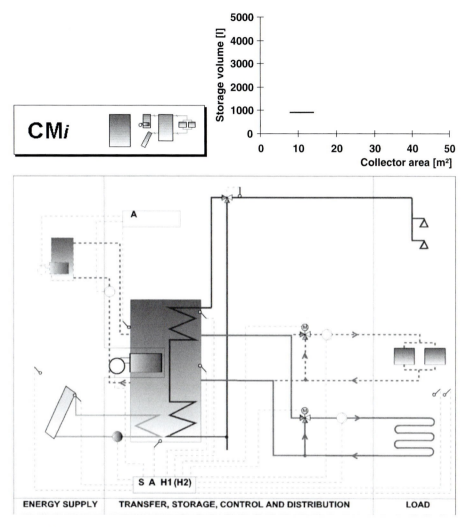

Figure 4.11. Hydraulic scheme System #8

During the course of Task 26 the performance of System #8 has been significantly improved by systematically reducing heat losses from the store (from 2760 kWh/a down to 1726 kWh/a). The burner and tank bottom insulation have been improved, siphon traps have been added on both space heating and collector loop pipe connections to the store, and a piece of wood has been placed under the tank.

Influence of the auxiliary energy source on system design and dimensioning

This system can be used with a gas or oil auxiliary burner. Alternatively, a wood boiler can be connected directly to the lower part of the storage tank. In such a case, the boiler should be used cautiously to avoid competition between solar and auxiliary energies in the commonly used, lower section of the storage tank.

Cost (range)
The total cost of the whole system with a gas or oil burner is about €20,000–23,000, for a collector area of 8–16 m². Installation costs and a heating floor are included in these figures. A similar reference system without solar heating costs about €11,000.

Market distribution
This system was introduced in Switzerland in 1998. By the end of 1999, 25 systems had been installed with a total collector area of about 300 m².

4.4.11 System #9: small DHW tank in space heating tank (Switzerland, Austria and Norway)

4.4.11.1 System #9a (Switzerland and Austria)
Main specific features
In this system, a DHW tank is built in the space heating storage tank. The space heating tank size and the DHW tank size can be independently chosen over a wide range. In the Swiss/Austrian system, the DHW tank has a characteristic, mushroom-like shape.
   A diagram of the system is shown in Figure 4.12.

Heat management philosophy
A simple differential controller controls the pump of the collector loop. A thermostat with a typical set-point temperature of 55°C controls the heating of the upper part of the storage tank by auxiliary energy.

Specific aspects
The failure of components like pumps and valves in earlier designs has led to a simple system design to minimize the risk of failure. Overheating is prevented by cooling the lower part of the storage tank after the sun has set, by using the collector as a heat sink.

Influence of the auxiliary energy source on system design and dimensioning
This system can be used either with a gas or an oil auxiliary boiler, or with a long-running-time boiler (e.g. wood in the form of logs).

Cost (range)
The total cost of the whole system in Switzerland is about €17,200, with a 12 m² collector, a 1200 litre storage tank, a gas or oil boiler and a heating floor. Installation costs are included in these figures. A similar reference system without solar heating costs about €11,000.

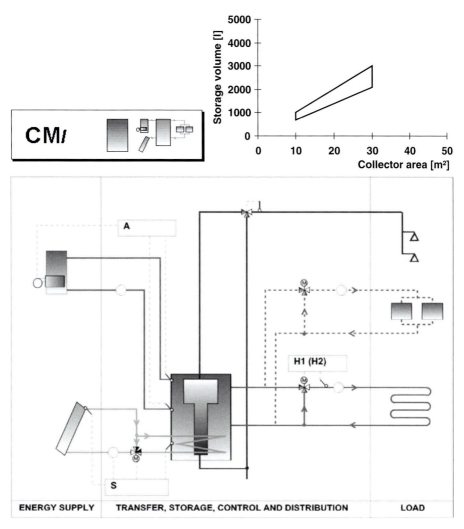

Figure 4.12. Hydraulic scheme System #9a

Market distribution
This system is common in Switzerland. Since 1976, more than 100,000 m² of collectors have been installed by about 10 companies.

In Austria, this system was introduced in 1994. About 3000 systems with more than 50,000 m² collectors have been installed by at least 10 companies.

4.4.11.2 System #9b (Norway)
Main features
In this system, a DHW tank is built in the space heating storage tank. The space heating tank size and the DHW tank size can be independently chosen over a wide

range. Water is used as the common heat transfer fluid in the solar collector loop, the space heating tank and the heat distribution loop, without any intermediate heat exchanger. Accordingly, all components are made of stainless steel, copper or plastic. The tank operates at atmospheric pressure. A special polymer flat-plate collector is used, filled with ceramic/clay granulates. Filling with granulates helps keep the water level stable in the space heating tank, independently of the collector loop pump status (operation or standstill), and secures a turbulent flow in the collector channels. The DHW tank located inside the space heating tank is operated at the usual domestic water pressure.

A diagram of the system is shown in Figure 4.13.

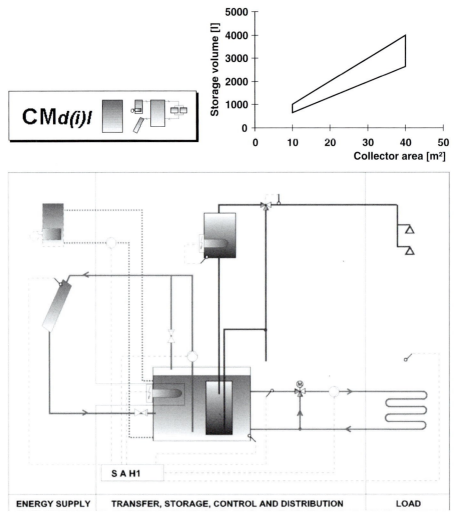

Figure 4.13. Hydraulic scheme System #9b

Heat management philosophy

All system functions except DHW auxiliary heating are controlled by a single control unit.

The pump of the collector loop is controlled according to the temperature difference between the collector sensor and the sensor at the bottom of the storage tank. For the start-up phase, a special control feature is provided to remove from the collector the air present during standstill.

The supply of auxiliary heat for space heating is basically under the control of a thermostat. Optionally, a dynamic thermostat function can be provided (thermostat setting dependent on the outdoor temperature). In the case of electricity as the auxiliary energy source, the controller is programmable in order to utilize off-peak electricity at night.

The heat transport to the space heating loop is controlled by an 'on/off' operation of the floor circulation pump, and/or thermostat valves at the manifold of the floor distribution lines. The control parameters are the outdoor temperature, the solar irradiance (through the windows) and, optionally, the wind speed (in coastal regions).

A separate thermostat controls the auxiliary heater for DHW.

Specific aspects

Overheating and freeze protection are provided by the drainback principle.

Influence of the auxiliary energy source on system design and dimensioning

This system can be used either with a gas or an oil auxiliary boiler, or with a long-running-time boiler (e.g. wood in the form of logs). Alternatively, an auxiliary electrical heater can be installed into the space heating storage tank.

Cost (range)

The total cost of the whole system in Norway is about €11,000, with a 20 m² collector, a 2000 litre storage tank, a gas or oil boiler and a heating floor. Installation costs are included in these figures. A similar reference system without solar heating costs about €8000.

Market distribution

This system was launched on the Norwegian market in 1997. About 4000 m² of collectors have been installed.

4.4.12 System #10: advanced small DHW tank in space heating tank (Switzerland)

Main features

In this system, a DHW tank is built in the space heating storage tank. A heat exchanger is series-connected to the built-in tank, for pre-heating cold water and stratification enhancement in the combitank. The total storage capacitance is 950 litres, with 250 litres used for the DHW tank. For space heating, the system works as a pre-heating system.

A diagram of the system is shown in Figure 4.14.

Heat management philosophy

A simple differential controller controls the pump of the collector loop. A thermostat with a typical set-point temperature of 55°C controls the heating of the upper part of the storage tank by auxiliary energy.

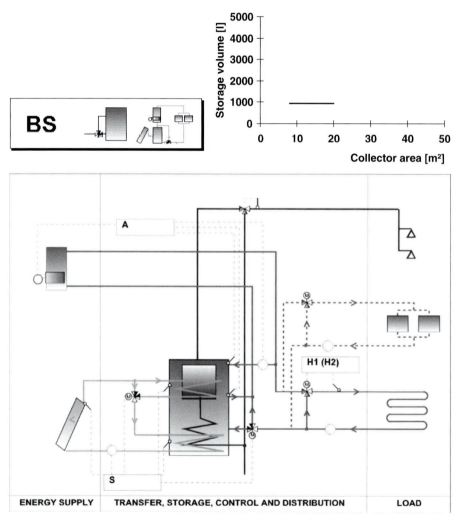

Figure 4.14. Hydraulic scheme System #10

Specific aspects
Overheating is prevented by cooling the lower part of the storage tank after the sun has set by using the collector as a heat sink.

Influence of the auxiliary energy source on system design and dimensioning
In this system, an auxiliary boiler with power modulation, i.e. with gas or oil as the auxiliary energy source, should be used. Modulation can also be by intermittent operation.

Cost (range)
The total cost of the system is about €17,700, for a 12 m² collector, a 950 litre storage tank and a heating floor. Installation costs are included in these figures. A similar reference system without solar heating costs about €11,000.

Market distribution
This system was introduced in Switzerland at the end of the 1990s. By the end of 1999, more than 100 systems with a total collector area of about 1000 m² had been installed.

4.4.13 System #11: space heating store with DHW load-side heat exchanger(s) and external auxiliary boiler (Finland and Sweden)

Main features
The tank in this system is fitted with an immersed horizontal finned-coil heat exchanger for DHW preparation and another heat exchanger in the bottom for the collector loop. An electric heater, operating on demand, heats the upper third of the tank. The optional use of a wood boiler or a pellet burner is very common in these systems. By 2002, a variant had become available with a pellet burner integrated into the store. In Sweden, an optional heat exchanger is generally used for DHW pre-heating as this significantly improves the thermal performance of the system. In Finland, this system is usually designed with a smaller collector area and a smaller storage tank (750 litres) than in Sweden.
A diagram of the system is shown in Figure 4.15.

Heat management philosophy
The pump of the collector loop is under the control of a differential controller. The pump is switched off when the temperature at the collector outlet reaches 95°C. No control for space heating and auxiliary boiler is included in the system. The electric heater is under control of a separate thermostat.

Specific aspects
Overheating is prevented by using a relatively small expansion vessel (10–30% of collector loop volume), and by allowing a high pressure of up to 6–9 bar. This high pressure ensures that the fluid in the collector does not boil. However, as a result of Task 26 work, at least one company moved to a low-pressure collector circuit

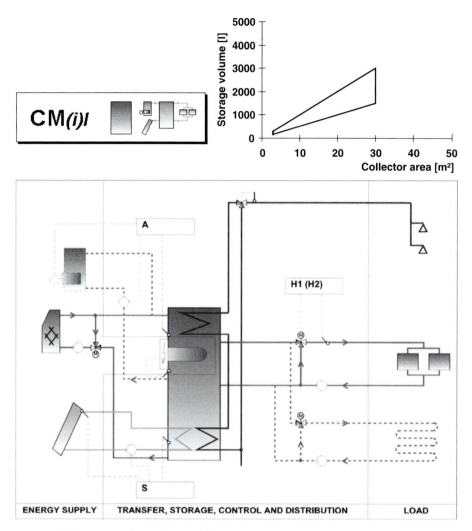

Figure 4.15. Hydraulic scheme System #11

where, during stagnation, the contents of the collector are pushed down into the expansion vessel.

As a result of the way in which DHW is prepared, there is no legionella risk. Some companies sell a variant with the internal DHW heat exchanger replaced with an external load-side heat exchanger unit.

Influence of the auxiliary energy source on system design and dimensioning

Depending on the type of auxiliary boiler used, the outlet connection is located at the bottom of the tank (as with a wood logs boiler) or in the middle of it (as with a pellet boiler). In the first case, the whole tank is heated when the boiler is used. In the second case, only the upper part is heated. One or more buffer tanks can be added in conjunction with a wood boiler. In this way, the boiler's requirement for a large volume is satisfied and the collector loop can still use a part of the whole volume, by manually or automatically connecting or disconnecting the buffer tanks.

An electric auxiliary heater is always included in the tank.

Cost (range)

In Sweden, a typical system with 10 m^2 of solar collectors and a 1500 litre storage with a wood boiler as auxiliary, costs about €12,300. A similar reference system without solar heating costs about €8600.

In Finland, a typical system with 7 m^2 of solar collectors and a 700 litre storage without boiler (all auxiliary energy with electricity) costs about €9100. A similar reference system without solar heating costs about €6100.

Market distribution

This system has been marketed in Sweden since 1990 and remains the dominant type on the Swedish market. Up to 2000, about five companies had installed between 10,000 and 20,000 m^2 of solar collectors. In Finland, this system is quite new. About 80 systems with 800 m^2 of solar collectors have been installed, from Helsinki to beyond the Arctic Circle.

In Sweden, three or four companies are manufacturing these storage tanks and about the same number of manufacturers produce the collectors. Marketing is by several companies. It is the preferred system among self-builders in Sweden, involving some 20 small companies.

In Finland, two companies are manufacturing and four companies are selling these systems.

4.4.14 System #12: space heating store with DHW load-side heat exchanger(s) and external auxiliary boiler (advanced version) (Sweden)

Main features

This system is very similar to the previous system but with greater sophistication in the collector loop, in the space heating loop and in the controller. Two immersed heat exchangers are connected to the collector loop to increase the thermal stratification in the storage tank.

A diagram of the system is shown in Figure 4.16.

Heat management philosophy

The collector loop pump is turned on under the control of the absorber plate temperature. The speed of this pump is then controlled by the temperature difference between the collector outlet and the temperature of either the top or bottom tank sensor, depending upon whether the DHW section or the space

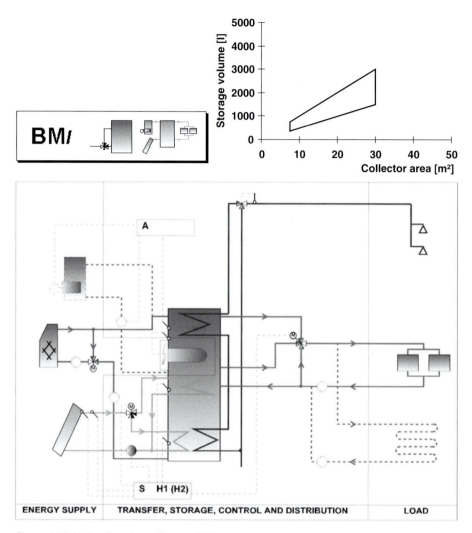

Figure 4.16. Hydraulic scheme System #12

heating section of the tank is to be heated. The space heating loop is connected to the tank with a four-way valve, enabling heat delivery from the central part of the tank.

The electric heater is under the control of a separate thermostat, but is locked out by the solar controller when the collector loop pump is running.

Monitoring capabilities and the ability to compute energy balances are included in the controller, which can be easily connected to a PC.

Specific aspects, influence of the auxiliary energy source on system design and dimensioning are identical to those of the previous system.

Cost (range)
A typical system with 10 m² of solar collectors and a 1500 litre storage tank with a wood boiler as auxiliary costs about €13,300. A similar reference system without solar heating costs about €8600.

Market distribution
One company in Sweden has marketed this system since 1993. By 2000, this company had installed about 2000 m² of solar collectors, but the market share of this system is decreasing. Separate companies generally produce the combitank and controller.

4.4.15 System #13: two stores (series) (Austria)

Main features
This is a two-store system in which the space heating and the DHW storage tank sizes can be independently chosen. The collector loop with 20–50 m² of solar collectors heats one or more storage tanks (typical main storage tank volume is 60–100 litres per m²). This space heating storage is stratified by means of an external valve that appropriately directs hot water from the collector heat exchanger to the middle or top of the tank. The upper part of this storage tank is connected to an auxiliary boiler. DHW is heated by running a pump that circulates space heating water through an immersed heat exchanger in the DHW storage tank (typical DHW storage tank volume is 200–500 litres depending on the expected draw-off profile).
   A diagram of the system is shown in Figure 4.17.

Heat management philosophy
If the temperature at the collector outlet is higher than the temperature at the bottom of the tank, the pump of the collector loop is started. The secondary pump only starts when the temperature at the heat exchanger is higher than the temperature at the bottom of the tank. The three-way valve is operated in accordance with the temperature at the heat exchanger.
   The DHW pump is started when the temperature in the DHW tank is lower than the set-point temperature, and if the temperature of the space heating store is high enough.
   If the temperature of the space heating store is lower than the set-point temperature, the auxiliary boiler starts.

Specific aspects
This system is designed for low-flow collectors.

Influence of the auxiliary energy source on system design and dimensioning
Because of the size of the storage tank, an auxiliary wood boiler can be easily used, but an auxiliary gas or oil boiler can also be connected to the system.

Cost (range)

A typical system with 30 m² of solar collectors, a 350 litre tank for DHW and a 2000 litre space heating store costs about €20,300, with a wood boiler as auxiliary. A similar reference system without solar heating costs about €10,700.

Market distribution

This system has been distributed in Austria since 1994. Four companies are marketing this system, with a total collector area of about 20,000 m² in operation by 2002.

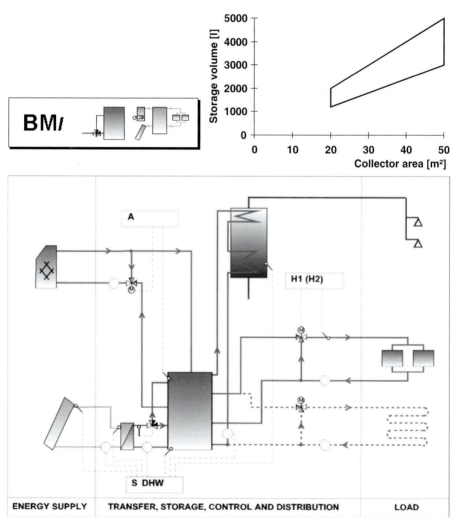

Figure 4.17. Hydraulic scheme System #13

4.4.16 System #14: two stores (parallel) (Austria)

Main features

This system is representative of a group of systems. All geometric parameters can be varied. Either immersed or external heat exchangers may be used, as well as stratifiers. Auxiliary boilers with either possible intermittent operation or long running times can be used. In the first case, the boiler can be connected directly to the heat emission loop. In the second case, the space heating storage tank is used as a buffer tank for the boiler.

Diagrams of the two systems are shown in Figures 4.18 and 4.19.

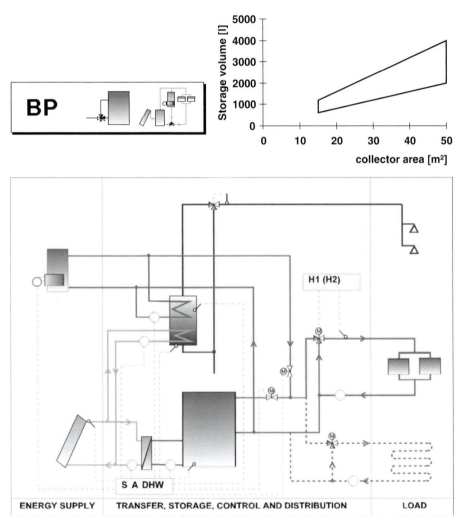

Figure 4.18. Hydraulic scheme System #14a

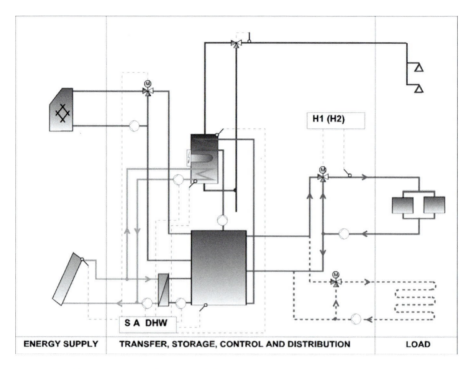

Figure 4.19. Hydraulic scheme System #14b

Heat management philosophy

In winter, the solar collectors deliver heat to the coldest tank. In summer, priority is given to the DHW tank, which is heated to the maximum temperature allowed before heating of the space heating tank begins. If a power-modulating auxiliary boiler is used, heat is delivered directly to the space heating loop, as long as the temperature at the top of the space heating tank is below the temperature needed for the space heating loop. Otherwise, the auxiliary boiler is switched off and heat is taken from the space heating tank.

Specific aspects

A large expansion vessel, dimensioned so that it is able to contain the fluid volume expelled from the collectors by the vapour produced in them when stagnation occurs, provides overheating protection.

Influence of the auxiliary energy source on system design and dimensioning
If an auxiliary solid-fuel boiler is used, the hydraulic scheme is modified as follows: the heat produced by the boiler is always delivered to the space heating tank in order to decouple the boiler and heat-load mass flows, and to guarantee a sufficiently long running time for the boiler. The auxiliary energy for the DHW tank is then delivered from the space heating tank. An electric heater is used during summer to prevent the boiler from switching on.

Cost (range)
A typical BP system (see Table 4.2 for classification) with 30 m^2 of solar collectors, 350 litres for DHW and a 2000-litre heating storage costs about €19,300, with a gas or oil boiler as auxiliary. A similar reference system without solar heating costs about €8000. A typical BM system with 30 m^2 of solar collectors, 350 litres for DHW and a 2000 litre heating storage costs about €20,300, with a wood boiler as auxiliary. A similar reference system without solar heating costs about €10,700.

Market distribution
This system has been distributed in Austria since 1994. Four to five companies are marketing this system, with a collector area of 15,000 m^2 installed yearly.

4.4.17 System #15: two stratifiers in a space heating storage tank with an external load-side heat exchanger for DHW (Germany)

Main features
This system is constructed as a compact unit, in which all components (auxiliary condensing gas burner, DHW flat-plate heat exchanger with its primary pump, solar loop, heat exchanger and solar hydraulic unit) are integrated. Consequently, the installation time is reduced because of the reduction in the number of connections needed. The solar storage tank works as an optimized energy manager for all types of incoming energy (from the solar collectors, a gas burner, etc.) and outgoing energy (domestic hot water, space heating water).
   A diagram of the system is shown in Figure 4.20.

Heat management philosophy
The speed of the collector loop pump is controlled to reach an optimal loading temperature in the storage tank and also to maintain a minimum flow rate in the collector to ensure good heat transfer. The DHW temperature is brought up to the

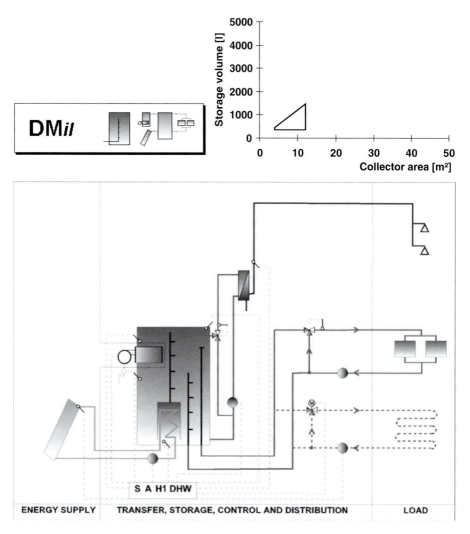

Figure 4.20. Hydraulic scheme System #15

set–point temperature by controlling the speed of the pump located in the primary loop of the heat exchanger. Heat delivered to the space heating loop is controlled by a pump with variable flow rate automatically controlled by the thermostatic valves of the radiators (to save pump energy and to make sure there is no noise produced by the radiator valves). The power of the gas burner can be modulated between 5 and 20 kW, depending on the temperature in the tank and the requested temperature of the space heating loop (calculated from the outside air temperature, the room temperature and the time of the day).

Specific aspects

Solar energy input to the storage tank is provided by an immersed low-flow heat exchanger in co-operation with stratifying tubes (low-flow technology).

Beginning in 2002, the external load-side heat exchanger for DHW has been located apart from the store; previously, it was located under the store insulation. Moreover, a new thermostatic valve has been mounted on the heat exchanger inlet line from the store, to limit the inlet temperature to 65°C. The new design facilitates maintenance and provides better protection against scaling of the heat exchanger.

Another change since 1999 has been the new controller with a provision for controlling two (instead of one) space heating loops with mixing valves. The integration of this additional control function saves €1340 for the customer, compared with the acquisition of a second separate control unit for the second space heating hydraulic loop.

Influence of the auxiliary energy source on system design and dimensioning

This system is designed with a condensing gas burner integrated into the storage tank. During the course of Task 26, the burner efficiency was improved by 1% in the heating period, by modifying the heat exchanger. All other auxiliary energy boilers (e.g. wood or pellet burners) can be easily connected to the storage tank without additional heat exchangers.

Cost (range)

The total cost of the system (space heating emission loop and installation included) is between €13,040 for a system with a 5 m² collector and a 400 litre storage tank, and €16,850 for a system with a 12 m² collector and a 750 litre storage tank. A similar reference system without solar heating costs about €9000.

Market distribution

This system has been marketed in Germany since 1997. About 22 sale offices in Germany are marketing this system directly to 800–1000 plumbers, with more than 3000 units and 20,000 m² of solar collectors sold to date.

4.4.18 System #16: conical stratifier in space heating store with load-side heat exchanger for DHW (Germany)

Main features

The collector loop of this system works on the drainback principle, using water as heat transfer fluid. The flow rate in the collector loop is variable. The system works as a pre-heating system for space heating.

A diagram of the system is shown in Figure 4.21.

Heat management philosophy

The flow rate in the collector loop can vary from 20–100% of the maximum flow. When the temperature at the middle of the storage tank is below 45°C, the flow

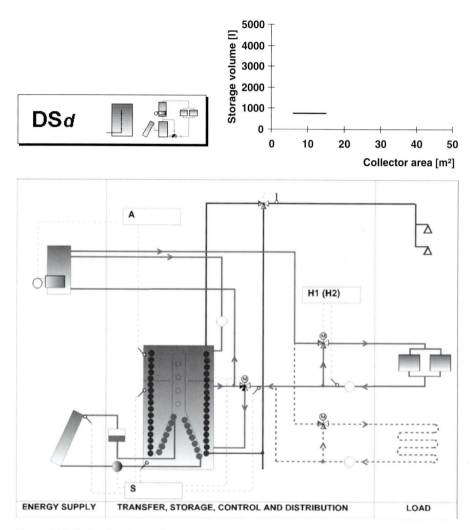

Figure 4.21. Hydraulic scheme System #16

rate in the collector loop is adjusted to give a difference of 30°C between the collector outlet and the middle of the tank. Otherwise, it is adjusted to 15°C. When the temperature at the middle of the storage tank exceeds 90°C, or if the temperature difference between the collector outlet and the bottom of the tank drops below 4°C, the collector loop pump is switched off. When the temperature at the top of the storage tank drops below 54°C, auxiliary heating is activated. When the temperature at the middle of the storage tank is 3°C higher than the space heating loop return temperature, the three-way valve is opened to allow circulation through the tank.

Specific aspects
The collector loop heat exchanger is placed in a conical stratifier surmounted by a vertical pipe with horizontal outlets at different levels to allow stratified charging of the store. As a result of the relatively large opening at the bottom of this stratification device, the flow rate on the secondary side is two to three times larger than the flow rate through the collector loop heat exchanger. For the preparation of DHW a smooth-tube heat exchanger is mounted on the inside of the tank wall. The upper part of the tank is only used to heat DHW and is separated from the lower part for space heating by a horizontal plate to maintain thermal stratification. The drainback construction gives protection from overheating and freezing.

Influence of the auxiliary energy source on system design and dimensioning
The storage tank works as a pre-heating device for the boiler. Hence, it is important that the boiler can be operated intermittently. To allow long periods of operation with resulting energy savings, the minimum heating power should be as low as possible.

Cost (range)
The total cost for this system with 10 m² of solar collectors (auxiliary boiler and radiator loop included) is about €18,450. A similar reference system, without solar heating, costs about €9000.

Market distribution
This system has been on the market since 1996. The total collector area in operation until 2000 was about 1000 m².

4.4.19 System #17: tank open to the atmosphere with three heat exchangers (Germany)

Main features
The heart of this storage tank comprises three thermosiphon heat exchangers with stratifiers, which allow charge and discharge without using pumps. The DHW is heated instantaneously in the upper heat exchanger. This method guarantees the hygienic quality of DHW from large volume tanks. The tank operates at atmospheric pressure and is constructed of long-lasting polypropylene material, which avoids corrosion problems. The insulation material is expanded polypropylene foam and complies with environmental requirements regarding production, usage and disposal. The system works as a pre-heating system for space heating.

A diagram of the system is shown in Figure 4.22.

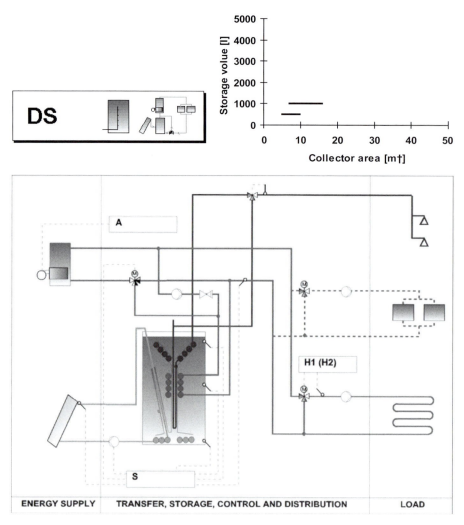

Figure 4.22. Hydraulic scheme System #17

Heat management philosophy

The system is operated in three different modes:

- summer mode 1: interval-pumping mode, when the collector temperature is higher than the temperature at the bottom of the storage tank (pump is run at intervals to give a usable water temperature)
- summer mode 2: permanent pumping mode, when the collector temperature is higher than a set-point temperature at the top of the tank (e.g. 60°C)
- winter mode: permanent pumping mode, when the collector temperature is higher than the temperature at the bottom of the storage tank.

An optional control feature is automatic change between summer and winter modes, based on the temperature in the space heating loop.

Specific aspects

The solar heat exchanger is placed at the bottom of the tank and the tank is charged via a stratifier with two outlets: the lower outlet allows pre-heating of the lower part of the tank and the upper outlet delivers solar-heated water for immediate use. The level of water in the store has to be checked every two to three years. Instantaneous heating of DHW in the heat exchanger eliminates the risk of legionella. The very light tank makes this system easy to install.

Influence of the auxiliary energy source on system design and dimensioning

The system is not suitable for wood-fired boilers burning logs because the buffer volume is too small. Electrical heating devices are offered as an option.

Cost (range)

The total cost of the system (auxiliary boiler and heating floor included) is €13,750–15,050, for a collector area of 6–10 m². A similar reference system without solar heating costs about €9000.

Market distribution

This system has been available since 1996, marketed by two companies. The total collector area in operation is about 14,400 m², with about 1800 systems installed by 450 companies in several countries: Germany, Austria, Italy, France, Switzerland, Spain and Belgium.

4.4.20 System #18: finned-tube load-side DHW heat exchanger in stratifier (Germany)

Main features

This system is a one-store system, in which DHW is instantaneously heated in a finned-tube heat exchanger with a maximum discharge power of about 50 kW. The DHW heat exchanger is placed at the top of the tank in a vessel with a vertical tube extending to the bottom of the tank. The water circulates by natural convection and a thermo-hydraulic valve regulates the flow rate in the tube. There is an external heat exchanger in the collector loop. Horizontal inlet pipes with two inlet positions – one for solar-heated water and one for the space heating return – enhance thermal stratification. Three different sizes of storage tanks are available: 500, 850 and 1200 litre, with typical collector areas of 10–25 m². The system works as a pre-heating system for space heating. All auxiliary boilers, with intermittent operation or with long running time, can be used.

A diagram of the system is shown in Figure 4.23.

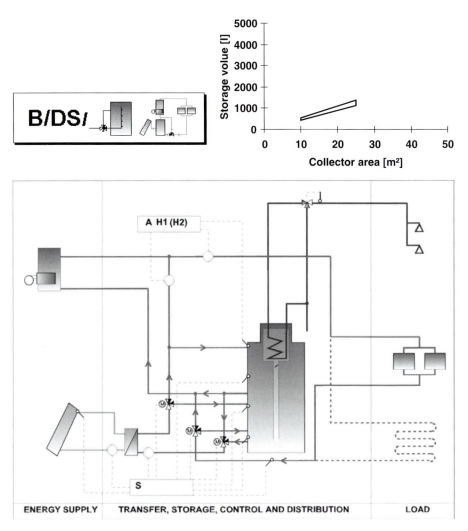

Figure 4.23. Hydraulic scheme System #18

Heat management philosophy

The collector pump is controlled by the temperature difference between the collector outlet and the bottom of the store. The boiler used for space heating also supplies auxiliary energy for the DHW cycle at the top of the tank, and is controlled by a thermostat with a typical set point of 55–60°C. When the temperature in the tank is too low, the boiler supplies heat directly to the space heating distribution loop, thus bypassing the tank and helping to reduce heat losses.

Specific aspects

In order to achieve a high degree of stratification in the storage tank, the flow of water through the vertical tube inside the tank is regulated by a thermo-hydraulic valve placed inside the tube beneath the heat exchanger. The valve is connected to expandable material at the DHW outlet. In this way, the DHW outlet temperature is almost constant, independent of the hot water demand and of the water temperature in the store. Any discharge of water via the DHW heat exchanger results in cold water (about 20–30°C) flowing through the tube to the bottom of the tank. A large expansion vessel, dimensioned so that it is able to contain the fluid volume expelled from the collectors by the vapour produced in them when stagnation occurs, provides overheating protection.

Influence of the auxiliary energy source on system design and dimensioning

This system can be used either with an auxiliary boiler capable of intermittent operation (gas or oil) or with a long-running-time boiler. In the latter case, the hydraulic scheme is slightly different; the tank is not series-connected in the return line of the space heating loop, but is used as a buffer tank for the boiler.

Cost (range)

The cost of the tank is between €2300 (500 litres) and €3225 (1200 litres). The total cost of the system (auxiliary boiler and radiator loop included) is €15,700 for a system with a 10 m² collector and a 500 litre storage tank, €17,800 for a system with a 14 m² collector and an 850 litre storage tank, and €18,100 for a system with a 14 m² collector and a 1200 litre storage tank. A similar reference system without solar heating costs about €9000.

Market distribution

One company in Germany has marketed this system since 1997, and several hundred systems have been sold. However, by 2002 it had disappeared from the market. The market trend is towards simpler and cheaper systems.

4.4.21 System #19: centralized heat production, distributed heat load, stratified storage (Austria)

Main features

The system is intended to supply estates of terraced houses or multi-family dwellings. For the best possible system operation, low-temperature heating systems (wall or floor heating with a maximum flow temperature of 50°C) are required. The individual houses or flats are supplied from the central storage tank via a local heating network operated at about 60°C. DHW is prepared in each individual house or flat by means of decentralized, once-through heat exchanger units connected to the local heating network. In a previous variant (1999), decentralized DHW storage tanks were provided instead of the once-through heat exchanger units. With this system configuration, the local network was periodically operated at 65–70°C to reload the decentralized stores, whereas the normal operational temperature was about 40°C for the supply of heat for space heating. During DHW reload (2–4 hours a day), the space heating was switched off.

A diagram of the system is shown in Figure 4.24.

Heat management philosophy

- *Collector loop*: the collector loop pump starts when the temperature at the collector outlet is higher than the temperature at the bottom of the tank. On the secondary side, the pump only starts when the temperature at the heat exchanger inlet is higher than the temperature at the bottom of the tank. Both pumps are switched off when the temperature at the heat exchanger inlet drops

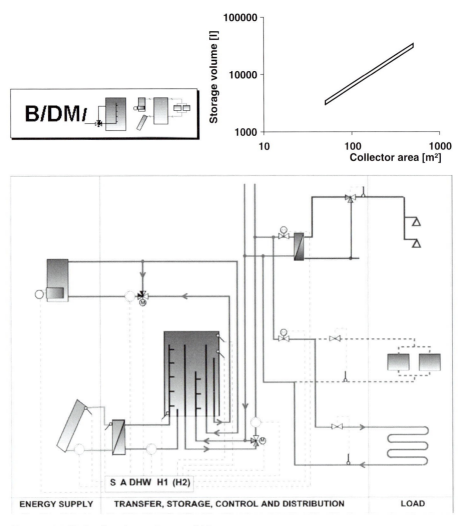

Figure 4.24. Hydraulic scheme System #19

below the temperature at the bottom of the tank. The two loops are operated on a low-flow principle.

- *Auxiliary boiler, auxiliary heat storage volume*: the biomass boiler starts up when the solar yields are insufficient to heat the tank above 60°C, and runs until the middle sensor reaches approximately 65°C. This temperature level in the upper part of the store is needed to provide about 50°C at the primary side of the DHW once-through heat exchangers. The volume for the storage of the auxiliary heat is calculated according to the expected peak heat load and the heat power of the auxiliary heater.
- *Space heating*: heat is supplied for space heating using one or two differential-pressure-regulated network pumps and regulated by the outside air temperature. In the case of two pumps, they are of different sizes and operate in parallel.
- *Preparation of DHW*: the DHW heat exchanger is maintained at a temperature of about 50°C at the inlet over the whole year, by a continuous small mass flow rate through the heat exchanger. If a DHW demand occurs, the valve on the primary side of the DHW heat exchanger opens and the DHW set-point temperature controls the mass flow through the valve. The heat exchanger is designed for a maximum DHW demand of up to 15 litres/minute.

Influence of the auxiliary energy source on system design and dimensioning

Biomass (woodchips or pellets) is usually used as auxiliary energy. Oil, gas or district heating could also be used.

Cost (range)

Because of the wide variety of plants, the costs, especially the cost for the heating loop, depend very strongly on the number and sizes of dwellings as well as on the collector size. Therefore, for easier comparison, both the total and the reference costs given for systems exclude the heating loop, and are related to the collector area. The cost for the solar heating system includes the roof-mounted collectors, collector piping with insulation, solar hydraulic equipment, antifreeze fluid and a woodchip boiler. The total cost varies between €720/m^2 for a small system (50 m^2 collector and a 3 m^3 storage tank) and €310/m^2 for a large system (500 m^2 collector and a 30 m^3 storage tank).

Reference cost for the same size of heating system without solar collectors varies between €220/m^2 and €60/m^2 (cost given per m^2 of solar collector in the corresponding solar heating systems), so that the solar-related additional cost varies between €500 and €250/m^2 of solar collector.

Market distribution

This system has been marketed in Austria since 2000 and several systems, with a total collector area of more than 4000 m^2, have been sold. (The first variant had been marketed since 1997 and five systems, with a total collector area of 450 m^2, had been sold.) Several companies manufacture and market this system. So far, it has only been installed in Austria.

4.4.22 Large systems for seasonal heat storage

Main features

These systems can be considered as long-term storage systems since the tank sizes may be several cubic metres. The goal is to achieve high solar fractions. Two systems are presented below. The first is already on the market, whereas the second is a prototype.

4.4.22.1 System #20: large tank-in-tank for seasonal heat storage (Switzerland)

Main features

This system is very similar to the Swiss system 'small DHW tank in space heating tank' (System #9a). A DHW tank with a characteristic shape is placed in the space heating storage tank. Three-way valves control heat charge to and discharge from the storage tank. A high solar fraction can be obtained in a single-family house with a collector area up to 100 m² and a storage volume up to 20 m³.

A diagram of the system is shown in Figure 4.25.

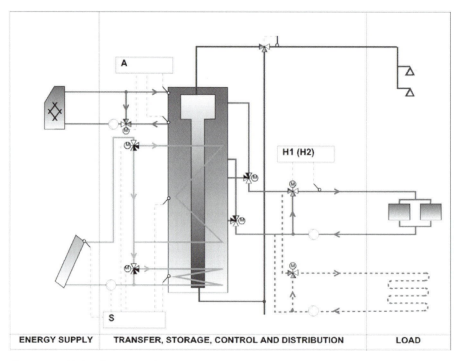

Figure 4.25. Hydraulic scheme System #20

Influence of the auxiliary energy source on system design and dimensioning

This system can be used either with an auxiliary boiler capable of intermittent operation (gas or oil) or with a long-running-time boiler.

Market distribution

About 40 systems, with a mean collector area of 60 m² and a mean storage volume of 15 m³, have been installed by 2000 in Switzerland. Some systems are also found in the South of Germany. One company produces the combitank.

4.4.22.2 System #21: large stratified tank for seasonal heat storage, air heating system (Germany)

Main features

This system, installed in a passive solar office building, can be considered as a prototype. It has 64 m² roof-integrated solar collectors and an 87 m³ storage tank.

A diagram of the system is shown in Figure 4.26.

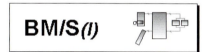

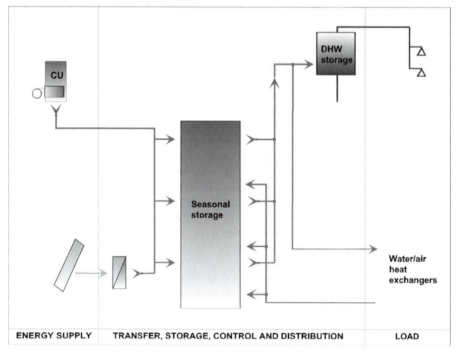

Figure 4.26. Hydraulic scheme System #21

Heat management philosophy

To maintain good stratification, heat can be charged to and discharged from the storage tank at different levels. The storage tank is charged by the solar collectors and a cogeneration unit (CU). The hydraulic scheme only indicates the energy flows within the system, without any detail on the hydraulics used for transferring heat.

Specific aspects

A mechanical heating and ventilating system delivers heat for space heating.

Influence of the auxiliary energy source on system design and dimensioning

In this prototype, a cogeneration unit provides auxiliary energy, but a conventional boiler could also be used.

REFERENCE

Suter J-M, Letz Th, Weiss W and Inäbnit J, 2000, *Solar Combisystems in Austria, Denmark, Finland, France, Germany, Sweden, Switzerland, the Netherlands and the USA – Overview 2000*, IEA SH&C Task 26 Solar Combisystems.

5 Building-related aspects of solar combisystems

Peter Kovács, Werner Weiss, Irene Bergmann, Michaela Meir and John Rekstad

The integration of a solar heating system into buildings becomes increasingly relevant with the trend towards large solar contributions. Appropriate surfaces have to be found by the architect for the large collector areas, and both aesthetics and building physics have to be taken into consideration. Roof and façade integration of collectors is discussed in Section 5.2. Large collector areas require correspondingly large storage volumes. Floor space requirements, especially for the heat store, are discussed in Section 5.1.

5.1 SPACE REQUIREMENTS

In the following, 'space requirement' will be discussed from different points of view, space requirement meaning the floor space that will be occupied by the system components placed indoors, traditionally in the boiler room, such as the storage tank, pumps, expansion vessels and a boiler. The heat distribution system, for instance, radiators, is not included in the space requirements in this context. After a short discussion of the benefits and drawbacks of a low space requirement, some hints on how to minimize this are given. Finally, 20 generic systems are rated with respect to their space requirements.

5.1.1 Is a low space requirement always desirable?

Obvious advantages of a low space requirement are that saved space is saved money, or space that can be used for other needs. Another, not so obvious, advantage is that a low space requirement also gives more freedom in the placement of the equipment. For example, it can in many ways be advantageous to put the storage tank and hydraulic equipment in the attic, near to the collector array, if this is possible. This will save piping length and reduce the cost of piping and installation, as well as reducing heat losses from the system. This option will of course be more feasible for a system with a small space requirement.

A low space requirement is often achieved through a high level of system integration, for example by integrating the auxiliary heater – a gas, pellet or oil burner – into the heat store, and by placing a number of small components inside the outer cover of the storage tank. There is obviously a risk that this will result in systems that are very impractical to maintain and repair. Such a risk should be considered in the design of a system, and also in planning the room where the system is to be placed. In the comparison that will follow, 0.2 metres on each side of a component was considered as a realistic 'installation and service space', in general. Some systems will require more, some less.

5.1.2 How to achieve a low space requirement?

Plenty of things can be done to reduce the space requirement of a system in general. Solid-fuel boilers (wood in the form of logs) are normally bigger than, for example, oil or pellet boilers, but, most of all, they will need a larger storage volume and thus require more floor space. As already mentioned, a well designed storage tank will reduce the space requirement without making installation and service a tough issue. On the contrary, assembling a number of components at the factory stage and integrating them with the tank will also facilitate the installation process, so that it can be carried out in a shorter time and with a reduced risk of error. Another quite obvious way to keep the space required low is to collect the required storage volume within one single vessel. Two 500 litre tanks may require up to 40% more floor space than one 1000 litre tank. Prerequisites for such an 'optimization' are, of course, that it does not interfere with the performance of the system, and that the optimized storage tank can still fit through the boiler room door. However, one store instead of two will in general also be an improvement with regard to storage losses.

Figure 5.1 shows an example of how both space requirement and installation time were reduced for a solar combisystem by combining several of the ideas discussed here. Finally, there is the possibility of completely removing the space heating store from the system or from the individual houses in a group of dwellings. Systems #1 and #3 show examples of the first option, where a concrete floor has

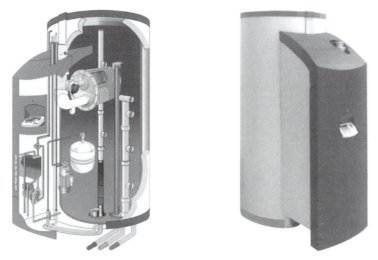

Figure 5.1. An example of fruitful minimization of space requirement and installation effort. Space heating store, condensing gas burner and hot water preparation, as well as the electronic control and hydraulic equipment, are packed into one compact unit (Source: SOLVIS, Germany)

taken over the role of the store. In a group of houses built close together, space in the individual houses can be saved at the expense of space in a common central heating plant. An example of how this can be solved is shown in System #19 in Chapter 4, and in Figures 5.7 and 5.8.

5.1.3 Space requirements of the 20 generic combisystems

In order to make the comparison of the generic systems more complete, the space requirements have also been compared. The comparison is mainly based on the following assumptions:

- a single-family house installation (except for System #19): one comparison is based on a typical size of the system, and one based on the range of sizes offered by the manufacturer for that system
- estimated space requirement, expressed as the floor area in the boiler room or similar, for storage tank(s), hydraulic equipment, expansion and drainback vessels, external boiler and all external heat exchangers (if provided)
- 0.2 metres of additional free space required for piping, on each side of any component that adds to the required space; exceptions may be storage tanks or boilers that are designed for minimum space requirement and therefore have all connections inside the nominal dimensions
- wall-mounted components that also take up floor space: if there is more than one in a system, only the largest (covering the largest floor area) is counted
- for systems that can be configured either for boilers with long running time (requiring large storage volume) or for boilers with intermittent operation (with smaller storage), only the latter is included in the comparison, as the space requirement for this option is more directly related to the collector area.

The space required for 20 of the generic combisystems is shown in Figures 5.2 and 5.3. In Figure 5.2, each system covers a range of collector areas frequently used in that system, corresponding to a range of space requirements. Some systems, e.g. System #1, have the same requirement independent of the collector area installed, because they use the heating floor as a heat sink instead of a water store for space heating. Most systems, however, show different amounts of increased space requirement as the collector area increases.

No simple rule of thumb could be derived from Figure 5.2, as the relationship between collector area and space requirement looks very different for different systems. In Figure 5.3, the systems are sorted by collector size and the space requirement for each generic system is calculated for the most frequently used size. The exceptions to space requirement being proportional to collector area are found in systems using a heating floor as a heat sink, highly integrated systems with the boiler and store in one single unit, and the multi-family house system, where the space requirement in the individual apartments is unaffected by an increase in the total collector area.

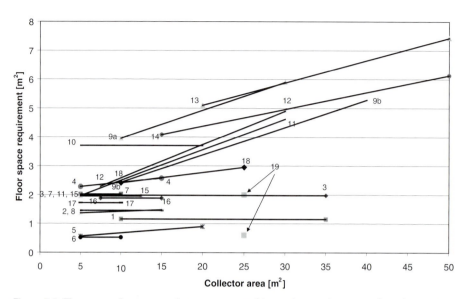

Figure 5.2. The range of space requirements covered by each generic system, from its smallest collector area to its largest. Note: for System #19, two figures are presented. For the higher figure the total space required has been divided by nine, thus referring to one of the nine apartments of the multi-family house supplied with heat by this system. The lower figure shows the actual space requirement in each apartment, excluding the boiler room space requirement

The following figures make the space requirements shown in Figure 5.3 a little clearer. The storage unit for the Dutch combisystem (System #6), as shown in Figure 5.4, is very compact and requires just 0.5 m² of floor space. This storage unit also contains the gas or oil burner for the auxiliary heating. Apart from the expansion vessel, all hydraulic and electronic components are also part of the compact unit. As a

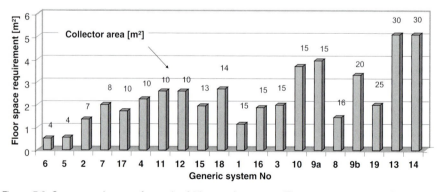

Figure 5.3. Space requirement for each of 20 generic systems. The systems are sorted by collector size (the figure on the top of the bar) and the size most frequently used in each system is the one used to calculate the space required. Note: for System #19, the figures have been divided by nine, thus referring to one of the nine apartments of the multi-family house supplied with heat by this system. If the space requirement does not include the boiler room space requirement, the figure will be much lower: only 0.6 m² per apartment. For System #1, no boiler space has been added because it should use a stove, which is normally placed in the living area

Figure 5.4. Compact storage–burner unit with very low space demand (Source: Daalderop, the Netherlands)

result of the design, it is also possible to install this unit in the living space should no cellar or attic be available. It should be mentioned that this storage unit is designed for small collector areas (4 m²), and accordingly for low fractional energy savings.

The storage unit and the boiler for the French System #3 is shown in Figure 5.5. The space requirement for this system, which is suitable for a collector area of 15 m², is about 1.8 m². Because of the high level of prefabrication of the storage unit, this system also has a relatively low space demand and requires only a reasonably small amount of work on site to connect the storage unit to the boiler and the collector array.

Compared to the space requirements shown above, the system shown in Figure 5.6 needs more space for the storage tank and the auxiliary boiler. It shows a system

Figure 5.5. Storage unit (foreground) and the boiler (background, left) for System #3 (Source: CLIPSOL, France)

Figure 5.6. Optimized version of System #14 (Source: AEE INTEC, Austria)

with a space heating store of 2.5 m³ and a wood boiler. Preparation of the domestic hot water is done with a load-side heat exchanger. The system is less compact, and also needs more work on site to assemble it. The space demand is 4–5 m².Because of the large space required for the heating store (2.5 m³), in the case shown it was also necessary to lower the floor. This system is designed for collector areas between 15 and 30 m².

Large solar combisystems for a group of houses, row houses or multi-family houses require less space relative to the living area of one house or flat compared to systems for single-family houses. For System #19, approximately 1.8 m² is needed per flat or house. Figure 5.7 shows the SUNDAYS housing estate in

Figure 5.7. General view of the SUNDAYS housing estate (Source: AEE INTEC, Austria)

Gleisdorf, Austria. It comprises six residential units and an office building, which is divided into three individual buildings; 210 m² of roof-integrated collectors were installed to supply the buildings with heat. A heat storage tank with a capacity of 14 m³ (Figure 5.8) was installed and connected to the solar heating system.

Figure 5.8. View of free-standing heat storage tank with a capacity of 14 m³ (Source: AEE INTEC, Austria)

5.2 ARCHITECTURAL INTEGRATION OF COLLECTOR ARRAYS

Normally, solar combisystems require large collector areas. The integration of solar collectors in the building skin, the roof or the façade, represents an obvious choice with several advantages. Section 5.2.1 shows examples of roof constructions with integrated collectors and the most important aspects of the building physics of a roof. Different principles are illustrated for mounting a collector roof. Nevertheless, certain problems exist concerning roof-collector installations and these are discussed. Façade-integrated collectors are less common today. Section 5.2.2 demonstrates the advantages of façade-integrated collectors, with regard to energetic performance, building physics and architectural aesthetics. Detailed studies have been carried out in Austria and the results are presented. In Section 5.2.3, many successful examples of architectural solutions for roof- and façade-integrated collectors are shown. Finally, in Section 5.2.4, a short overview is given of the aspects that have to be considered by the architects and planners in the early planning phases of a building with solar heating.

The growing interest in solar combisystems brings new challenges for architects, building services, engineers and the solar industry. The collector area needed for these systems is substantially larger than for solar domestic hot water systems. The usual range of collector areas of a solar combisystem is between 10 and 30 m² for a single-family house, and can go up to several hundred square metres if the system is designed for multi-family houses. At this size, the collector array becomes a dominant architectural element. It is therefore necessary to improve the appearance of the collectors, which can be regarded as multifunctional building elements that provide both shelter and heat. As solar collectors involve both technology and architecture, and also demonstrate social and ecological awareness, the concerted professional efforts of engineers and architects are needed to make a success of the integration of solar collectors into the building envelope.

In most cases, solar collectors installed on a flat roof look like a foreign body on the building (Figure 5.9). As a result of the structure that is needed to support the collectors, this type of installation is one of the most expensive solutions.

Figure 5.9. Collectors installed on a flat roof are not the most aesthetically pleasing solution for a solar collector array. Because of the cost of the supporting structure, this approach is also more expensive than a building-integrated solution (Source: SOLTOP Schuppisser, Switzerland)

If the architect integrates the collector array into the overall design, it is possible to find good solutions, even if the collectors have to be mounted on buildings with flat roofs or roofs sloping to the north. Nevertheless, these solutions have the disadvantage that the pipes and the reverse side of the collectors are exposed to ambient temperatures and the wind, and, especially during the winter, have higher losses than collectors integrated into the building envelope. Last but not least, the full market penetration of solar combisystems may even be more dependent on a successful building integration than on prices and technology; see, for example, Figure 5.10.

In principle, there are two main options for integrating solar collectors into the building envelope: integration into the roof and the integration into the façade.

Figure 5.10. 87 m² of solar thermal collector in a south-orientated façade for domestic hot water preparation and space heating for an office and factory building in Vorarlberg, Austria (Source: AKS DOMA, Austria)

5.2.1 Roof integration

A building is a complex system that is exposed to varying external and internal loads. The primary task of the roof is to protect the building interior from the effects of various weather conditions. One of the main requirements of the roof is that it should be watertight. If a roof is not made watertight from the start, it is very difficult to find leaks. This is also the case for a collector roof. If the details of integration are not correct, the leakage risk will be higher. As well as the details of the roof integration, it is strongly recommended that the solar collectors themselves are tested and confirmed to be watertight before they are used on the roof.

Conventional roof-mounted collectors of solar domestic hot water systems are small, external installations with little influence on the physical performance of the roof. However, the larger and building-integrated collector arrays required for solar combisystems have a certain impact on the physical performance of the roof or the façade.

5.2.1.1 Cold roof

A common roof construction in central and northern Europe is the 'cold roof', where the space under the roof cover is thermally insulated from the interior of the building (Figure 5.11). The cold roof is normally well ventilated and the temperature under the roof closely follows the daily and seasonal variations of the ambient temperature. As shown in Figure 5.11 (right), the most straightforward way of obtaining roof integration is replacing the tiles with solar collectors, which consist of a transparent cover, absorber and insulation.

For most of the time, the collector array has a higher temperature than the standard roof and adds no additional risk of condensation and increased humidity.

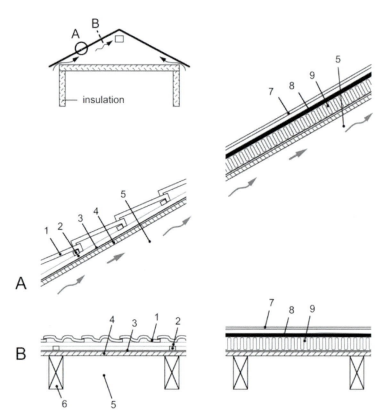

Figure 5.11. Cross-section of a 'cold roof' construction without (left) and with (right) integrated collectors, seen from the side (A) and from the bottom (B). Good ventilation is ensured. 1 – roof tiles; 2 – battens/counter battens; 3 – waterproof membrane; 4 – roof boarding; 5 – attic; 6 – rafters; 7 – solar collector cover; 8 – absorber; 9 – thermal insulation of the collector

As collectors are normally lighter than standard roofing materials, an integrated collector roof adds no extra load to the load-bearing construction.

5.2.1.2 Warm roof

As a result of the increasing specific costs of the living area, the 'warm roof' has become more common because it increases the living space. While the cold roof is built rather simply, the warm roof is a more complex construction, which has to balance the physical processes caused by the variations in temperature and humidity during the year. Figure 5.12 (left) shows a warm-roof construction with thermal insulation between the rafters. Several variations of the warm-roof construction exist (Lutz *et al.*, 1997). The principle of this system is to allow a constant flow of cold air above the insulation but below the roofing material. The vapour barrier toward the warm side of the building, the vapour-permeable barrier above the insulation layer and the ventilation gap all prohibit warm and humid air from inside being trapped in the insulation layer and the load-bearing roof construction during

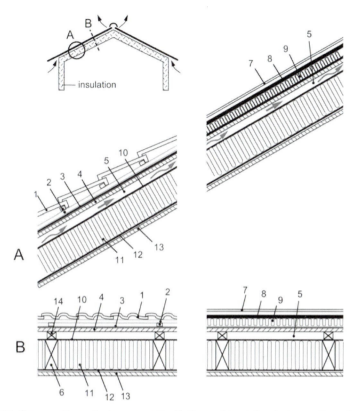

Figure 5.12. Cross-sections of a 'warm roof' with thermal insulation between the rafters and with a vented space. Construction without (left) and with (right) integrated collectors, seen from the side (A) and bottom (B). The integrated collectors improve the total thermal insulation of the roof. 1 – roof tiles; 2 – battens/counter battens; 3 – watertight membrane; 4 – roof boarding; 5 – vented space; 6 – rafters; 7 – solar collector cover; 8 – absorber; 9 – collector insulation; 10 – waterproof membrane (diffusion open); 11 – thermal insulation; 12 – vapour barrier; 13 – ceiling; 14 – battens

cold periods. Because of the presence of the ventilation gap, the temperature of the roof boarding is almost the same as the ambient temperature, which minimizes risk of condensation and of ice building up under the roof boarding. Replacing the tiles in a warm roof with solar collectors (Figure 5.13) increases the temperature of the roof cover and reduces the risks mentioned. Hence, the need for ventilation between the roof boarding and the roof insulation becomes less significant (NBI, 1991). The change of the thermal properties by roof-integrated collectors can, in many cases, justify simplification of the roof construction and lead to cost reductions.

Figure 5.14 shows an integrated collector array located on the upper part of the roof with conventional tiles on the roof below the collectors. As a result of the higher temperature and lower surface friction than roof tiles, snow will more easily slide down the collector roof. Under certain weather conditions, snow and ice can be trapped on the tiles below the collector array and can melt. The transitions between

Figure 5.13. Integration of the collector array into a warm-roof construction (Source: AEE INTEC, Austria). See colour plate 3.

different roof covers are weak points, leading to a higher risk of leaks. With regard to architectural design, working effort and costs, better results are normally obtained when the architect designs the building in such a way that the complete roof or natural divisions of the roof are covered by a solar collector array. All transitions between different roof covers require additional measures for safe rainwater transport, ventilation and avoiding accumulation of snow; all these cause additional costs.

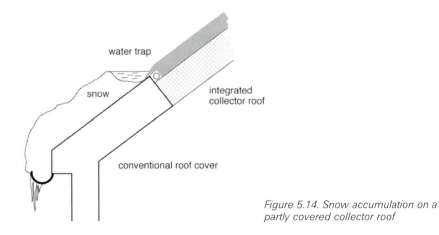

Figure 5.14. Snow accumulation on a partly covered collector roof

If the whole roof area is not needed for the collector array, the solution that is most aesthetic and most economic may be to cover the remaining roof area with a dummy collector. This dummy consists simply of a glass cover and a black–covered insulation layer. Visually, it is very similar to the solar collector (Figure 5.15).

The glass cover of the collectors is the waterproof layer and it replaces the roof tiles. To make the plumbing between the collector elements as easy and cheap as possible, chimneys and other building elements should be avoided in the collector roof.

Figure 5.15. Roof-integrated collectors. The far left and far right sections of the roof are dummies. As they are the same colour as the centre section, there is a uniform look to the whole roof. In this case two roof windows have also been integrated into the collector roof (Source: AEE INTEC, Austria). See colour plate 4.

5.2.1.3 Roof installation

Traditionally, HVAC (Heating, Ventilation and Air Conditioning) tradesmen install solar heating systems. This is natural for solar domestic hot water systems in which the solar components are extensions of the conventional heating installations. However, a problem for the distribution of solar heating systems is that the HVAC tradesmen do not traditionally work on the roof.

The installation of large collector areas, in particular the roof integration of collectors, requires consideration as to which tradesmen should install the collector roof. The best solution, however, is for specialized solar companies to be responsible for installing the whole system, including the integration of the collector array into the roof. This is more and more common in countries like Germany and Austria, in which a relatively big solar thermal market has already been established.

Another possibility is to transfer the responsibility for the installation of collector roofs to roofing companies, provided that the design of the collector is adjusted to their requirements. The interface between the solar heating system installer and the roofing company can then be at a convenient point between the roof and the boiler room. A local separation of the installation tasks will clearly define the areas of responsibility and the period when each contractor has to be present on the building site.

5.2.1.4 Roof integration and mounting process

Figure 5.16 shows common processes of mounting an integrated collector roof:

- collectors with on-roof assembly
- collectors as roof cover modules
- collectors as roof modules
- collectors as factory-prepared roof units ('solar roof').

The collector integration by on-roof assembly (Figure 5.16a) exists because of the 'do-it-yourself' market from the pioneer days of solar heating systems. The solar

(a) On-roof assembly

Source: AEE INTEC, Austria

(b) Collector as roof cover modules

Source: SolarNor, Norway

(c) Collector module with framing

Source: S.O.L.I.D., Austria.

(d) Collector as factory built unit

Source: Wagner & Co, Germany

Figure 5.16. Different types of roof-integrated solar collectors. See colour plate 5

collector with frame, insulation, absorber units and the collector cover is to a large extent assembled on the roof in stages. This solution offers a large degree of freedom to adapt to given architectural frames. However, it binds specialized and costly installers to an extensive mounting process on the roof. As any work on the building envelope is very exposed to the weather and is seasonally dependent, factory prefabricated collector units might be preferable.

In the examples of Figure 5.16b–c, the on-roof assembly of collector components is increasingly reduced. The collector modules are to a large extent prefabricated and their size allows integration in most roof sizes and shapes. For the collector as a roof-cover module (Figure 5.16b), the thermal insulation and the wooden frame are part of the roof construction. Here, a factory-built roof module of 1–3 m^2 includes the absorber and the collector cover with a metal frame. Also common are roof modules of 6–18 m^2 with wooden or metal framing, including the collector cover, absorber and insulation (Figure 5.16c). Certain collectors offer the possibility for on-roof and roof-integrated installation. These are normally provided with a metal casing.

Similar to the elements of prefabricated houses, the so-called 'solar roof' is a factory-built, load-bearing roof unit. The solar roof is a rather elegant solution and the work of the HVAC tradesmen on the roof is reduced to a minimum. The production of a solar roof involves a rather complex industrial process and flexibility in dimensions may be limited. Naturally, the construction of the building and the production of the solar roof require good planning and co-ordination between different contractors; this should include the construction of the north-facing roof and the warranty for the entire roof.

5.2.1.5 Evacuated tube collectors

Even though evacuated tube collectors have a slightly higher performance than flat-plate collectors, the proportion of this collector type used in solar combisystems is rather small. This is mainly because the price of this collector type is higher and it is not possible to integrate evacuated tube collectors into roofs or façades. If evacuated tube collectors are installed on roofs, it is always necessary to have an ordinary waterproof roof underneath. The collector array cannot substitute for the roofing material, and tube collectors may be the source of problems at snow-rich locations.

5.2.2 Façade integration

Façade-integrated photovoltaic systems have become increasingly familiar, although solar collectors are generally confined to rooftops. However, where large collector areas provide energy for space heating as well as for hot water production, façade integration has much to offer – although it makes considerable demands on system manufacturers.

In the main, solar heating systems are used to prepare hot water in small-scale plants. However, when it comes to applications such as solar space heating, there is sometimes a lack of suitably oriented roof area for solar collectors. What is more, when collectors are installed on existing roofs, including flat roofs, the plants are not an integral part of the architectural design, and can stand out on the roofline. For this reason solar collectors are still rejected by some architects and town planners.

In order to reach a wider market, therefore, collector systems are needed that can be integrated into building façades; see Figure 5.17. As the development of façade systems for photovoltaic modules has shown, this opens up a large, new market sector.

Figure 5.17. Design can enable a façade-integrated collector to receive maximum irradiation (Source: Sonnenkraft, Austria). See colour plate 6

5.2.2.1 Solar irradiation on façade collectors

In central Europe, the annual solar irradiation on the façade is about 30% less than the irradiation on a south-facing roof with a 45° slope. A characteristic of façade-integrated collectors is the regular profile of the solar irradiation, with just small peaks in spring and autumn (see Figure 5.18). This leads to a more or less balanced collector yield throughout the year.

The energy demand has to be looked at in relation to the irradiation on the collector area – in the case of solar combisystems, this is the demand for hot water

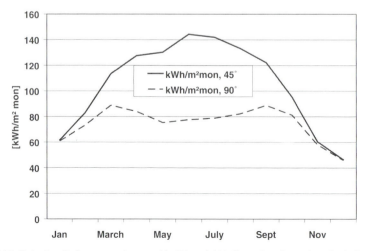

Figure 5.18. Solar irradiation on surfaces with 45° and 90° tilt angles, Graz, Austria; latitude: 47°

and space heating. Whereas the demand for domestic hot water is more or less constant over the year, the space heating demand varies very much depending on the season. Moreover, most of the energy for space heating is needed when the irradiation is lowest.

Solar combisystems for hot water and space heating often have large collector areas – 15–30 m² for a single-family house. On one hand, collector areas of this size give high solar fractions, but, on the other hand, can lead to stagnation problems during summer. Depending on the location of a house, the standard of the building insulation, the passive solar gains, the airtightness of the house and the room temperature preferred by the inhabitants, the heating season ends between March and May. During summer, when there is no, or just a very small, demand for space heating, more energy is available as a result of the higher irradiation. This leads to the stagnation of the solar collectors.

Thus the irradiation curve on the façade meets the needs of combisystems rather well: during the heating season, the irradiation falling on the façade and on a 45° inclined surface are quite similar. During the summer, however, the advantage is on the side of the collector in the façade, because the danger of overheating the solar heating system is significantly reduced as a result of the lower irradiation. Yet the relatively large collector area of a combisystem is sufficiently large to meet the domestic hot water requirement.

As shown above, the solar irradiation on the façade is less than on a surface with 45° tilt angle, reducing the annual collector yield, so a larger collector area is needed in the façade to meet the same energy demand as a system with inclined collectors.

Simulations have been carried out to obtain the collector yield of façade collectors compared with collectors with a tilt angle of 45°. Calculations have been carried out for a combisystem providing domestic hot water and space heating, and for a domestic hot water (DHW) system (space heating demand 14,500 kWh, DHW demand 2700 kWh). The assumed combisystem had a 2000 litre stratified space heating storage tank and a 300 litre DHW storage tank. The DHW system had a 300 litre DHW storage tank. The collector area was varied to simulate different solar fractions from 20–60%.

Figure 5.19 shows the results of these simulations. The higher the solar fraction of a combisystem, the smaller the additional collector area needed for façade collectors to reach the same solar fraction as a system with collectors at a 45° tilt. For example, for a combisystem with collectors tilted at 45° and a solar fraction of 60%, only about a 20% larger collector area is required to reach the same solar fraction. If the solar fraction is 20% for the solar collector with 45° tilt, then the collector area required for the façade-integrated collector is approximately 55% larger.

The opposite applies if the comparison is made for systems that only heat domestic hot water. In this case, the additional collector area in the façade increases with the increased solar fraction. Therefore, at central and northern European latitudes, façade collectors offer their greatest advantage when used in combisystems for hot water and space heating, as a result of the irradiation on the façade as described above.

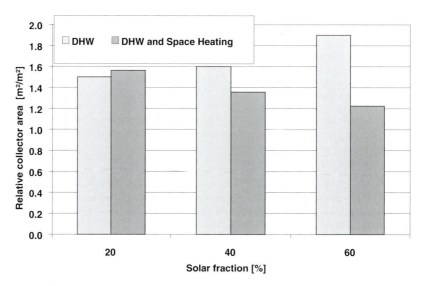

Figure 5.19. Collector area in the façade compared to a collector area with a 45° tilt angle for different solar fractions for a DHW system and a combisystem for a single-family house

The U-value of the collector

What has not been taken into account in these simulations is that the U-value of the collector is improved when it is mounted vertically, because the heat losses caused by convection of air between the absorber and the glazing are reduced. If there is no air gap for ventilation between the collector and the building, the insulation of the building also functions as the insulation of the collector. This further improves the U-value of the collector. Therefore the real additional collector area required in the façade is less than the calculated values from the simulation above, which is another advantage of façade-integrated collectors.

The transport of heat between the absorber and the glazing caused by the convection of air decreases as the tilt angle increases. This leads to a reduction of the U-value of the collector and a higher collector efficiency of vertical collectors at higher temperatures. The results of calculations are shown in Figure 5.20 and Table 5.1.

Table 5.1. Influence of the tilt angle on the characteristic values of the efficiency of a selective-coated collector. For the symbols, see EN 12975–2: 2001 (2001)

Tilt angle β	Absorptance α	Emissivity ϵ	Insulation mm	η_0	a_1 W/m²K	a_2 W/m²K²
45°	0.95	0.05	40	0.800	3.37	0.005
90°	0.95	0.05	40	0.807	3.05	0.004

Reflected radiation

The radiation on a surface is composed of the direct radiation and the diffuse radiation, as well as radiation reflected from the ground and the surroundings. This

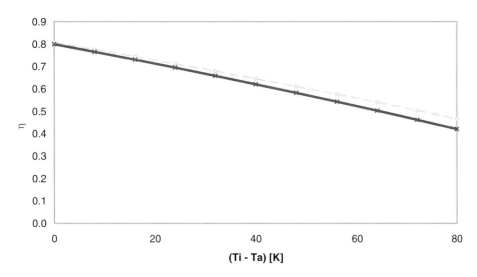

Figure 5.20. Influence of the tilt angle on the efficiency curve for a collector with a selective absorber at an irradiance level of 800 W/m² and no wind; upper line – tilt angle 90°; lower line – tilt angle 45°

reflection depends very much on the surface. Reflected radiation from a light-coloured building façade is about three times as high as the reflection from grass or pebbles, for example, and, if there is snow or ice, the reflection from the ground is up to four times as high as the reflection from grass (Figures 5.21 and 5.22):

$$G = G_b \cdot R_S + G_d \cdot \frac{(1+\cos \beta)}{2} + (G_b + G_d) \cdot \frac{(1-\cos \beta)}{2} \cdot \text{re} \qquad (5.1)$$

where G (W/m²) is the hemispherical solar irradiance on the collector plane, G_b (W/m²) is the direct solar irradiance on the horizontal surface, R_S is the conversion factor from a horizontal to a tilted surface, G_d (W/m²) is the diffuse solar irradiance on the horizontal surface, β is the tilt angle and 're' is the reflection factor.

Figure 5.21. In regions with snow, façade-integrated collectors for solar combisystems have several advantages: no snow cover on the collectors and high irradiation on the façade due to reflection from snow (Source: AKS DOMA, Austria). See also colour plate 7.

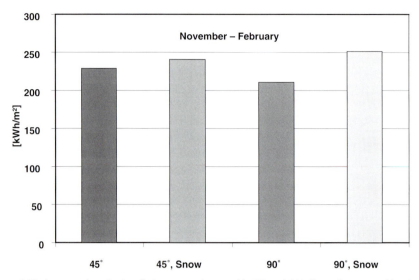

Figure 5.22. Increase in solar irradiation on surfaces with 45° and 90° tilt angles caused by the reflection of the snow on the ground from November to February; Graz, Austria

Solar radiation reflected onto the collector from the ground increases the collector yield. The influence of reflection grows with the collector's tilt angle. Reflection is therefore important when it comes to façade integration of solar collectors. Simulations have shown that during the heating season the irradiation on the façade is higher than on a surface with a 45° tilt angle, as a result of the reflection from snow.

5.2.2.2 Direct façade integration

As with roof integration, there are two ways of integrating a collector array into the façade: the collectors can be mounted either with or without an air gap (ventilation gap) between the collector and the wall. From the point of view of building physics, the installation with a ventilation gap is unproblematic and has the same characteristics as a warm roof.

In a collector element directly integrated into the façade, the thermal insulation is a component of both the building and the collector – there is no thermal separation between the collector and the wall in the form of rear ventilation (see Figure 5.23). As building physics has to be considered for a direct façade-integrated collector, this type of integration will be the main focus in the following.

Consequently, the collector, which comprises an absorber, a transparent cover, glass bearer profiles, sealants and sheet metal cover strips, assumes different functions:

- it acts as a flat-plate collector
- it improves the building's thermal insulation
- it provides weather protection
- it acts as a structural design element for the façade.

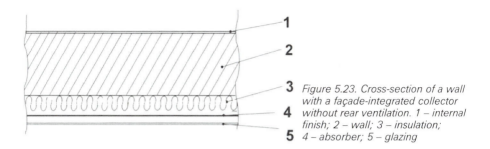

Figure 5.23. Cross-section of a wall with a façade-integrated collector without rear ventilation. 1 – internal finish; 2 – wall; 3 – insulation; 4 – absorber; 5 – glazing

Façade-integrated collectors therefore offer certain advantages:

- cost savings, as building components have more than one function
- replacement of the conventional façade
- suitability both for new buildings and for the refurbishment of old buildings.

Façade collectors are therefore both an integral part of the architectural design and an energy converter. Another advantage of façade collectors is the possibility of a high level of prefabrication, as shown in Figure 5.24. Prefabrication shortens the working hours on the building site, which reduces costs. It also prevents the collectors from getting dirty or wet during installation on the building.

Figure 5.24. Installation of prefabricated wall elements with façade-integrated collectors (Source: AKS DOMA, Austria). See also colour plate 8

The façade-integrated collector helps reduce heat losses from the wall, and in periods of low irradiation, when the collector loop pump is switched off, the collector functions as a 'passive solar' element. Simulations have shown that the U-value of a wall with a façade collector is reduced by up to 90% during cold winter days with high irradiation and by up to 45% during days with low irradiation, because the temperature of the outer layer of the wall – the collector – is higher than the ambient temperature outside. Monitoring of the test façades confirmed the simulations.

5.2.2.3 What architects look for

Façade collectors can be used as a design element for buildings. Changing the surface grid dimensions, the type and colour of the glazed cover and the colour of the absorber can vary the appearance of the façade. A survey was carried out to see what architects and town planners require from the collectors, including their priorities for use of façade-integrated collectors, the colour of the absorber, standardization of absorber grid dimensions and the design of the glazing cover strip.

Of the architects questioned, 86% thought that façade-integrated collectors would be best used in new buildings, while the rest would use them for refurbishment of old buildings. The differences in the two uses are obvious: in refurbishment, the designer has to consider the limitations of an existing building, whereas in new buildings the designer has more design freedom. Figure 5.25 shows the successful thermal renovation of a youth hostel in Austria, while integration of collectors into the façade of a new building is seen in Figure 5.26.

Figure 5.25. Solar heating system with a façade-integrated collector of area 112 m² for a youth hostel in Dornbirn, Austria. The façade-integrated collectors were installed as a part of the thermal renovation of the building (Source: AEE INTEC, Austria). See also colour plate 9

Figure 5.26. Solar heating system with a façade-integrated collector of area 22.7 m² for domestic hot water and space heating in a new single-family house (Source: AEE INTEC, Austria). See also colour plate 10

With regard to the shape and the colour of the absorber, it was shown that the architects would prefer more freedom in design. Only 15% are satisfied with black as the collector colour, and most would prefer a choice of different colours (Figure 5.27) – even if that means a reduction in the yield of the collector. A good example with a bright blue absorber is a solar combisystem for DMW preparation and space heating for a restaurant in the Tyrolean Alps in the Tyrol, Austria (Figure 5.28). A project launched with institutes and companies in Germany, Slovenia and Austria is developing and testing selective colours for absorbers. This EU CRAFT project will run until the end of 2003.

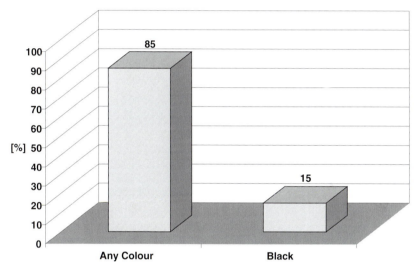

Figure 5.27. Result of an inquiry regarding the preferred absorber colour by architects. 85% of the architects would prefer colours other than black (even if there is a lower collector yield)

Figure 5.28. Restaurant at an altitude of 2400 metres in a skiing area in the Tyrol, Austria, with a blue collector of area 120 m² (Source: AKS DOMA, Austria). See also colour plate 11

Only 29% of the architects think that it is sufficient to provide collectors with standard dimensions – most would prefer to adapt the size of the collector to the dimensions of the building, or even to choose any dimensions they want. This is clearly a challenge for the manufacturers.

Metal flashings (cover strips) for the glazing of the collector form an important part of the design for façade collectors. 92% of the architects thought that the available cover strips do not entirely meet their requirements – presenting the manufacturers with another challenge.

It is rarely possible to use standard-sized collectors because of the way that collectors are architecturally integrated into façades: the architect determines the size and appearance of the façade! In most cases this does not correspond to the size of the absorber. (However, a large absorber can be divided visually with the help of cover strips.)

For optimum façade design, architectural integration also requires co-operation between the architect, the HVAC engineer and the façade manufacturers from the very early stages of a project.

5.2.2.4 The thermal and humidity behaviour of walls with façade collectors

In order to evaluate the thermal and humidity behaviour of systems, AEE INTEC in Austria has measured two systems with façade-integrated collectors. One test façade was erected on a lightweight timber frame wall construction, and the other on a brick wall so that the different behaviour of the system 'collector/wall' in these different situations could be recorded. The results revealed different problems in the two systems. Whereas the main question in solid wall constructions is the fixing of the collector without thermal bridges, in lightweight wall constructions the problem is the removal of humidity. The two solar engineering companies participating in this project have used these results as the basis for the production of test façades and subsequently for the transfer to manufacturing and series production.

Figure 5.29 shows the test façade mounted on the timber frame wall. The total collector area is 55 m². The collector consists of three collector arrays, each 18.3 m². The arrays were prefabricated and were mounted with the help of a crane.

Figure 5.29. Two-family house with a collector area of 55 m² on the south-facing façade (Source: AEE INTEC, Austria). See also colour plate 12

METEONORM 4.0

Global Irradiation: year [kWh/m^2]

■	640 .. 900
■	900 .. 1050
■	1050 .. 1200
■	1200 .. 1350
■	1350 .. 1500
■	1500 .. 1700
■	1700 .. 1900
■	1900 .. 2100
■	2100 .. 2300
■	> 2300
□	non-study area

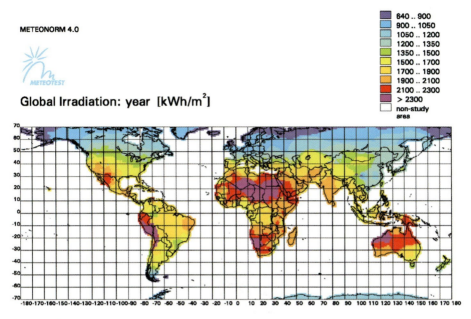

Plate 1. World map of yearly average global irradiation (on a horizontal surface) in kWh/m²a. (Source: METEOTEST, Berne, Switzerland, http://www.meteonorm.com). See also Figure 2.1, page 11

METEONORM 4.0

Temperature: year [°C]

■	< -20
■	-20 .. -10
■	-10 .. -5
■	-5 .. 0
■	0 .. 5
■	5 .. 10
■	10 .. 15
■	15 .. 20
■	20 .. 25
■	25 .. 27.5
■	> 27.5
□	non-study area

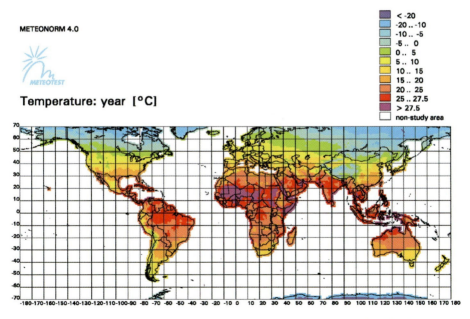

Plate 2. World map of yearly average ambient temperature in °C. (Source: METEOTEST, Berne, Switzerland, http://www.meteonorm.com). See also Figure 2.2, page 11

Plate 3. Integration of the collector array into a warm-roof construction (Source: AEE INTEC). See also Figure 5.13, page 104

Plate 4. Roof-integrated collectors. The far left and far right sections of the roof are dummies. As they are the same colour as the centre section, there is a uniform look to the whole roof. In this case, two roof windows have also been integrated into the collector roof (Source: AEE INTEC, Austria). See also Figure 5.15, page 105

*(a) On-roof assembly. (*Source: *AEE INTEC, Austria)*

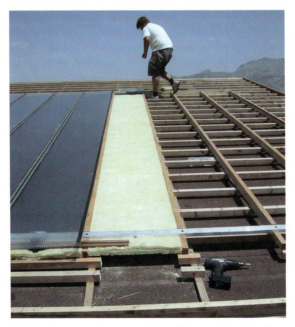

*(b) Collector as roof cover modules. (*Source: *SolarNor, Norway)*

Plate 5. Different types of roof-integrated solar collectors. See also Figure 5.16, page 106

(c) Collector module with framing. (Source: S.O.L.I.D., Austria)

(d) Collector as factory built unit. (Source: Wagner & Co, Germany)

Plate 5. continued

Plate 6. Design can enable a façade-integrated collector to receive maximum irradiation (Source: Sonnenkraft, Austria). See also Figure 5.17, page 108

Plate 7. In regions with snow, façade-integrated collectors for solar combisystems have several advantages: no snow cover on the collectors and high irradiation on the façade due to reflection from snow (Source: AKS DOMA, Austria). See also Figure 5.21, page 111

Plate 8. Installation of prefabricated wall elements with façade-integrated collectors. (Source: AKS DOMA, Austria). See also Figure 5.24, page 113

Plate 9. Solar heating system with a façade-integrated collector of area 112 m² for a youth hostel in Dornbirn, Austria. The façade-integrated collectors were installed as a part of the thermal renovation of the building (Source: AEE INTEC, Austria). See also Figure 5.25, page 114

Plate 10. *Solar heating system with a façade-integrated collector of area 22.7m² for domestic hot water and space heating in a new single-family house. (Source: AEE INTEC, Austria). See also Figure 5.26, page 114*

Plate 11. *Restaurant at an altitude of 2400 metres in a skiing area in the Tyrol, Austria, with a blue collector of area 120m² (Source: AKS DOMA, Austria). See also Figure 5.28, page 115*

Plate 12. Two-family house with a collector area of 55 m^2 on the south-facing façade (Source: AEE INTEC, Austria). See also Figure 5.29, page 116

Plate 13. Test collector on a brick wall of the south-west façade of an office building. The collector forms a square of 25 m^2 (Source: AEE INTEC, Austria). See also Figure 5.32, page 118

Plate 14. Collector roof with integrated roof windows (Source: AEE INTEC, Austria). See also Figure 5.33, page 120

Plate 15. Ranten Mountain Resort, Nesbyen, Norway – solar combisystem for DHW, space and swimming pool heating; collector area 200 m²; storage volume 4 m³; pool volume 90 m³ (Source: Solarnor, Norway). See also Figure 5.34, page 120

Plate 16. Collectors used as a design element – the collector array is duplicated in the shape of the winter garden glazing (Source: AEE INTEC, Austria). See also Figure 5.35, page 121

Plate 17. When integrating collectors into the façade, shading of the collectors by other building elements during summertime should be very carefully taken into consideration (Source: AKS DOMA, Austria). See also Figure 5.36, page 121

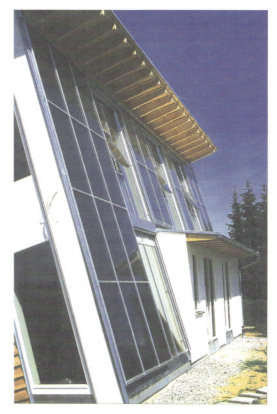

Plate 18. Another good example of façade integration (Source: Wagner & Co., Germany). See also Figure 5.37, page 121

Plate 19. A successful example of roof integration (Source: AEE INTEC, Austria). See also Figure 5.38, page 122.

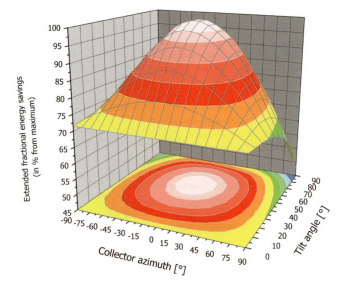

Plate 20. Dependency of the extended fractional energy savings on tilt angle and azimuth of the collector (climate: central Europe, 100% = 39% of $f_{sav,ext}$) (Heimrath, 2002). See also Figure 8.1, page 193

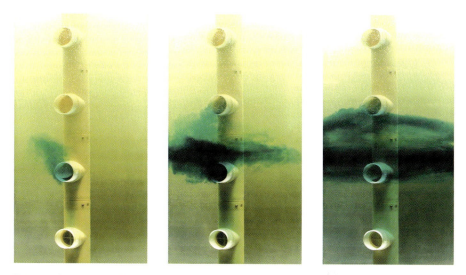

Plate 21. Stratifying unit for hot water stores showing outlet into the middle of the store (Source: Solvis, Germany). See also Figure 8.13, page 205

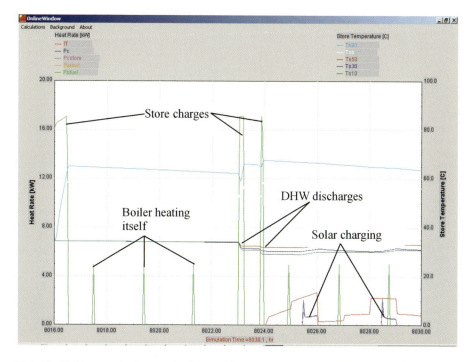

Plate 22. Plot for one day from a simulation of System #11 using TRNSYS. See also Figure 8.21, page 220

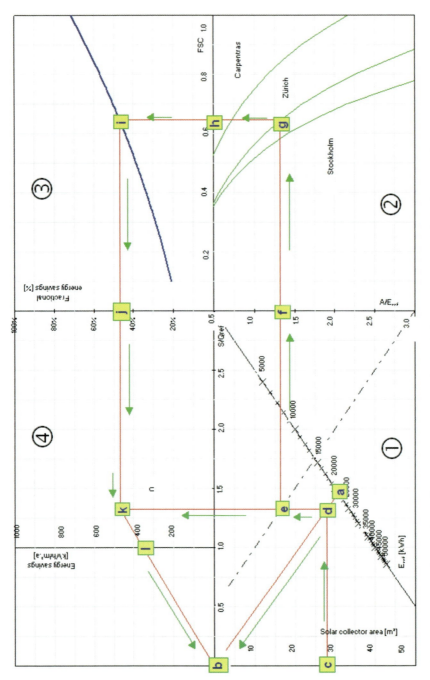

Plate 23. The four diagrams of the FSC nomogram and an example of its use. See also Figure 8.16, page 214.

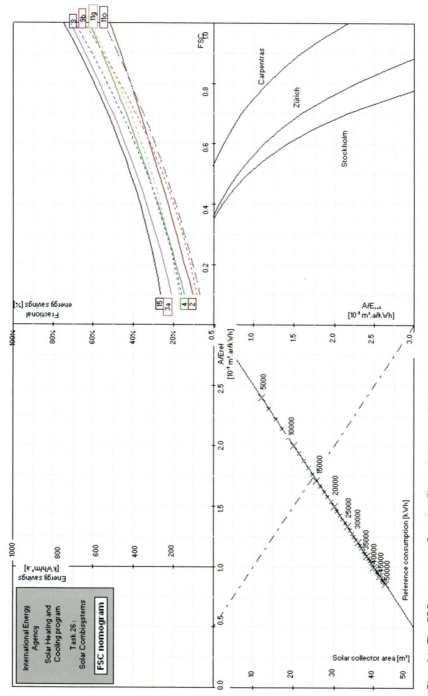

Plate 24. The FSC nomogram. See also Figure 8.17, page 215

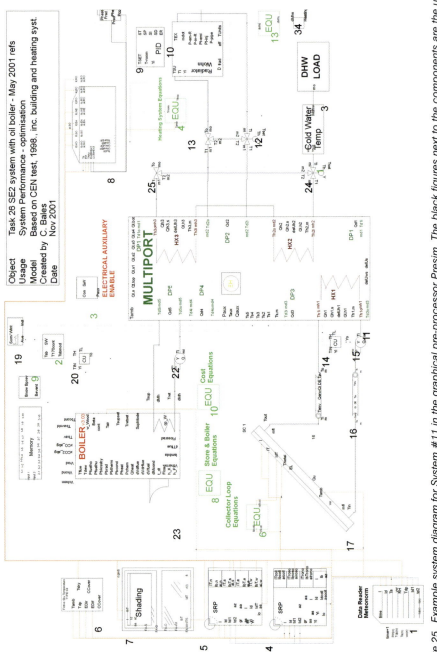

Plate 25. Example system diagram for System #11 in the graphical pre-processor Presim. The black figures next to the components are the unit number (sequential number) and the green next to some of the boxes is the number of the relevant equation set. See also Figure 8.22, page 225

The wooden back wall of the collector was fixed to the timber frames with steel angles. Then, the insulation of the building (mineral wool) was applied (Figure 5.30). There are only about 10 steel angles for fixing each 18.3 m² collector array. This type of fixing has almost no effect on thermal bridging.

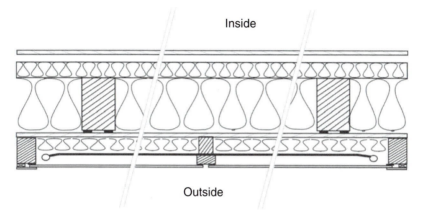

Figure 5.30. Cross-section of the timber frame wall with attached façade collector. Collector insulation – 40 mm mineral wool; insulation of building – 160 mm mineral wool; inner-wall heating layer – 50 mm wood fibreboard

The solar heating system consists of a 3570 litre stratifying space heating storage tank and a 500 litre DHW storage tank. A pellet boiler provides the auxiliary heat – the house is therefore heated 100% by renewable energy.

Measuring instruments were installed in every layer of the wall to record the temperature and humidity profile of both wall and collector. The measurements started in March 2001. The building's occupants moved in in June 2001, and the solar heating system was initiated at the same time.

The monitoring results showed that it is necessary to ensure dry construction material from the beginning. Moreover, the trapping of the timber wall between two vapour-tight layers – the collector on the outside and a vapour barrier on the inside – has to be avoided, or the wood will be damaged within a very short period of time due to the growth of mould. To ensure the drying of the timber construction it must be possible to dry it out to the inside of the building. If a vapour barrier is used it must be relatively vapour-permeable.

At the beginning of the monitoring, high levels of relative humidity were detected in the wall. This was caused by the high humidity of the wood used for the wall construction and the insulation material. Figure 5.31 shows monthly mean values of the relative humidity in the layers of the collector and the wall. The measurements show that the relative humidity in the wall decreased significantly during the period of the measurements from March 2001 to January 2002. This was possible because the construction was vapour-permeable on the inside.

As a wall with a façade collector cannot dry out to the outside, it must be possible to dry out to the inside of the building. Therefore, the inner layers of the wall must

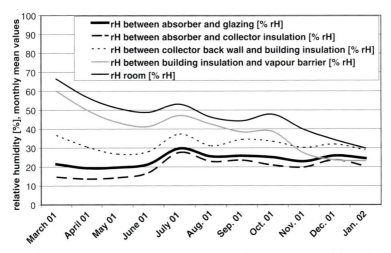

Figure 5.31. Monthly mean values of the relative humidity (rH) in the layers of the collector and the wall from March 2001 to January 2002

be relatively vapour-permeable. This should be considered in the planning of the building. Bathrooms should not be positioned behind a façade collector if tiles may be used on the interior wall, as they form a vapour-tight layer. If there is no way of avoiding tiles, wall heating is a possibility for raising the temperature level in the wall and minimizing the danger of condensation.

The second test façade was installed on the south-west façade of an office building in June 2001, with the collector attached to a brick wall (Figure 5.32). The total collector area is 25 m^2. Before constructing the façade collector, simulations were made to optimize the construction in terms of thermal bridging. Stationary calculations were made using the THERM program (multidimensional thermal bridge program).

Figure 5.32. Test collector on a brick wall of the south-west façade of an office building. The collector forms a square of 25 m^2 (Source: AEE INTEC, Austria). See also colour plate 13

In general, the mounting of a solar collector on a solid wall and also the fixing of the glazing cover strip should always be free from thermal bridges, otherwise the U-value of the whole wall will be significantly lowered and this will lead to high heat losses.

5.2.2.5 Conclusions

Façade collectors are both an energy converter and an integral part of the architectural design, so it is important for architects and planners to co-operate from the very beginning of a project to achieve a successful outcome.

Vertical collectors receive less solar irradiation than those systems on an inclined surface. On the other hand, vertical collectors have a better U-value than inclined collectors, because heat losses from the collector are reduced as a result of lower convection levels between the absorber and the glazing. If there is no thermal separation between the collector and the wall construction in the form of rear ventilation the U-value is lowered even more, because of minimization of heat losses from the rear of the collector. This also leads to an improvement of the U-value of the whole wall.

If the collector is mounted without an air gap for ventilation, it must be possible for the wall to dry out to the inside of the building. Therefore, inner layers of the wall must be vapour-permeable. When collectors are mounted on massive walls, it is important to avoid thermal bridges, otherwise heat losses from the building in winter are significant.

5.2.3 Aesthetic aspects

Building-integrated collectors have to fulfil the various demands of the building envelope and have to fit into the overall concept of the building design. Maybe, except for the solar enthusiasts priorities, the aesthetics of a building is one of the most important aspects when solar collectors are integrated into the building envelope. The collectors have often been considered as separate elements placed on the building and the architecture of the building itself disregarded. For architects, the most common reason for unacceptable solar energy systems is their disharmony with the design of the roof or façade. The placement of the architecturally 'foreign' components without any relation to the scale of the roof or façade leads to a fragmentation of homogeneous spaces (Herzog and Krippner, 1998; Krippner and Herzog, 2000).

The integration of collectors should be consistent with the design of the roof and façade of a building. The first approaches towards building integration show that 'integration' was considered synonymous with 'invisibility'. The aim was to maximize integration, and to hide the fact that solar energy systems were different from other building elements. This practice has changed and architects have started to use solar energy systems in order to enhance the aesthetic appeal of a building by providing variation or contrast (Hestnes, 2000).

Solar collectors enlarge the range of materials and components that may be used in building construction. However, architects show a certain lack of 'solar design'.

One reason for this, among others, may be that the design and planning of buildings (by an architect) is carried out separately from research and development on the components (by an engineer) (Krippner and Herzog, 2000).

Roofs and façades play an important role in the appearance of towns and villages. The shapes are influenced by regional differences, by climate and by the materials used. For certain forms, it seems to be easier or more suitable to integrate large collector arrays, with the fact that collectors are usually rectangular in shape taken into account. More appropriate integration options are, for example, possible for single pitched roofs and double pitched roofs than for hipped or mansard roofs. The latter roof types provide less rectangular space for the components. The placement and design of windows in a collector roof is another important aspect (Figure 5.33).

Figure 5.33. Collector roof with integrated roof windows (Source: AEE INTEC, Austria). See also colour plate 14

As has already been mentioned, one way of achieving integration is to cover a complete roof or façade surface with collectors. In many cases this may also be the most cost-effective approach. Figure 5.34 shows a Norwegian example of such a collector roof. The uniformity of such a solar roof can be 'broken' by architectural means such as building extensions, winter gardens (Figure 5.35) and by using natural divisions in a roof or planes of different level.

Figure 5.34. Ranten Mountain Resort, Nesbyen, Norway – solar combisystem for DHW, space and swimming pool heating; collector area 200 m²; storage volume 4 m³; pool volume 90 m³ (Source: Solarnor, Norway). See also colour plate 15

Figure 5.35. Collectors used as a design element – the collector array is duplicated in the shape of the winter garden glazing (Source: AEE INTEC, Austria). See also colour plate 16

Furthermore, a 'good design' is a question of personal taste or of the influence of a style of architecture. The pictures in Figures 5.36–5.38 may give some ideas for building integration of large collector arrays for solar combisystems. A competent judgement on successful design may be left to architects.

Figure 5.36. When integrating collectors into the façade, shading of the collectors by other building elements during summertime should be very carefully taken into consideration (Source: AKS DOMA, Austria). See also colour plate 17

Figure 5.37. Another good example of façade integration (Source: Wagner & Co., Germany). See also colour plate 18

Figure 5.38: Two successful examples of roof integration. Left – Germany (Source: Wagner & Co.); right – Austria (Source: AEE INTEC, Austria). See also colour plate 17

5.2.4 Project planning and boiler room

Usually, the first actors involved in the planning process are the architects and the building services consultants, who begin the process based on a client's requirements. This may be to reduce the total purchased energy rather than to use a certain type of technology (Herzog and Krippner, 1998). The challenge for the solar thermal industry is to interest architects and building consultants in the important issues in the planning of solar heating systems. There are many examples of elegant solutions where this interest has been evident, but unfortunately there are also numerous negative experiences, caused by ignorance on the part of one or several of those involved.

An integrated solar collector array, which takes up a substantial part of the roof or façade, represents an architectural element that has to be incorporated in the overall building design at an early planning stage. Conflicts frequently occur between the location of chimneys, roof windows, ventilation openings and the solar collectors, and compromises stand as monuments to poor planning. Usually there is sufficient space available and suitable results are a matter of good planning. Not only the aesthetic aspects, but also technical or practical issues make good planning mandatory.

A boiler room is needed for the other equipment of the solar combisystem. The feasibility of a combisystem depends on the heat storage tank(s). Typical storage volumes vary between 0.3 m^3 and 3 m^3 depending on the system type and the size of the single-family house. Normally the space for the boiler room requires approximately 2% of the heated floor area. From a functional and economical point of view, the boiler room should be placed at the shortest possible distance from the solar collectors. The path for the pipes between these elements should be well planned.

Attention must be paid to the transport of large units into the boiler room. Standard door dimensions, narrow corridors, stairs and halls limit where the boiler room equipment can be placed and when during the building process the boiler room equipment can be installed. From the point of view of the building costs, the boiler room should occupy a low-value area of the building. Figure 5.39 shows examples of how a boiler room can be placed in different building designs with a

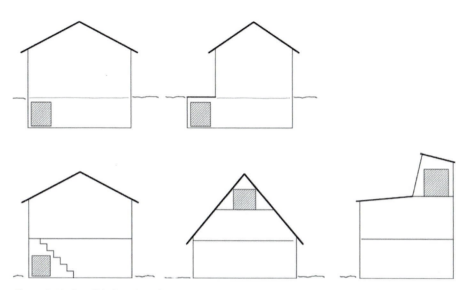

Figure 5.39. Possible locations for a boiler room in buildings with and without basements

minimum of inconvenience.

Drainback systems, which are usual in the Netherlands and Norway, place additional demands on the position of the heat storage tank and the paths of the piping. This system type requires that water can run back to the store by the force of gravity. Furthermore, the pipes have to be mounted in such a way that the air and water can change places during the start-up and drainback phases.

REFERENCES

EN 12975–2:2001, 2001, *Solar thermal systems and components – Collectors. Part 2: Test methods.* Available from the national standardization institutes.

Herzog T and Krippner R, 1998, 'Synoptic description of decisive subsystems of the building skin, Proceedings Building a New Century', in *5th European Conference Solar Energy in Architecture and Urban Planning*, Bonn, Germany.

Hestnes A G, 2000, 'Building integration of solar energy systems', in *Solar Energy*, 67(4–6), 181–187.

Krippner R and Herzog T, 2000, 'Architectural aspects of solar techniques – Studies on the integration of solar energy systems', in *Proceedings EuroSun 2000, 3rd ISES-Europe Solar Congress, Copenhagen, Denmark.*

Lutz P, Jenisch R, Klopfer H, Freymuth H, Krumpf L, Pelzold K, 1997, *Lehrbuch der Bauphysik*, 4th edn, Stuttgart, B.G. Teubner.

Norwegian Building and Research Institute, 1991, *Vannbaserte solfangere – Funksjon og energiutbytte*, Byggforskserien: Byggforskdetailjer A 552.455.

FURTHER READING

Bartelsen B, Kiermasch M and Rockendorf G, 1999, 'Wärmeverluste von Flachkollektoren in Abhängigkeit vom Kollektorneigungswinkel', 9. Symposium Thermische Solarenergie, Staffelstein, Ostbayerisches Technologie-Transfer-Institut e.V., Regensburg, Germany.

Bergmann I, 2001, Fassadenintegrierte Kollektoren – Konstrucktion, Bauphysik und Messresultate zweier Systeme, IEA-SHC Task 26 Solar Combisystems, Industry Workshop Rapperswil, Switzerland, http://www.iea-sch.org/task26

Butters C and Østmo F, 2002, *Bygg for en Ny Tid ('Towards Environmental Architecture')*, NABU-NAL (Norwegian Architects for Sustainable Development – Norwegian Association of Architects), Oslo, http: //byliv.vindheim.net/nabu.html

Diem P, 1996, *Bauphysik im Zusammenhang*, 2nd edn, Bauverlag, Wiesbaden.

NBI – Norwegian Building and Research Institute, 1999, *Isolerte skrå tretak med kombinert undertak og vindsperre – Byggforskserien: Byggdetailjer 525.102.*

Rockendorf G and Janßen S, 1998, Façade-integrated solar collectors, *Proceedings Gleisdorf Solar 1998*, http://www.aee.at

Stadler I, 2001, Fassadenintegration von thermischen Sonnenkollektoren ohne Hinterlüftung, *11. Symposium Thermische Solarenergie*, Staffelstein, Ostbayerisches Technologie-Transfer-Institut e.V., Regensburg, Germany

Suter J-M, Letz T, Weiss W, Inäbnit J (ed.), 2002, *Solar Combisystems – Overview 2000*, IEA SHC Task 26, http://www.iea-shc.org/task26

Internet site

http://www.hausderzukunft.at

6 Performance of solar combisystems

Ulrike Jordan, Klaus Vajen, Wolfgang Streicher and Thomas Letz

One of the targets of Task 26 was to compare different combisystem designs by means of annual system simulations. To describe the performance of solar combisystems and to carry out an adequate comparison with detailed simulation models, it needs to be recognized that the result of a comparison depends on the chosen **reference conditions** concerning energy demands, energy sources, parameter settings, and standard components, and the **output or target function** of the annual system simulation that serves as a measure of the combisystem performance (e.g. the saved gas consumptions of a combisystem compared to the gas consumption of a non-solar reference heating system). In order to carry out a comparison between combisystems that do not correspond to the reference conditions defined in Section 6.1, these non-complying combisystems were additionally characterized in a way that allows comparisons of different system designs for various climates and system sizes. A description of a **characterization method** developed in the framework of Task 26 is given in Section 6.3.

6.1 REFERENCE CONDITIONS

System simulations were carried out with the simulation tool TRNSYS (Klein *et al.*, 1998; see also Sections 8.3 and 8.4). TRNSYS consists of a main program file, together with subroutines for the simulation control and calculation of component models. Subroutines of component models (**types**) are calculated separately in a certain sequence. The values of variables, for instance, temperatures and mass flow rates, are transferred from one component to another each time a subroutine is called. These variables, which can change their values in each time step, are called **inputs** and **outputs** of the components, and serve as the connection between the component models. Values for constant properties of the component models (**parameters**) are defined for a whole simulation. Whereas some parameters were defined as fixed reference values for all calculations carried out in the framework of Task 26, other parameters were optimized for certain combisystem designs or were varied in order to carry out sensitivity analysis. Some of the reference parameter settings are described in the following.

As described in Chapter 4, a wide variety of system hydraulics (regarding, for example, the connections of stores and heat exchangers) and various ways to enhance the stratification in the storage tank (e.g. the stratification pipe in the storage tank) are found in the various combisystems. In addition to these system-specific differences, there is a wide variety of parameters, components, and input data that are *not* characteristics of the specific system design, but which nevertheless influence the system performance:

- the magnitude and yearly distribution of the energy delivery to a domestic heating system (e.g. solar radiation and auxiliary heat supply) and the heat demands for domestic hot water (DHW) and space heating (SH)
- parameters of components that are *not* characteristic for the specific system design (e.g. the length of pipe connections between the collector and storage tank)
- standard components that can be applied in the same way for most of the investigated systems (e.g. a gas boiler as the auxiliary energy source, the collector type and the components of the conventional heating system).

The SH demand depends not only on the building design, but also on the interactions between the solar heating system and the building. For example, both the thermal mass of the building and the control of the solar loop can have an impact on the SH demand. Therefore, the final energy consumption of the boiler was calculated in each combisystem simulation. The SH demand was simulated for four different buildings (Chapter 3) in each of three climates (Chapter 2). Furthermore, input files for DHW profiles were used (Chapter 3). The remaining parameter reference settings for various system components are described in the following. Parameter sets were defined for the standard components, i.e. boiler, solar collector, piping, storage tank and electrical components.

Because the boiler efficiency and heat losses from the storage tank differ for conventional and solar heating systems, the energy demand of a conventional heating system cannot be evaluated as the sum of the solar and auxiliary energy contributions of a combisystem. Therefore, the same parameter sets were applied for both combisystems and conventional **reference systems**, to calculate the amount of fossil fuels that can be saved by a combisystem as a result of the active solar contribution.

The simulation results of the energy consumption of the **reference systems** are given in Section 6.1.6 for all sets of weather data and building models. For investigations in which the interaction between the thermal mass of the building and the solar heating system is neglected, 'standard' SH-load profiles were generated. If the thermal mass of the house is used as the main heat store, a larger thermal mass is integrated into the building design. Therefore, some of the reference conditions have not been applied for the basic direct solar floor system.

6.1.1 Boiler parameters

In the framework of Task 26, a wide variety of different boiler models was used to describe the auxiliary energy source of solar combisystems. Nevertheless, two boiler models, a gas boiler model and a biomass boiler model, were defined as **standard** boiler models. These boiler models were applied for combisystems where no specific type of boiler is given as an integrated part of the system design. To model these **standard** boilers, the TRNSYS **type 170** was applied, combined with the TRNSYS **type 123** PID-controller. More details about the boiler models can be found in Section 8.4.1.4.

The energy demand for refining and transportation of fuels was not taken into account. Therefore, the final energy consumption of the boilers (E_{boiler}), calculated with the lower heating value of the combustibles consumed by each heating system, was used for the analysis of the energy consumption of the systems in Task 26. Simulation results of the mean annual boiler efficiencies (η_{boiler}) of the standard boilers for typical solar combisystems, as well as the power range and minimum operation and standstill times, are given in Table 6.1.

Table 6.1. Reference data for the standard boilers

	Gas boiler	Biomass boiler
Nominal burner power, $P_{nom,burner}$	15 kW (single-family house) 24 kW (multi-family house)	
Power range	25–100%	30–100%
Mean annual boiler efficiency	90%	80%
Minimum operation time	1 minute	30 minutes
Minimum standstill time	1 minute	30 minutes

The final energy consumption (E_{boiler}) of an auxiliary boiler in a solar combisystem can also be expressed as the thermal energy load of the auxiliary boiler (Q_{boiler}) divided by the mean annual efficiency of the boiler (calculated with the lower heating value):

$$E_{boiler} = \frac{Q_{boiler}}{\eta_{boiler}} \tag{6.1}$$

Model descriptions and model parameters for specific boilers that are included in some systems (e.g. with external oil and gas burners and different internal burners) are given in the Task 26 technical reports (Bales *et al.*, 2002).

Because hydroelectric power plants are widely used in Norway, System #9b is specially designed for an electrical heating element as the auxiliary heater. As a result of this special situation in Norway, an annual electricity generation efficiency ($\eta_{el.heater}$) of 90 % was defined for this heating element supplied with renewable energy sources. For electrical heating elements that are supplied by non-renewable energy sources, an annual electricity generation efficiency ($\eta_{el.heater}$) of 40% was considered. Nevertheless, the electricity generation efficiency for the electricity supply of other devices (e.g. pumps and valves) was set to 40% for all systems (see Section 6.1.5).

The primary energy consumption of an electrical heating element is defined in Equation 6.2 as the thermal energy load of the electrical heating element ($Q_{el.heater}$) divided by the annual electricity generation efficiency ($\eta_{el.heater}$):

$$E_{el.heater} = \frac{Q_{el.heater}}{\eta_{el.heater}} \tag{6.2}$$

with $\eta_{el.heater}$ = 40% for systems that do *not* apply solely renewable energy sources (mean European electricity generation efficiency) and $\eta_{el.heater}$ = 90% for systems that apply solely renewable electrical energy sources.

For systems that include both a boiler and an electrical heating element, the combined auxiliary energy consumption (E_{aux}) of a solar combisystem is defined as the sum of the final energy consumption of the auxiliary boiler (E_{boiler}) and the primary energy consumption of the electrtical heating element ($E_{el.heater}$):

$$E_{aux} = E_{boiler} + E_{el.heater} \tag{6.3}$$

Since the boiler model was not included in the simulation models of the reference systems, the thermal energy demand of the reference boiler ($Q_{boiler,ref}$) was defined as the sum of the energy demands for DHW preparation (Q_{DHW}) and SH (Q_{SH}) and the heat losses of the storage tank $Q_{loss,ref}$ (see Section 6.1.4):

$$Q_{boiler.ref} = Q_{SH} + Q_{DHW} + Q_{loss.ref} \tag{6.4}$$

A mean annual boiler energy efficiency ($\eta_{boiler,ref}$) of 85% was then used to calculate the final energy consumption of the reference system boiler:

$$E_{ref} = \frac{Q_{boiler.ref}}{\eta_{boiler.ref}} \tag{6.5}$$

6.1.2 Collector parameters

A typical flat-plate collector with optically selective coated absorbers was used for all simulations within Task 26. The collector parameters are shown in Table 6.2. The TRNSYS **type 132** was used as collector model.

Table 6.2 Collector parameters (data with respect to the aperture area)

Parameter	Value	Unit
η_0	0.8	–
a_1	3.5	W/m^2K
a_2	0.015	W/m^2K^2
Incident angle modifier ($\theta = 50°$)	0.9	–

6.1.3 Pipe parameters

The thermal losses from pipes were simulated only for the collector loop of solar combisystems, not for the reference systems. Following EN 12976–2, 2000, the following pipe parameters were assumed:

Length:	30 metres (total, single-family house)	
Insulation:	< 12 mm inner pipe diameter:	200% of inner pipe diameter
	> 12 mm diameter:	100% of inner pipe diameter
Ambient temperature:	15°C	

6.1.4 Storage parameters

For most of the storage tanks investigated, the model parameters were determined using parameter identification methods based upon experiments conducted at various research institutes. For variations of the storage geometry that were not specifically tested, functions for the volume/diameter ratio, thermal losses and vertical thermal conductivity, as well as the ambient temperature of the store, were defined as shown in Table 6.3.

Table 6.3 Parameters of the storage tank

		Unit	Valid for
Storage height (Vajen, 1996)	$h_{store} = \max\left[\min\left(2.2, 1.78 + 0.39 \cdot \ln \dfrac{V_{store}}{m^3}\right), 1.25\right]$	m	$V_{store} = 0.6 - 2.5\ m^3$
Thermal conductivity of the insulation λ	0.04 (sensitivity analysis for top and bottom insulation)	W/mK	Insulation thickness: 0–15 cm
Thermal losses (Vajen, 1996)	$\dot{Q}_{loss}/\dot{Q}_{loss,theor} = \max\left[1.1, \left(1.5 - \dfrac{V_{store}/m^3}{10}\right)\right]$		V_{store} in m^3
Vertical thermal conductivity (Vajen, 1996)	$\lambda_{vertical} = \max\left[0.7, \left(1.3 - \dfrac{V_{store}/m^3}{10}\right)\right]$	W/mK	V_{store} in m^3
Ambient temperature	15	°C	

Reference storage heat losses

The reference system is equipped with a DHW storage tank. Space heating water is not stored in the reference systems. The yearly heat loss of the DHW store of the reference system $Q_{loss,ref}$ is given by:

$$Q_{loss,ref} = (UA)_{store,ref} \cdot (\overline{T}_{store} - T_{store,amb}) \cdot 8760 \frac{hr}{a} \qquad (6.6)$$

According to ENV 12977–1, 2000, the size of the store $V_{store,ref}$ is defined as 0.75 times the daily DHW discharge volume, with the heat loss rate:

$$(UA)_{store,ref} = 0.16 \sqrt{V_{store,ref}/litre}\ W/K \qquad (6.7)$$

With a mean storage temperature of $\overline{T}_{store} = 52.5°C$ and a storage ambient temperature of $\overline{T}_{store,amb} = 15°C$, the storage losses for the SFH (single-family house) with a mean daily DHW draw-off volume of 200 litres are:

$$Q_{loss,ref,SFH} = 644\ kWh/a$$

For the MFH with a mean daily DHW draw-off volume of 1000 litres, (5 x 200 litres) – the storage losses for the MFH (multi-family house) are five times as high as the storage losses for the SFH:

$$Q_{loss,ref,MFH} = 3220 \ \text{kWh/a}$$

6.1.5 Electricity consumption of system components

The parasitic electricity demand of a combisystem, W_{par}, and of a reference heating system, $W_{par,ref}$, is defined as the sum of the annual electricity consumption of all electrical system components other than for heating (pumps, boiler devices, valves and controllers):

$$W_{par//par,ref} = W_{pumps} + W_{boiler} + W_{valves} + W_{controller} \qquad (6.8)$$

For solar combisystems that are sold as a package with specific pumps, the actual electricity consumptions of these pumps were used in the simulations. For the other solar combisystems, as well as for the reference system, typical electricity consumptions as described in the following sections were used.

6.1.5.1 Electricity consumption of pumps: W_{pumps}

Pumps are typically placed in the heat distribution system and in the collector loop. If external heat exchangers are used in the collector, DHW or SH loop or in additional circulation loops (e.g. when several storage tanks are applied), the increased pump energy consumption needs to be taken into account. The final annual energy consumption of the pumps is calculated as the product of the power consumption of all pumps installed in the heating system and their annual operation time. It is assumed that there is no energy transfer from the pump into the fluid.

$$\qquad (6.9)$$

$$W_{pumps} = \Delta t_{solar} \cdot P_{el,pump,solar,int/ext} + \Delta t_{SH} \cdot P_{el,pump,SH} + \Delta t_{DHW} \cdot P_{el,pump,DHW} + \sum_{i} \Delta t_{pump,i} \cdot P_{el,pump,others,i}$$

The values for the operation times, Δt, are calculated for each solar combisystem and reference system.

Pumps in the collector loop

The pump power for the primary (and secondary) collector loop, $P_{el,pump,solar,int/ext}$, was estimated for collector areas up to $A_{col} = 75 \ \text{m}^2$ by an Austrian inquiry into 16 different solar heating systems (Schröttner, 2000; Figure 6.1) and for a collector area range of $A_{col} = 100–400 \ \text{m}^2$ by Streicher *et al.*, 2002 (Figure 6.2). According to the results of the inquiry, the collector pump power can be calculated with the following equations:

For internal heat exchangers:

$$P_{el,pump,solar,int} = \left[0.3 \left(\frac{A_{col}}{\text{m}^2} \right)^2 - 2.5 \cdot \frac{A_{col}}{\text{m}^2} + 50 \right] W \qquad (6.10)$$

For external heat exchangers the sum of the electrical pump power consumption of both the *primary and secondary* loops is:

$$P_{el,pump,solar,ext} = \left[78.3 \cdot \exp\left(0.0156 \cdot \frac{A_{col}}{m^2} \right) \right] W \text{ for } A_{col} < 75m^2 \qquad (6.11)$$

$$P_{el,pump,solar,ext} = \left[196 \cdot \exp\left(0.0046 \cdot \frac{A_{col}}{dy} \right) \right] W \text{ for } A_{col} \geq 75m^2$$

whereas the electrical pump power consumption in the *primary* loop only, for small collector areas, can be calculated with:

$$P_{el,pump,solar,ext} = \left[44.6 \cdot \exp\left(0.0181 \cdot \frac{A_{col}}{m^2} \right) \right] W \text{ for } A_{col} < 75m^2 \qquad (6.12)$$

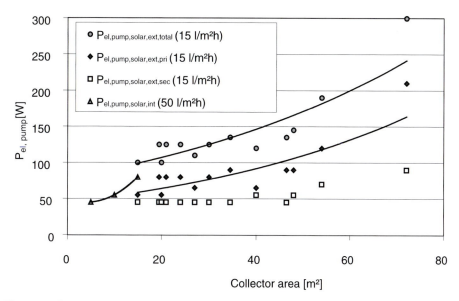

Figure 6.1. Specific electrical power consumption of collector loop pumps for relatively small collector areas – Austrian inquiry by AEE INTEC (J Schröttner, 2000) and product information (Grundfos, 2000)

Pumps placed in the space heating distribution system

The electrical power consumption of pumps in the space heating distribution system, $P_{el,pump,SH}$, and in the primary loop of a DHW storage tank, $P_{el,pump,DHW}$, were evaluated by Gertec (1999) for about 200 solar heating systems. In Figure 6.3, trend curves are shown for the power consumption of the pumps as a function of the nominal burner power. According to these evaluations, the electrical power consumption of the space heating pumps for the reference case is assumed to be:

$$P_{el,pump,SH} = 90W + 2 \cdot 10^{-4} \cdot P_{nom,burner} \qquad (6.13)$$

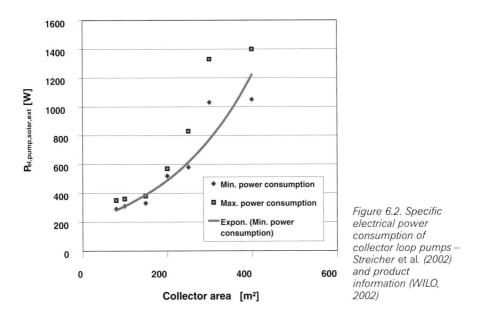

Figure 6.2. Specific electrical power consumption of collector loop pumps – Streicher et al. (2002) and product information (WILO, 2002)

According to Equation 6.6 for the reference buildings SFH and MFH, the following power demands were taken into account:

$P_{el,pump,SH}$ = 93 W for a nominal burner power of 15 kW and

$P_{el,pump,SH}$ = 95 W for a nominal burner power of 24 kW

Pumps of the reference system used to load the DHW store with auxiliary energy

The electricity demand of the pump to load a DHW store was evaluated with the following correlation (see Figure 6.3):

$$P_{el,pump,DHW} = 49.4\,W \cdot \exp(0.0083 \cdot \frac{P_{nom,burner}}{W}) \tag{6.14}$$

According to Equation 6.7, the pump power demands for the reference buildings are assumed to be:

$P_{el,pump,DHW}$ = 55 W (SFH, nominal burner power: 15 kW) and

$P_{el,pump,DHW}$ = 60 W (MFH, nominal burner power: 24 kW)

Other pumps

If any other pumps are installed in the combisystem, the electric power demand is assumed to be:

$P_{el,pump,others}$ = 50 W

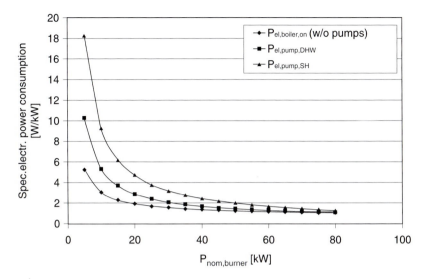

Figure 6.3. Specific electrical power consumption of condensing gas boilers and DHW and SH pumps; trend curves of about 80 values each (Gertec, 1999)

6.1.5.2 Electricity consumption of the boiler: W_{boiler}

The electricity consumption of the boiler is calculated according to Equation 6.8 as:

$$W_{boiler} = \Delta t_{boiler,on} \cdot P_{el,boiler,on} + \Delta t_{boiler,stby} \cdot P_{el,boiler,stby} \tag{6.15}$$

In Figure 6.3, a trend curve for the specific electric power consumption of 200 condensing gas boilers, evaluated by Gertec (1999), is shown. According to Gertec, the electricity demand for boiler operation can be described by Equation 6.9 as:

$$P_{el,boiler,on} = 22.3W + 8.4 \cdot 10^{-4} \cdot P_{nom,burner} \tag{6.16}$$

For nominal burner powers of 15 kW and 24 kW, the electricity demands for boiler operation are $P_{el,boiler,on}$ = 35 W and $P_{el,boiler,on}$ = 42 W, respectively. The electrical power demand for stand-by operation was assumed to be $P_{el,boiler,stby}$ = 9 W. Only for clearly stated periods, in which the power of the boiler is switched off, is the electricity demand of the boiler neglected.

6.1.5.3 Electricity consumption of controllers: $W_{controller}$

For each output of the controller, an electrical power consumption of 1 W was assumed. Therefore, the total electrical energy consumption of the controller was assumed to be:

$$W_{controller} = \text{no. of el.controller outputs} \cdot 8760 \text{ Wh/a}$$

The electrical energy consumption of the controller in the reference systems was not taken into account.

6.1.5.4 Primary parasitic energy consumption: E_{par}

The primary parasitic energy consumption is then calculated using an electricity generation efficiency (η_{el}) of 40% in Equation 6.17:

$$E_{par//par,ref} = \frac{W_{par//par,ref}}{\eta_{el}} \tag{6.17}$$

with η_{el} = 40%.

6.1.6 Combined total energy consumption

The combined total energy consumption of the solar combisystem (E_{total}) is defined as the sum of the combined auxiliary energy consumption (E_{aux}; see Equation 6.3) and the primary parasitic energy consumption (E_{par}; see Equation 6.17):

$$E_{total} = E_{aux} + E_{par} \tag{6.18}$$

For the reference system, the combined total energy consumption ($E_{total,ref}$) is defined as the sum of the final energy demand of the boiler (E_{ref}; see Equation 6.5) and the primary parasitic energy consumption of the reference system ($E_{par,ref}$; see Equation 6.17):

$$E_{total,ref} = E_{ref} + E_{par,ref} \tag{6.19}$$

Note that for the reference and auxiliary boilers, the final energy consumption (the lower heating value of the consumed fuel) was taken into account, whereas for parasitic energy and electrical heating elements, an electricity generation efficiency was applied.

Tables 6.4–6.8 show the values for Q_{SH}, Q_{DHW}, the specific space heating demand $Q_{SH,spec}$ (Q_{SH} per m² of floor area of the building), the annual operation time of the space heating pump, the final energy demand of the reference boiler (E_{ref}), the primary parasitic energy consumption ($E_{par,ref}$), and the combined total energy consumption of the reference system ($E_{total,ref}$). All values were calculated for the building models as described in Chapter 3 with a specific annual mean space heating demand of 30 kWh/m²a (SFH 30), 60 kWh/m²a (SFH 60), 100 kWh/m²a (SFH 100), and 45 kWh/m²a (MFH 45), in Zurich and for three different climates, respectively. The DHW load differs for different locations as a result of different cold water inlet temperatures.

Table 6.4. Annual space heating energy demand, Q_{SH}, and DHW energy demand, Q_{DHW}, of the reference system

	Q_{SH} (kWh/a)				Q_{DHW} (kWh/a)	
	SFH 30	SFH 60	SFH 100	MFH 45	SFH	MFH
Carpentras	1565	3587	6925	9320	2723	13568
Zurich	4319	8569	14283	22543	3040	15208
Stockholm	6264	12227	19773	31850	3122	15656
	$Q_{SH,spec}$ (kWh/m²a)					
Carpentras	11.2	25.6	49.5	18.6		
Zurich	30.9	61.2	102.0	45.1		
Stockholm	44.7	87.3	141.2	63.7		

Table 6.5. Annual operation time of the space heating pump (in hours)

	SFH 30	SFH 60	SFH 100	MFH 45
Carpentras	2945	3840	4908	4277
Zurich	4827	5206	5568	5289
Stockholm	5328	5810	6094	5857

Table 6.6. Final energy demand of reference system, E_{ref} (in kWh/a)

E_{ref}	SFH 30	SFH 60	SFH 100	MFH 45
Carpentras	5806	8183	12,100	31,786
Zurich	9411	14,410	21,130	49,967
Stockholm	11,790	18,770	27,670	61,629

Table 6.7. Primary parasitic energy consumption of the reference system, $E_{par,ref}$, in kWh/a

	SFH 30				SFH 60			
	W_{boiler}/η_{el}	W_{DHW}/η_{el}	W_{SH}/η_{el}	$W_{par,ref}/\eta_{el}$	W_{boiler}/η_{el}	W_{DHW}/η_{el}	W_{SH}/η_{el}	$W_{par,ref}/\eta_{el}$
Carpentras	219	31	685	934	227	31	893	1151
Zurich	232	34	1122	1388	250	34	1210	1494
Stockholm	241	35	1239	1514	266	35	1351	1652

	SFH 100				MFH 45			
	W_{boiler}/η_{el}	W_{DHW}/η_{el}	W_{SH}/η_{el}	$W_{par,ref}/\eta_{el}$	W_{boiler}/η_{el}	W_{DHW}/η_{el}	W_{SH}/η_{el}	$W_{par,ref}/\eta_{el}$
Carpentras	242	31	1141	1414	290	105	1016	1411
Zurich	275	34	1295	1603	343	115	1256	1715
Stockholm	299	35	1417	1750	377	118	1391	1886

Table 6.8. Combined total energy consumption of the reference system, $E_{total,ref}$, in kWh/a

$E_{total,ref}$	SFH 30	SFH 60	SFH 100	MFH 45
Carpentras	6740	9334	13,520	33,200
Zurich	10,800	15,900	22,730	51,686
Stockholm	13,310	20,420	29,420	63,522

6.2 FRACTIONAL ENERGY SAVINGS

The result of a comparison of solar combisystems depends not only on the system design and reference conditions chosen, but also on the measure that is actually compared, the target function. For example, if the energy consumption of combisystems is examined, a combisystem with a higher solar energy delivery might be less favourable compared to another system with significantly lower parasitic energy consumption. In Section 6.2.1, several types of target functions are defined, by comparing the performance of a solar combisystem with the performance of a non-solar reference heating system.

In order to evaluate the amount of fossil fuels saved by a solar heating system in comparison with a conventional heating system, the following aspects need to be taken into account:

- Because of the larger storage tank in a solar combisystem, the heat losses are increased compared to a conventional heating system.
  - The heat losses should be taken into account for both the solar and the reference heating system, for each set of reference conditions.
- The electricity demand of a solar heating system increases compared with a conventional heating system.
  - The electricity demand of the investigated systems needs to be evaluated and an average electricity generation efficiency needs to be applied.
- The desired DHW and room temperatures are not usually met exactly. However, the average performance of a solar heating system depends strongly on the deviations from the desired temperatures. Therefore, a fair comparison of the technological options is only possible on the basis of the same comfort level. Furthermore, optimization methods that are based on the target function should not lead to the least comfortable configuration.
  - Penalty functions need to be defined in such a way that increased deviation from the set DHW temperature and/or set room temperature interval is accompanied by an increase in the target function.

On one hand, a simple definition of the target function is desired. On the other hand, a complex target function is necessary for a fair overall evaluation. In addition, a penalty function is necessary to carry out optimization procedures on certain design parameters. Therefore, three target functions were defined in the framework of Task 26 to evaluate the fractional savings of a solar combisystem. The definitions are in accordance with the terminology introduced since the 1980s, by both the European standardization committee CEN/TC 312 and the international standardization committee ISO/TC 180, in charge of standards for solar heating technology.

6.2.1 Target functions

The **fractional thermal energy savings** ($f_{sav,therm}$) are defined as the saved combined auxiliary energy consumption of the solar combisystem (E_{aux}) compared with the final energy consumption of a reference system (E_{ref}) when no electrical devices other than a heating element are taken into account:

$$f_{sav,therm} = 1 - \frac{\dfrac{Q_{boiler}}{\eta_{boiler}} + \dfrac{Q_{el.heater}}{\eta_{el.heater}}}{\dfrac{Q_{boiler,re}}{\eta_{boiler,ref}}} = 1 - \frac{E_{aux}}{E_{ref}} \qquad (6.20)$$

with $\eta_{el.heater}$ = 40% for systems that do *not* apply solely renewable energy sources and $\eta_{el.heater}$ = 90% for systems that apply solely renewable electrical energy sources. Thus, if the electrical heater installed is operated with renewable energy, an annual electricity generation efficiency ($\eta_{el.heater}$) of 90% is assumed. Otherwise, the efficiency of the electrical energy generation is assumed to be η_{el} = 40%. With this definition of $f_{sav,therm}$ the boiler efficiencies of both the investigated solar combisystem and the reference system have a strong impact on the values of $f_{sav,therm}$.

The **extended fractional energy savings** ($f_{sav,ext}$) are defined as the saved combined total energy consumption of the solar combisystem, compared to the combined total energy consumption of a reference system (refer to section 6.1.6), taking into account parasitic energy consumptions as well as boiler efficiencies:

$$f_{sav,ext} = 1 - \frac{\dfrac{Q_{boiler}}{\eta_{boiler}} + \dfrac{Q_{el.\,heater}}{\eta_{el.\,heater}} + \dfrac{W_{par}}{\eta_{el}}}{\dfrac{Q_{boiler,ref}}{\eta_{boiler,ref}} + \dfrac{W_{par,ref}}{\eta_{el}}} = 1 - \frac{E_{total}}{E_{total,ref}} \qquad (6.21)$$

with $\eta_{el.heater}$ = 40% for systems that do *not* apply solely renewable energy sources, $\eta_{el.heater}$ = 90% for systems that apply solely renewable electrical energy sources and η_{el} = 40% for all systems. In the definition of $f_{sav,ext}$ the electricity consumption of all system components, such as pumps and controllers, is included as described in Section 6.1. With this definition of $f_{sav,ext}$, systems utilizing fewer electrical devices, more efficient pumps, and more efficient control systems are favoured.

The definition of the **fractional savings indicator** (f_{si}) extends the definition of $f_{sav,ext}$ by the addition of penalty functions if the solar combisystem does not supply the required DHW or room temperatures. For comparison reasons, an additional energy demand is assumed to compensate the reduction of comfort for the user:

$$f_{si} = 1 - \frac{E_{total} + Q_{penalty,red}}{E_{total,ref}} \qquad (6.22)$$

With this indicator, comfort is taken into account as a quantified measure in an optimization process. The definitions and implementation of penalty functions are described in Section 6.2.2.

6.2.2 Penalty functions

If the investigated heating system is not able to fulfil the user demand for the room temperature and DHW supply temperature, an additional energy demand, the penalty, is calculated and interpreted as an auxiliary energy demand of the heating system. The penalty energy was defined as the difference between the penalty of the investigated solar combisystem and that of the reference system; the latter occurs as a result of overheating of the reference building during summer:

$$Q_{penalty,red} = Q_{penalty} - Q_{penalty,ref} \qquad (6.23)$$

The difference between the penalty energies is then added to the numerator of the fractional savings indicator (see Equation 6.22). With this penalty, systems that do not provide the same user comfort can be compared. Furthermore, an optimum for the parameter configuration of a heating system can be evaluated by taking into account user demands.

The set DHW temperature is always met for all of the reference systems. Therefore, the penalty function for the reference DHW supply system is set to zero and only the heat demand of the space heating system needs to be taken into account to calculate the reference system penalty. The penalty function $Q_{\text{penalty,red}}$ can be evaluated as:

$$Q_{\text{penalty,red}} = Q_{\text{penalty,SH}} + Q_{\text{penalty,DHW}} - Q_{\text{penalty,ref}} \qquad (6.24)$$

6.2.1.1 Penalty function for DHW demand

If the set temperature for domestic hot water preparation cannot be delivered by a heating system, a penalty is calculated for every simulation time step, Δt, by:

$$ \qquad (6.25)$$

$$Q_{\text{penalty,DHW},\Delta t} = \Delta t \cdot \dot{C} \left[\text{MAX}\left(0; \frac{T_{\text{set}} - T_{\text{DHW}}}{K}\right) + \left(\text{MAX}\left(0; \frac{T_{\text{set}} - T_{\text{DHW}}}{K}\right) + 1\right)^{x_{\text{DHW}}} - 1 \right] K$$

$Q_{\text{penalty,DHW},\Delta t}$ has the units of Wh.

A heating system that does not supply the domestic hot water set temperature required by the reference conditions delivers less energy to the consumer than an ideal system. This energy lack is added to the target function as a penalty with the first MAX function given in Equation 6.25. To set an extra penalty for not supplying the users' comfort demands, the second term on the right-hand side of Equation 6.25 is given as an exponential function. If a high value of the exponent x_{DHW} is chosen, a system design that delivers large deviations of T_{DHW} from the set temperature is avoided when parameters are identified in an optimization procedure.

In order also to create a monotonic exponential penalty function if $T_{\text{set}} - T_{\text{DHW}}$ < 1, the value of 1 is added to the delivered temperature deviation given in the second MAX function in Equation 6.25. Finally, the value of 1 is subtracted from the exponential function, in order to create a continuous function at $T_{\text{set}} - T_{\text{DHW}} =$ 1. The set temperature for DHW preparation was defined to be $T_{\text{set}} = 45°C$. For the investigations carried out in Task 26, the exponent x_{DHW} was set to 4.

To calculate the annual penalty of the DHW supply system, Equation 6.25 needs to be summed over the one-year period:

$$Q_{\text{penalty,DHW}} = \sum_{\text{number of time steps}} Q_{\text{penalty,DHW},\Delta t} \qquad (6.26)$$

In Figure 6.4 the penalty energy $Q_{\text{penalty,DHW},\Delta t}$ divided by the average heat demand $Q_{\text{demand,DHW},\Delta t}$ is shown as a function of the domestic hot water temperature. The average heat demand is defined as the energy needed to heat water from 10°C to 45°C:

$$Q_{\text{demand,DHW},\Delta t} = \Delta t \cdot \dot{m} c_p \cdot (T_{\text{set}} - T_{\text{in}}) = \Delta t \cdot \dot{m} c_p \cdot 35K$$

6.2.1.2 Penalty function for space heating demand

The penalty function for the space heating system delivers positive values if the mean air temperature in the building, T_{room}, decreases below 19.5°C or rises above

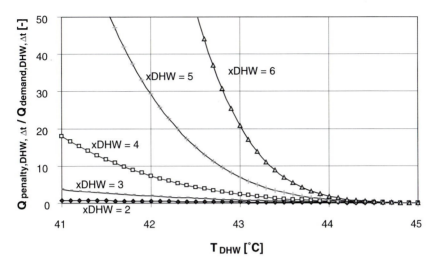

Figure 6.4. Penalty functions for the DHW temperature

24°C within a time step. These two cases, of exceeding the set interval at the lower and higher limits, are described by the following equations. If T_{room} < 19.5°C:

$$Q_{penalty,SH,\Delta t} = (UA)_{building} \cdot \Delta t \cdot MAX\left[0; MAX\left(0; 19.5 - \frac{T_{room}}{°C}\right) + \right. \tag{6.27}$$

$$\left.\left\{MAX\left(0; 19.5 - \frac{T_{room}}{°C}\right) + 1\right\}^{x_{SH}} - 1\right]K$$

If 19.5°C ≤ T_{room} ≤ 24°C:

$$Q_{penalty,SH,\Delta t} = 0 \tag{6.28}$$

If T_{room} > 24°C:

$$Q_{penalty,SH,\Delta t} = (UA)_{building} \cdot \Delta t \cdot MAX\left[0; \left\{MAX\left(0; \frac{T_{room}}{°C} - 24\right) + 1\right\}^{x_{SH}} - 1\right]K \tag{6.29}$$

where $(UA)_{building}$ is the heat loss rate of the zone to be heated; see Table 6.9.

Table 6.9. Penalty functions for space heating demand and the UA values for the reference buildings

	SFH 30	SFH 60	SFH 100	MFH 45
	Reference building: $Q_{penalty,SH}$ for T_{room} > 24°C in kWh/a			
Carpentras	27338	31807	28129	39312
Zurich	7101	6208	3766	5624
Stockholm	6247	5091	2453	4065
	UA value for the building in W/K			
	94	165	243	465

In the case where the room temperature falls below the lower limit of the set room temperature, the difference between the energy required by the consumer and the energy supplied by the heating system is added in form of a penalty. In order to be expressed in terms of energy, the penalty is defined as the product of $(UA)_{building}$ and the difference between required room temperature and the supplied room temperature, as given in the first MAX function of Equation 6.27. In the case of overheating of the building, a penalty function term proportional to a linear temperature difference does not need to be taken into account. However, exponential terms of the penalty functions are defined for both cases, exceeding the interval at the lower temperature limit and at the higher temperature limit, in order to take into account the users' comfort demands. Again, monotonic exponential functions are used in Equations 6.27 and 6.29; see the explanation below Equation 6.25.

The annual penalty for the space heating system is calculated as the sum of the penalties for the single time steps as:

$$Q_{penalty,SH} = \sum_{\text{number of time steps}} Q_{penalty,SH,\Delta t} \qquad (6.30)$$

In Figure 6.5, the penalty energy $Q_{penalty,SH,\Delta t}$ divided by the mean building energy demand, $Q_{mean,\Delta t}$, is shown as a function of the room temperature for $x_{SH} = 1.5, 1.8$ and 2. The mean building energy demand is defined as the heat loss from a building at 20°C, at a mean ambient temperature of 9°C:

$$Q_{mean,\Delta t} = (UA)_{building} \cdot \Delta t \cdot (T_{set,room} - T_{amb,mean}) = (UA)_{building} \cdot \Delta t \cdot (20°C - 9°C)$$

For the investigations carried out in Task 26 the exponent x_{SH} was set to 2.

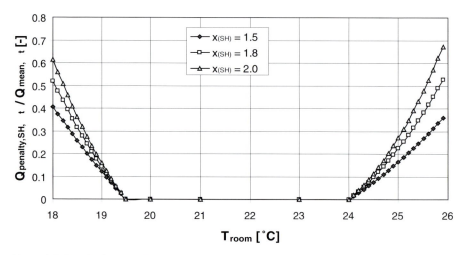

Figure 6.5. Penalty functions for the room temperature

6.2.1.3 Penalty function of the reference system for SH

The space heating penalty functions were calculated for the reference heating systems for each building and climate (see Table 6.9). They consist of a (zero) penalty for the heating case (for $T_{room} < 19.5°C$) and a high value of summer overheating (for $T_{room} > 24°C$). The penalty function of the reference case will be subtracted from the penalty function of the solar heating system. In this way, the penalty for overheating due to passive solar gains is eliminated.

6.3 COMBISYSTEMS CHARACTERIZATION

Characterization of solar combisystems with proper evaluation of performance is difficult. For example, is a solar combisystem with a 10 m² solar collector providing fractional energy savings of 50% for a well insulated house in Carpentras 'better' than another with a 20 m² solar collector that 'only' provides fractional energy savings of 20% for a badly insulated house in Stockholm? What if the first system has a lifetime of 15 years and costs 30% less than the second one, which has a lifetime of 25 years?

A number of questions arise:

- Are some solar combisystems better adapted to particular climates?
- Are some solar combisystems better adapted to particular loads?
- What is the influence of the collector size?
- How can one compare a solar combisystem which has a collector range between 5 and 12 m², with a solar combisystem which has a collector range between 10 and 30 m²?
- Is it possible to develop a method that removes all external parameters (climate, load, collector size) and makes it possible to characterize a solar combisystem in an intrinsic way?

6.3.1 FSC method

Within the framework of Task 26, a new method has been developed to characterize solar combisystems in a simple way. This method makes it possible to compare systems built in different locations, with different collector areas and delivering heat to different space heating and domestic hot water loads. The basic concept is to compare the actual fractional energy savings of the system with the maximum theoretical fractional energy savings. The method is appropriate for the representation of the two main target functions:

- the fractional *thermal* energy savings $(f_{sav,therm})$
- the *extended* fractional energy savings $(f_{sav,ext})$.

6.3.1.1 FSC definition

The monthly final energy demand for heating $(E_{ref,month})$ in an example house is shown in the first line of Table 6.10. The data include store and boiler losses as well as boiler efficiency, giving the so-called **reference consumption**. This monthly reference consumption without a solar combisystem, $E_{ref,month}$ (kWh), is calculated in the same way as the annual reference consumption (Equations 6.4 and 6.5) with the following equation:

$$E_{ref,month} = \frac{(Q_{SH}+Q_{DHW}+Q_{loss,ref})}{\eta_{boiler,ref}} \tag{6.31}$$

Table 6.10. Example calculation of FSC value, in kWh

	Jan	Feb	Mar	Apr	May	Jun	Jul	Aug	Sep	Oct	Nov	Dec	Total
Reference consumption	2659	2131	1477	989	412	320	237	226	359	1230	1905	2494	14,415
Solar irradiation available	716	991	1477	1740	1989	2017	2335	2183	1769	1230	663	558	17,668
Usable solar energy	716	991	1477	989	412	320	237	226	359	1230	663	558	7943
													FSC 0.57

The solar irradiation on the collector area is calculated by multiplying the solar collector area A (m²) by the monthly hemispherical solar irradiation in the collector plane H (kWh/m²). The monthly reference consumption and the solar irradiation are shown on Figure 6.6, where they define three zones:

1. Final energy consumption of the building, that exceeds the available solar radiation.
2. Final energy consumption of the building that could be saved by solar energy. This is called **usable solar energy** $(Q_{solar,usable})$.
3. Solar radiation that exceeds the final energy consumption of the building.

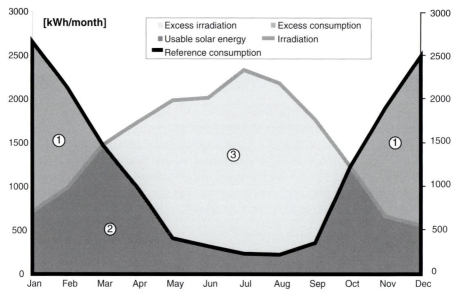

Figure 6.6. Monthly plot of final energy consumption for a reference system and solar radiation for a specific collector area, azimuth and slope

$Q_{solar,usable}$ is calculated on a monthly basis in a simple way, using the solar collector area A (m²), the monthly solar irradiation in the collector plane H (kWh/m²) and the monthly reference consumption $E_{ref,month}$ (kWh). The minimum of this reference consumption and the available irradiation is taken for each month and then summed over the year:

$$Q_{solar,usable} = \sum_{1}^{12} \min(E_{ref,month}, A \cdot H) \qquad (6.32)$$

The yearly **reference consumption** E_{ref} is the sum of the monthly reference consumptions $E_{ref,month}$:

$$E_{ref} = \sum_{1}^{12} E_{ref,month} \qquad (6.33)$$

Dividing the usable solar energy $Q_{solar,usable}$ (area 2 in Figure 6.6) by the reference consumption of the house E_{ref} (areas 1 and 2 in Figure 6.6), a new parameter, called **Fractional Solar Consumption (FSC)** is defined. FSC can be considered as the *maximum theoretical fractional energy savings* that could be reached if the solar combisystem had no losses:

$$FSC = \frac{Q_{solar,usable}}{E_{ref}} \qquad (6.34)$$

FSC is a dimensionless quantity, which simultaneously takes into account the climate, the building (space heating and domestic hot water loads) and the size of the collector area and its orientation and tilt angle, but which *does not depend on the choice of any particular solar combisystem.*

Table 6.10 shows an example of the calculation procedure, resulting in a FSC of 0.57.

Comparing the real fractional energy savings to FSC gives a good indication of the 'effectiveness' of a solar combisystem; the closer f_{sav} is to FSC, the better the solar combisystem converts the usable solar energy into real auxiliary energy savings.

6.3.1.2 Relation between fractional energy savings and fractional solar consumption

Analysis of simulations made in the framework of Task 26 has shown that plotting the target functions, real fractional energy savings (thermal or extended), against FSC gives a cloud of points with a parabolic shape. Thus the target functions can be expressed by a *very simple parabolic equation in FSC*, and the coefficients for it can be identified with a very good regression coefficient (close to 1):

$$f_{sav} = a \cdot FSC^2 + b \cdot FSC + c \qquad (6.35)$$

The fractional thermal energy savings and the extended fractional energy savings are calculated according to the equations given in Section 6.2.

Figure 6.7 is an example of the relationship between $f_{sav,therm}$ and FSC. Points have been calculated for the three reference climates and the three reference houses

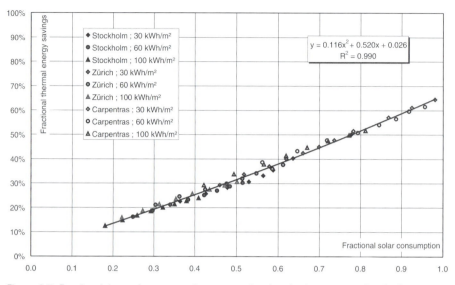

Figure 6.7. Fractional thermal energy savings versus fractional solar consumption for System #3a, calculated with PSD-MI (CSTB, 1998)

defined by Task 26 and for several collector sizes. For this diagram, a French design tool for System #3a, called PSD-MI (CSTB, 1998), has been used. The reference values (domestic hot water tank losses and boiler efficiency) are not exactly the same as those defined in Task 26, but this does not matter: what is important to consider is the distribution of points. It can be seen that the points are close to the mean parabola (regression factor very close to 1).

Points for the $f_{sav} = f(\text{FSC})$ curve can be obtained in different ways:

- simulations using TRNSYS
- simulations using other simulation programs or design tools
- measurements: if the same system is installed in various locations or with different sizes, then several points can be plotted on the $f_{sav} = f(\text{FSC})$ diagram
- laboratory tests.

However, if the points come from different sources, the reference conditions should be the same because both f_{sav} and FSC are dependent on the reference conditions.

As the FSC method is a simplified method, it is important to have in mind the main assumptions. These are summarized in Table 6.11.

6.3.1.3 How to use the FSC concept

The FSC characteristic ($f_{sav} = f(\text{FSC})$) can be used in different ways:

- If the FSC is calculated for different loads and climates, and all representative points are fitted with one parabolic equation, a characteristic curve of the

Table 6.11 Major assumptions of the FSC method

Assumptions	Implications
Exactly the same reference conditions must be used for the solar combisystems and reference systems	With results coming from different design tools, correction of the calculation of both FSC and the fractional energy savings is needed to be consistent with Task 26 reference values
$E_{ref,month}$ depends on the definition of the reference system and specifically on its heat source; in Task 26, a gas boiler was used, with constant efficiency of 85%	
Simulations have to be done in the same way; for comparison of curves coming from different programs, it has to be assumed that the programs deliver identical (or very similar) results	
No large spread in the values; the regression factor R^2 has to be close to 1	Elimination of the points where FSC = 1 and where the comfort criteria are not reached
There are some limitations to the use of the method:	
• orientation only up to 45° from south • tested only for DHW 100 – 300 litres/day • not valid for FSC = 1	• only for houses with permanent occupation • limitation for possible collector sizes • limitation of DHW load to 150–300 litres/day

system is obtained. This allows easy visualization of the global behaviour of the system and makes it possible to compare different systems directly. For example, Figure 6.8 shows the result of the optimization of System #4; fractional energy savings have increased by about 3–5 percentage points.

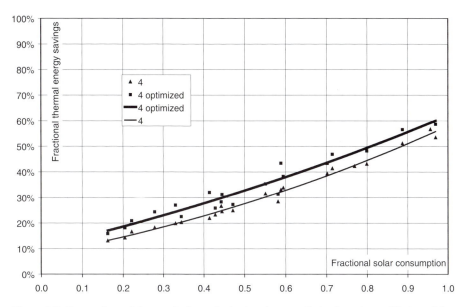

Figure 6.8. Comparison of the results for optimized and non-optimized versions of System #4

- If the representative points are sorted by climate, the various parabolae will show the behaviour of the system according to the climate.
- If the representative points are sorted by load, the various parabolae will show the behaviour of the system according to the load. In Figure 6.9 it can be seen that for System #2 performances are lower in well insulated houses. As a result of the very low load and the fact that there is no storage for space heating, the system is quickly 'saturated'.

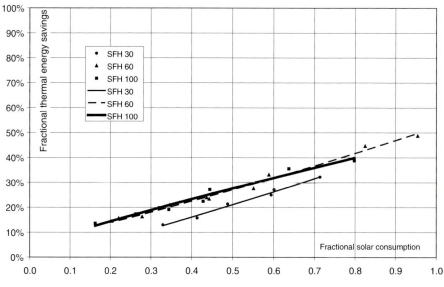

Fig. 6.9: Influence of load for System #2

With the FSC approach, each target function is defined by the specific parameter values of Equation 6.35 (a, b, c), which characterize the global behaviour of the solar combisystem, taking into account the quality of the solar collector, the efficiency of the auxiliary boiler, the insulation of the heat store, the behaviour of the controller and so on.

Equation 6.35 is very simple, but the accuracy of the simplified formula can be increased and the splitting of points can be decreased by introducing a storage-size correction factor. However, to quickly compare different systems in a simple way, the method without storage-size correction factor is preferable, because it can be represented graphically and the visual intercomparison is easy.

As it is easy to calculate the **fractional solar consumption** of a solar combisystem from the meteorological data, the heat load of the house and the collector area, the method presented gives a simple way to calculate quickly the yearly performance of a solar combisystem, provided that the house is occupied continuously all through the year. The FSC method forms the base of the 'Combisun' program, presented in Section 8.2.2.

6.3.1.4 Systems intercomparison using the FSC concept

Nine systems have been simulated in the framework of Task 26. Figure 6.10 presents the range of collector areas and storage sizes for seven of the systems.

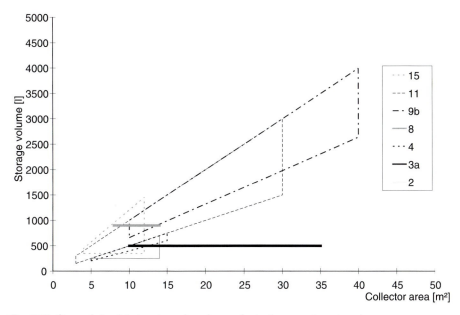

Fig. 6.10: Sizes of simulated systems (numbers refer to the generic systems)

System #9b usually uses a polymer flat-plate collector, which is less efficient (and potentially less expensive) than the reference collector used for simulations. This is why collector areas up to only 30 m² have been simulated, although areas up to 40 m² can be installed.

System #19, usually designed for multi-family houses, could not be represented in this diagram; collector areas vary between 25 and 250 m², and the specific storage volume varies between 40 and 370 l/m².

Major assumptions of the comparison

The major assumptions of the comparison are as follows:

• All use the same reference collector, defined in section 6.1.2. This was necessary for system concepts, including hydraulic design and control strategies, to be compared. The results cannot be used directly for intercomparison of commercial systems, because the solar collectors in commercial systems have different characteristics from those of the Task 26 collector.
• The boiler is part of the system and thus varies from system to system, as do the store losses (see Table 6.13)

Table 6.12 gives an overview of the results. Many other simulations have been performed for the sensitivity analysis, but for this intercomparison, only points with FSC less than 1 have been taken into account. A few points have also been eliminated because the comfort criteria were not achieved.

In columns 3–6 and 8–11, the parameters of the parabolic equation (Equation 6.35) are given for the fractional energy savings $f_{sav, therm}$ and $f_{sav, ext}$ respectively, along with the regression factor R^2. The closer the regression factor is to 1, the better the correlation, and the smaller the scatter of the points.

Table 6.12 Parameter values for the quadratic equation in FSC identified from the detailed system simulations

System	Number of points	$f_{sav, th}$ a	b	c	R^2	E_{aux} R^2	$f_{sav, ext}$ a	b	c	R^2	E_{total} R^2
#2★	18	0.073	0.377	0.065	0.980	0.999	0.047	0.308	0.056	0.971	0.999
#3a	31	0.244	0.292	0.178	0.966	0.995	0.199	0.324	0.178	0.969	0.995
#4	20	0.145	0.368	0.107	0.948	0.994	0.100	0.337	0.093	0.960	0.996
#8	23	0.315	0.245	0.131	0.979	0.998	0.212	0.292	0.105	0.978	0.998
#9b	46	0.342	0.246	0.048	0.967	0.996	0.258	0.238	0.031	0.971	0.997
#11 oil	23	0.212	0.301	0.035	0.963	0.998	0.196	0.232	0.029	0.969	0.999
#11 gas	45	0.306	0.153	0.155	0.950	0.993	0.237	0.142	0.131	0.959	0.997
#15	86	0.322	0.182	0.243	0.985	0.996	0.143	0.252	0.224	0.985	0.998
#19	100	0.161	0.390	0.036	0.957	0.998	0.119	0.379	0.014	0.944	0.984

★ Only for loads SFH 60 and SFH 100, according to Figure 6.9: System #2 should not be installed in low-energy houses like SFH 30. Therefore, for further analysis, points for SFH 30 have been omitted

To get a better idea of the accuracy of the FSC method, the estimated and simulated combined auxiliary energy used by the solar heating systems is compared. The estimated values were calculated using fractional energy savings from Equation 6.35. The simulated values were obtained from TRNSYS. Column 7 of Table 6.12 shows the regression factors for the combined auxiliary energy used only for heating purposes, whereas column 12 includes the primary parasitic energy consumption.

Figure 6.11 shows a comparison between 392 estimated and simulated values of the combined auxiliary energy demand used by the solar heating system for the nine simulated systems.

It can be seen that estimated results, i.e. those estimated from the FSC characteristic, are very close to simulated ones: 84% of the estimated values deviate by less than 5% from the simulated ones. 12% deviate by between 5% and 10%, and only 4% deviate more than 10%. For the multi-family house, the points are a little more scattered because of a wider range of collector areas and storage tanks than used for solar combisystems in single-family houses.

Figure 6.12 presents the FSC characteristics for systems simulated in the frame of Task 26, with all systems using the same collector.

Figures 6.10 and 6.12 can be used for a rough intercomparison. They also show some other interesting aspects:

- Some systems can be installed with a wide range of collector areas (Systems #3a, #9b and #11). Others can only be installed with a limited collector area (Systems #8 and #15). This has to be considered when comparing the $f_{sav} = f(FSC)$ curves.

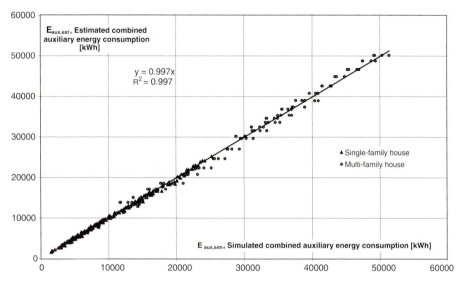

Figure 6.11. Accuracy of the FSC method

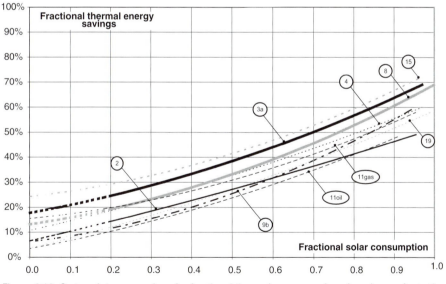

Figure 6.12. System intercomparison for fractional thermal energy savings (numbers refer to the generic systems)

- Direct comparison between systems using a heating floor for the space heating loop (Systems #3a and #9b) and others using radiators has to be made cautiously. The two types of system do not provide the same comfort for identical inside air temperatures. Systems using large heat emitters, like heating floors or heating walls, can use a lower inside air temperature, and consequently require less energy. On the other hand, they create higher losses from the floor than in houses using standard radiators in the space heating loop, resulting in an increase in the energy consumption. These two phenomena compensate one another more or less, so it is not unrealistic to take the same reference space heating loads for low-temperature heating systems and for conventional, radiator-based heating systems.

- Systems #3a and #9b have been simulated with the same air set-point temperature as the other systems. So it can be reasonably considered that, for these systems, the real auxiliary energy consumption would be a little lower than the calculated one, and consequently the fractional energy savings would be a little larger; f_{sav} values are a little underestimated, especially for small FSC values. Therefore, the slope of the curves $f_{sav} = f(\text{FSC})$ is also steeper for Systems #3a and #9b than for the other systems.
- If only the thermal performance is considered, System #15 is obviously better than all the others, especially for small FSC values. Then come System #3a and System #8. Systems #4 and #11 (gas) behave in a similar manner.
- The four other systems seem to have a poorer performance, but their performance has to be analysed cautiously:
  - System #2 shows a worse behaviour when the FSC value is increased. The slope of the curve is the smallest of all curves. This is caused by the lack of storage capacity for space heating: excess solar energy cannot be stored and is thus 'wasted'. Comparison between Systems #2 and #4 shows the improvement given by the space heating storage. Both systems have very similar hydraulic layouts, except for the bigger DHW tank in System #4 that is used for heat storage for space heating. The difference in fractional energy savings for these two systems is between 5 points for small FSC values and 10 points for larger FSC values, where System #2 is 'saturated'. Simulation results in the technical report (Letz, 2002) on System #2 show that increasing the heat capacity of the radiators makes it possible to improve the performance for larger solar collector areas by storing energy in the heat emission system. It is expected that this effect can often be implemented in practice, as the system is often used in houses with floor heating in the bathroom.
  - System #9b uses electricity as auxiliary energy, with an electrical heater integrated into the storage tank. An efficiency of 90% has been used for the electric heater. When comparisons are made with other systems using oil or gas auxiliary boilers, the efficiency of these boilers has to be kept in mind.
  - The effect of using a gas boiler instead of an oil boiler can be seen by looking at System #11. The gas boiler increases the fractional energy savings by only 7–8%, whereas its annual efficiency is approximately 10% greater than that of the oil boiler.
  - System #19 is designed for multi-family houses. It has been simulated for a house with five flats. Heat losses for the connection pipes between the solar collector and the heat storage tank, and especially for the distribution loop, are much higher than for single-family houses. Therefore, System #19 is not directly comparable with the other systems.

- The f_{sav} value for FSC = 0 (no solar collector), obtained by extrapolation of the curves to the y axis, gives an indication of the quality of the system compared with the reference one, particularly concerning the boiler efficiency and heat losses from the storage tank(s). All systems studied perform better than the reference system. Once again, System #15 is best. To provide a deeper understanding of this, Table 6.13 shows some key data for the different systems concerning the boiler and store(s). The data are all for the Zurich climate, the SFH 60 house and a collector area near 10 m², except for System #19, where the MFH 45 and a collector area of 50 m² was used.

Note that the so-called 'standard type 170' boilers are theoretical boilers, the parameter values of which have been derived from data on actual boilers but have been adjusted somewhat. The values are reasonable for a moderate-efficiency condensing gas boiler and for a high-efficiency non-condensing oil boiler. Only the models of the burners in Systems #8 and #15 have been derived directly from measured data.

Some of the important data from Table 6.13 are:

- The main parameter in this comparison is the boiler efficiency, which differs by about 10% between the standard gas and biomass boilers, and from 90% to 105% for different gas boilers (based on the lower heating value). Systems using specific condensing gas boilers (Systems #8 and #15) or systems using the standard Task 26 gas boiler with a low-temperature space heating loop (System #3a) are the best. At the opposite extreme, System #11 (oil) is handicapped by the poor efficiency of the auxiliary boiler.
- Systems #2 and #11 have an auxiliary electrical heater integrated into the storage tank, which allows the auxiliary boiler to be turned off in summertime. Turning off the boiler increases the fractional energy savings by up to a couple of percent, and the annual boiler efficiency by about 1% for the simulated gas boiler. As explained above, an increased degree of condensing, either through good design of the boiler (Systems #8 and #15), or through the use of a low temperature from the space heating loop (System #3a), is much more significant for the mean annual efficiency of the main boiler.
- The analysis of the effect of the store losses is more difficult because the losses are related to the insulation as well as to the temperature and volume of the auxiliary heated part of the store. This depends on the integration of the set temperature for the auxiliary heater, as well as the heat management philosophy, especially in summer. However, it seems that the heat storage losses play a secondary role, except when the tank is particularly badly insulated.
- When Systems #2 and #4 are compared, it can be seen that they have similar heat storage losses. However, auxiliary boiler efficiency for System #2 is a little smaller than that for System #4. This is probably due to the lack of storage for space heating, resulting in a more frequent use of the auxiliary boiler when the solar energy delivered by the solar loop is less than the space heating load. The possibility of turning off the auxiliary boiler and using the integrated electric heater in summer, which should theoretically improve the annual efficiency, does not seem to be able to compensate for this effect.

Table 6.13 Data for the Zurich climate; SFH 60 load for Systems #2–#15 and MFH45 for System #19

System	Mean annual efficiency of the main boiler	Main auxiliary energy source	TRNSYS boiler type	Electricity used during the summer period	Annual storage losses	Storage tank size	Specific storage size	Heat loss rate from the store	Set temperature for the auxiliary heater	Volume of the part of the store heated by the auxiliary heater
Unit	%			kWh (primary energy)	kWh	litres	l/m²	W/K	°C	litres
#2	88.3	Gas	Standard type 170	365	453	280	28	1.9	53	98
#3a	100.4	Gas	Standard type 170	–	1178	500	50	4.48	50	150
#4	90.8	Gas	Standard type 170	–	594	750	50	1.94	50.5	75
#8	98.8%	Gas	Integrated burner	–	1833	830	69	6.3^1	60	415
#9²	90.0%	Electricity	Integrated heater	–	353	1000	100	1.79	Adapted to the space heating demand³	352
#11 (oil)	82.2%	Oil	Standard type 170	25	780	700	70	2.36	60	140
#11 (gas)	92.1%	Gas	Standard type 170	25	780	700	70	2.36	60	140
#15	105.1%	Gas	Integrated burner	–	997	635	63	2.37	57	158
#19⁴	95.1%	Gas	Standard type 170	–	4369	5500	50	13.9	70	500

1 Integrated burner losses taken into account

2 Values are given for the space heating storage tank. Auxiliary energy for domestic hot water is brought in a separate small tank (80 litres), with a heat loss rate of 1 W/K and a set-point temperature of 47.5°C

3 35°C for the coldest day for the SFH 60 building in the Zurich climate

4 Values are given for the space heating storage tank. Domestic hot water is heated in five separate small tanks (250 litres), with a heat loss rate of 2.8 W/K and a set-point temperature of 60°C. The additional annual storage losses are 2864 kWh for these five tanks

- Although System #3a is using the standard Task 26 gas boiler, its mean annual efficiency is high because the exhaust gas can condense most of the time because of the low return temperatures from the space heating floor. Therefore, low-temperature heat emitters, like floor heating or wall heating systems should be preferred. Moreover, stand-by losses are reduced because the boiler is actually turned off by the controller when there is no demand for auxiliary energy. However, the insulation of the storage tank in this system could be improved, thus slightly increasing the fractional energy savings.
- Integrated burners show higher efficiencies than external boilers, because part of the heat losses are actually gains to the storage tank. On the other hand, systems with integrated auxiliary burner (System #8) may have greater storage tank losses than others.
- If Systems #15 and #3a are compared, it can be seen that they have similar storage tank losses. The difference between the two f_{sav} curves is mainly related to the difference in the boiler efficiencies.
- Systems #8 and #3a have similar boiler efficiencies. The difference between the two f_{sav} curves is mainly related to the difference in the storage tank losses. In System #8, the auxiliary heated volume is nearly three times as large as in System #3a, and is maintained at a temperature 10 K higher.
- Systems #4 and #11 (gas) have comparable performances because of the similar boiler efficiencies and storage tank losses.
- System #9b has low storage tank losses. The insulation of the store is thick, and the set-point temperature is varied so as to supply the floor heating system and not domestic hot water. On the coldest day for the Zurich SFH 60 building the temperature of the tank is only 35°C, considerably lower than for other combisystems. When this is taken into account, together with other favourable features such as a high efficiency for the auxiliary electrical heater and the lack of heat exchangers, it can be concluded that the average value of fractional energy savings compared to other systems can be explained by the introduction of simple, unsophisticated heat stratification management.
- In spite of having high boiler efficiency, the performance of System #19 is a little worse than the others. This is due to the relatively high pipe losses in the collector loop and the losses in the long heat distribution pipes in the multi-family building. In addition, heat-store losses are relatively high as a result of the high set temperature for the auxiliary heater in the space heating storage tank and of additional losses in the individual domestic hot water tanks.

When parasitic electricity is also considered, things change a little; Figure 6.13 presents the results for the $f_{sav, ext}$ target function:

- For all systems except System #3a, $f_{sav, ext}$ is lower than $f_{sav, therm}$ by approximately 2% for small FSC values and 7–10% for larger FSC values. This means that System #3a uses less parasitic electricity than others, especially when the collector area increases.
- Systems #3a and #15 are close together, with System #15 better at low FSC values and System #3a better for large FSC values.

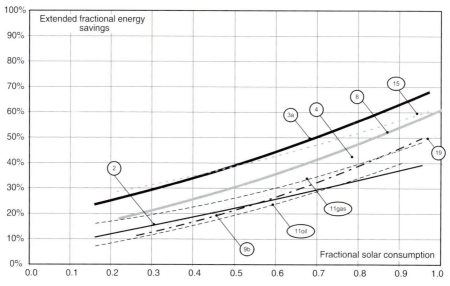

Figure 6.13. System intercomparison for extended fractional energy savings

- System #8 also has a better behaviour than others with regard to parasitic electricity.
- The difference in parasitic electricity consumption becomes greater at high FSC as the collector pump is being used more during the year.

6.3.2 Cost analysis

6.3.2.1 Cost range of the different solar combisystems

In Section 4.4, typical costs of the solar combisystems have been given. In practice, these costs may be subject to large variations in each particular case. Therefore, in order to make a fair comparison between systems, the following methodology has been adopted.

For each generic solar combisystem, the total cost without taxes includes the following components and their installation:

- solar collectors mounted into the roof (integrated collectors)
- collector piping with insulation
- solar hydraulic equipment (storage tanks, pump, valves, controllers, etc.)
- auxiliary boiler
- boiler piping with insulation
- antifreeze fluid
- space heating loop (heat distribution lines and heat emission devices) designed for heating rooms with a total floor area of 130 m².

The total cost of a reference system in the country of origin is given for comparison. The difference between the cost of the solar combisystem and the cost of this reference system, called 'additional' cost, is believed to be more reliable for system intercomparison than the total cost itself, even within a single country.

However, when comparing figures, the reader should remember that the economic background of the manufacturer, the differences in purchasing power in each country, and the national market structure and price level, as well as the level of comfort offered by the systems under consideration, are also reflected in the cost information.

The choice of the reference system depends on the generic system under consideration. The reference system has no solar collector, but has the same auxiliary energy source, the same heat distribution lines and heat emission devices, and a comparable DHW production unit, as well as a similar controller. The heating services delivered to the inhabitants in the form of space heating and domestic hot water by both the solar combisystem and its reference system are supposed to be equivalent.

Typical system costs are given for collector sizes varying between 4 and 30 m². In order to have a rough intercomparison of costs, the following approach has been adopted:

• Costs have been corrected taking into account the Comparative Price Levels (CPL) given by OECD (2000) (Table 6.14). These correction factors are supposed to eliminate the difference in purchasing power in the different countries. Corrected costs are obtained by dividing the national costs by CPL and multiplying by 100.

Table 6.14. Comparative Price Levels used in the comparison (Source: OECD, 2000)

Country	CPL
Austria (A)	104
Switzerland (CH)	130
Denmark (DK)	125
France (F)	107
Germany (D)	109
Norway (N)	123
The Netherlands (NL)	99
United States (US)	100
EU 15	102
Euro zone	100
Finland (SF)	109
Sweden (S)	117

• The specific total cost (€/m² of solar collector) and of the specific additional cost (€/m² of solar collector) have been calculated.

Figure 6.14 shows the specific costs as a function of the collector area.

The following observations can be made:

• Even if representative points are rather scattered, a general decrease of both the total and the additional specific costs can be observed when the collector area increases.

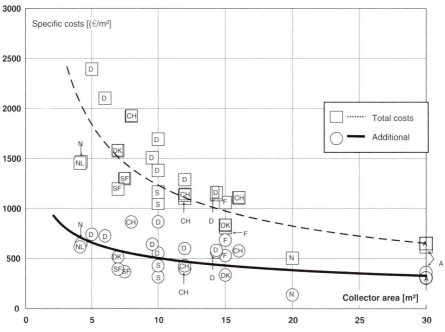

Figure 6.14. Combisystem-specific costs

- Additional costs are rather high in Germany, France and Switzerland, near the average in the Netherlands, Denmark and Austria, and a little lower than the average in Sweden and Finland.
- Additional and total costs of the Norwegian system are very low, because of its simple design (e.g. drainback technology, no heat exchangers) and the use of a plastic solar collector.

This intercomparison gives only trends. In order to get a better evaluation of the systems, costs have to be compared with the thermal performance taken into account. For this purpose, a new indicator and a new diagram have been introduced (Suter, 1991).

6.3.2.2 The cost performance indicator (CPI) diagram
Figure 6.15 shows the **'annual energy savings'** (**thermal or extended**) as a function of the **'additional investment'**, each of which can either be absolute or calculated per m^2 of solar collector. The slope of the line between a point in the diagram and the origin is the reciprocal of the **Cost Performance Indicator (CPI)**. This indicator ($€$ year/kWh) is defined as the additional investment divided by the annual energy savings. The lower the CPI, the better the solar combisystem is. For the example shown on the diagram, an additional investment of $€560/m^2$ and annual energy savings of 700 kWh/m^2 lead to a CPI of $€0.8$ year/kWh.

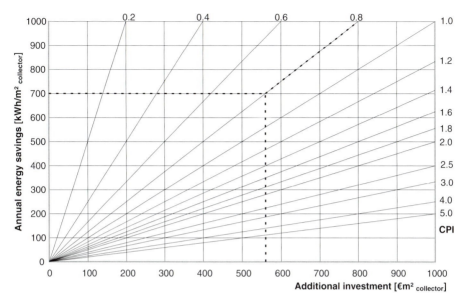

Figure 6.15. Diagram showing definition of the cost performance indicator

The CPI diagram can be used for different types of comparisons between the solar combisystems, for example:

- basic case: several solar combisystems with the same load and the same climate
- effect of load on one system: several loads for the same climate
- effect of climate on one system: several different climates for the same load.

It can also be used to visualize the effect of a particular change for a chosen system. The CPI can also be interpreted in two different ways:

- CPI is the product of the simple payback time in years (no inflation or interest rates considered) and the price of the auxiliary energy used (€/kWh). For example, with a CPI equal to 1 € year/kWh, and a constant energy price of €0.05/kWh, the payback time is 20 years (1/0.05).
- CPI is also the product of the lifetime of the installation and the cost of the saved energy. For example, if the solar combisystem has a lifetime of 25 years and the CPI value is 0.8, the cost of the saved energy is €0.032/kWh (0.8/25). This cost can be compared with the price of the auxiliary energy used to evaluate the economic interest of a project.

For a chosen system, if points are plotted for different climates, loads and collector areas, a cloud of points will be obtained on the CPI diagram. This cloud shows the range in which the cost performance indicator can vary.

6.3.2.3 System intercomparison using the CPI method

In this section, all costs have been corrected using the Comparative Price Levels (CPL) given in Table 6.14.

The CPI diagram is used to make a rough comparison of six simulated solar combisystems (Systems #2, #3a, #4, #8, #11 (gas) and #15).

The additional cost is the difference between the total cost of the solar combisystem and the total cost of an equivalent reference system. It has been assumed that the additional cost can be represented by a linear equation:

$$\text{Additional cost} = A + B \cdot \text{collector area} \tag{6.36}$$

where A is the fixed part of the additional cost (€) and B is the cost per square metre of solar collector (€/m²).

In order to obtain valid cost functions for these systems, the following method has been used:

- Typical costs for the different systems, given in Chapter 4, have been used as inputs.
- Each country has been asked for the cost of 1 m² of solar collector included in the typical cost, and also an estimate of the cost of 1 m² of a collector equivalent to that used in the simulations.
- The fixed part of the additional cost for each system has then been derived.
- If necessary, an extra cost for the boiler has been added to this fixed part, in order to correct the difference between the simulated boiler ('type 170' boiler) and the boiler used in the typical system.
- Then the Cost Price Level correction has been applied in order to obtain comparable costs.
- Finally, a 'mean Task 26 collector cost' has been defined, by calculating a mean value for the reference collector used in the simulations, from estimations given by the different participating countries (DK, F, CH, D, S). This cost is €287/m², including installation costs.

Table 6.15 summarizes the characteristic figures describing each system, together with the fixed part of the additional costs.

Table 6.15 System cost figures for CPI analysis

System	Size of space heating storage tank litres or litres/m²	Size of DHW tank litres	Collector area m²	Fixed part of the additional cost €
#2	–	280	5–14	2565
#3a	–	500	10–35	3460
#4	–	750	15	2620
#8	830	–	8–14	3300
#11 (gas)	75 l/m²	–	7.5–20	1400 for a 750 litre tank
#15	750	–	10–12	3310

Collector areas have been chosen according to Figure 6.10, with the given storage tank capacities. This does not mean that other configurations are not allowed, but to perform a fair CPI analysis, cost functions and performance curves ($f_{sav} = f(\text{FSC})$) have to be given for similar size ranges.

Systems #8 and #15 are factory-made and have an auxiliary burner integrated in the storage tank. The simulated systems therefore correspond to those that are sold. Thus, no cost corrections for boiler costs have been taken into account and a realistic cost function could be determined directly.

For System #3a, the auxiliary boiler is sold by the manufacturer of the system. Because of the optimization process, the simulated auxiliary boiler is more efficient than the standard boiler, especially with regard to the internal heat exchanger. So an additional cost of €300 (before CPL correction) has been added to the solar system cost to take this into account.

For System #11 (gas), it has been assumed that the cost of the simulated gas boiler is equivalent to the cost of the wood boiler included in the typical costs given in Section 4.4. However, as the CPI analysis is performed for a nominal specific storage size of 75 $1/m^2$, an additional cost of €32/m^2 (before CPL correction) is added to the costs in order to take into account the variation of the storage size with collector area.

Systems #2 and #4 are often installed in retrofit houses using the existing boilers. The systems have therefore not been optimized with regard to the boiler. For that reason, the yearly efficiency for the simulated boilers is near to what can be obtained in reality. Thus, no corrections for boiler costs have been added to the typical costs.

Comparison of Systems #9 and #19 with others is hazardous: System #9 uses very different collectors and the determination of a significant cost function is much more difficult. Moreover, System #9 uses electricity as auxiliary energy where the other systems use gas. System #19 is designed for multi-family houses. Therefore Systems #9 and #19 were not included in the CPI analysis.

Major assumptions of the comparison

The major assumptions made in the comparison were as follows:

- The CPI comparison is based on the additional investment, defined as the difference between the cost of the solar combisystem and the cost of a reference system, as explained in Chapter 4. In this chapter, a reference cost for each system has been given. This reference cost is assumed to be valid for the arbitrary reference boiler with an annual efficiency of 85%.
- Costs used in the CPI analysis are not necessarily real costs, but corrected costs taking into account the differences between simulated systems and real systems, with regard to the solar collector and the auxiliary boiler.

In Figures 6.16 and 6.17, the ranges of CPI are given for the six systems studied, with the three reference climates and the three reference single-family houses. *An intercomparison of CPI values with such a diagram implicitly considers that all systems have the same lifetime.*

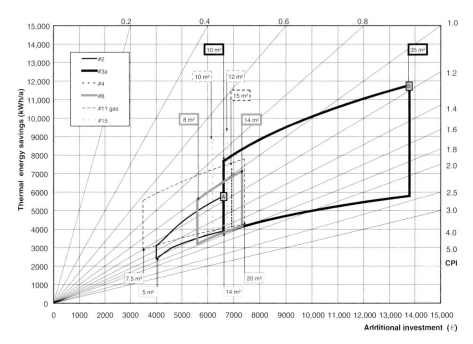

Figure 6.16. Cost Performance Indicator diagrams for six systems (thermal energy savings)

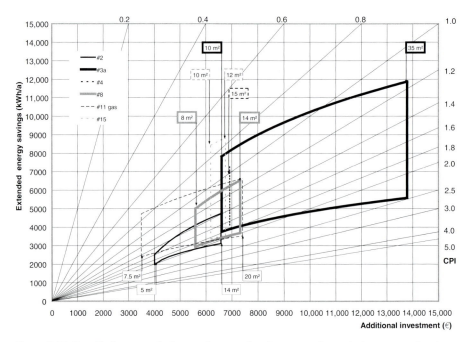

Figure 6.17. Cost Performance Indicator diagrams for six systems (extended energy savings)

The energy savings are defined analogously to the fractional energy savings as:

Thermal energy savings: $E_{sav,therm} = E_{ref} - E_{aux}$ (6.36)

Extended energy savings: $E_{sav,ext} = E_{total,ef} - E_{total}$ (6.37)

Figure 6.16 shows the CPI diagram using thermal energy savings, while Figure 6.17 uses extended energy savings, which also take parasitic electricity into account.

The very different ranges of collector area lead to a range of CPI values:

- between 1.14 and 1.69 for System #2
- between 0.86 and 2.18 for System #3a
- between 0.95 and 1.69 for System #4
- between 1 and 1.76 for System #8
- between 0.63 and 1.74 for System #11 gas
- between 0.70 and 1.55 for System #15.

However, if we considered the same collector ranges (10 to 12 m²) for all systems except System #4, CPI values become much closer:

- between 1.12 and 1.69 for System #2
- between 0.82 and 1.7 for System #3a
- between 1 and 1.75 for System #8
- between 0.7 and 1.40 for System #11 (gas)
- between 0.7 and 1.55 for System #15.

These results demonstrate that the systems are not too different, when performance and financial aspects are considered simultaneously.

From Figure 6.16, it can be seen that CPI values can be similar even with very different sizes and systems. For example, points A and B are obtained for the same house (SHF 100) and the same climate (Stockholm). These points are for Systems #2 and #3a, with collector areas of 14 m² and 35 m² respectively, both leading to a CPI value very close to 1.15. If System #2 is chosen, the collector size cannot exceed 14 m², providing annual thermal savings of 5800 kWh for an investment of €6600. With System #3a, up to 35 m² collector can be installed, providing annual thermal savings of 11,800 kWh for an investment of €13,800. This means that it is as cost-effective to invest a large amount of money for System #3a as to invest a smaller amount of money for System #2.

If the parasitic electricity needed is taken into account (Figure 6.17), System #3a has similar CPI values to System #15, while the relative positions of Systems #2, #8 and #15 do not change much. Even if System #2 has a lower thermal performance than Systems #3a, #8 and #15, the cost is €700–900 lower and leads to a similar CPI value.

However, it should not be forgotten that these figures are only indicative, because there are some uncertainties for the given values. The costs of a solar combisystem in a particular country not only depend on the complexity of the system, but also reflect the state of development of the market. In addition, attention should also be paid to other factors such as the space requirements (see Section 5.1), which could be converted to additional costs for a fairer intercomparison. The lifetime of the systems, which is related to the durability and the reliability of the system (see Section 7.1) could also lead to greater variety in the costs of saved energy.

REFERENCES

Bales C, Bony J, Chèze T, Ellehauge K, Heimrath R, Jaehnig D, Papillon P, Pittet T and Shah L J, 2002, *SHC Task 26: Solar Combisystems, Subtask C, Reports on the Simulation, Optimisation and Analysis of Solar Combisystems*, http://www.iea-shc.org/task26.

CSTB, 1998, *PSD-M: monthly method for evaluating the thermal performances of Direct Solar Floors*, CSTB, Sophia Antipolis, France, http://www.cstb.fr

DIN 4701: 1990, 1990, *Regeln für die Berechnung der Heizlast von Gebäuden.*

EN 12976–2: 2000, 2000, *Thermal Solar Systems and Components – Factory Made Systems – Part 2: Test Methods.*

ENV 12977–1: 2000, 2000, *Thermal Solar Systems and Components – Custom Built Systems – Part 1: General Requirements.*

Gertec, 1999, CO_2-Minderung durch stromsparende Pumpen und Heizungsantriebe, Untersuchung an 136 Gas Brennwertkesseln, Gertec, Essen.

Grundfos, 2000, product information.

Klein S A, Beckmann WA, Mitchell JW, Duffie JA, Duffie NA, Freeman TL, Mitchell JC, Braun JE, Evans BL, Kummer JP, Urban RE, Fiksel A, Thornton JW, Blair NJ, 1998, *TRNSYS, A Transient System Simulation Program – Version 14.2* (as used in this project), Solar Energy Laboratory, University of Wisconsin–Madison, USA.

Letz, T., 2002, *Validation and background information on the FSC procedure, A Technical Report of IEA SHC – Task 26 Solar Combisystems.* http://www.iea-shc.org/task26.

OECD, 2000, *Purchasing Power Parities – Comparative Price Levels, Main Economic Indicators*, July, OECD, http://www.oecd.org

Schröttner J, 2000, *Inquiry on electric power demand of pumps of solar collector fields up to 75 m^2*, AEE-Intec, Gleisdorf.

Streicher W, Fink C, Riva R, Heimrath R, Heinz A, Kaufmann H and Purkarthofer G, 2002, *Solarunterstützte Wärmenetze, Endbericht zum gleichnamigen Projekt in der Forschungsausschreibung 'Haus der Zukunft' im Auftrag des BMVIT*, Institut für Wärmetechnik, TU Graz.

Suter J-M, 1991, 'Kosten/Nutzen-Vergleich thermischer Solaranlagen in der Schweiz', *Proceedings of the Conférence internationale Energie solaire et Bâtiment CISBAT'91, Ecole polytechnique fédérale de Lausanne, Lausanne*, 10–11 October.

Vajen K, 1996, *Systemuntersuchungen und Modellierung solarunterstützter Warmwasserbereitungssysteme in Freibädern*, Dissertation. Universität Marburg.

WILO, 2002, product information.

7 Durability and reliability of solar combisystems

Jean-Marc Suter, Peter Kovács, Robert Hausner, Huib Visser and Markus Peter

Of major importance to the competitiveness of solar thermal systems, however rarely assessed, is the reliability and durability of these systems. As the cost structure of a solar heating system is a high cost but low initial operating costs, it is essential to the owner that the system maintains its high performance for many years. This is why durable materials and a reliable system operation are of great importance in a solar heating system. When different concepts are compared, durability and reliability therefore have to be carefully considered in order to reach a true optimum.

There are two parts in this chapter. First, general considerations related to durability and reliability are given for materials and system features. Then, the system stagnation behaviour is considered in detail, including new research results on how to design even more reliable systems.

7.1 GENERAL CONSIDERATIONS

In this section, the durability and reliability aspects relevant for solar combisystems are summarized. It has to be emphasized that with proper design, durability and reliability are today no longer problems. A number of manufacturers can look back at more than a decade of experience. Standards are available and quality tests are performed as a routine activity by a number of accredited testing institutes. Product labelling is common. The present section is intended to give the reader an overview of the facts 'behind the scene', to enable him or her to make a more informed judgement on these important features.

7.1.1 Durable materials

In the early history of solar thermal utilization there are many examples of failures due to a lack of knowledge about the requirements these installations have to meet in a long-term perspective. Fortunately, these bad examples have become much less common, but it is essential that new designers and manufacturers are aware of them in order to avoid these pitfalls in future installations. Long-lasting high performance requires durable components that are manufactured with the use of high-quality materials, appropriately chosen for the particular application.

In the case of solar heating systems, there are some special aspects to be aware of, most of them related to the high temperatures that can occur. The solar collector itself is, of course, the component exposed to the highest stress. (In Chapter 7, 'stress' is used to mean everything associated with high temperature: real temperature-induced stress, possible high pressure, material degradation, thermal shock and more.) However, the more conventional components should also be considered. As the stress on these sometimes gets much higher than on the corresponding components in a conventional heating system, there is a greater need to check their durability.

In the standard EN 12975–1:2001, requirements for solar collectors are specified. The qualification tests a collector has to pass in order to fulfil these requirements are designed in such a way that, within a reasonable period of time, the tests are able to identify the most serious and the most frequent failures that may occur during the lifetime of a collector. Thus, a number of tests are performed, e.g. high-temperature resistance, exposure test, rain penetration and mechanical load tests. Nevertheless, as the requirements on collector tests are a compromise between test cost and quality assurance level, there are still some important properties the qualification tests of EN 12975–1 do *not* address; they may be tested separately. The two most important of these are absorber surface long-term durability, addressed in ISO/DIS 12592:1997, and the long-term durability of transparent (polymer) covers, addressed in ISO/DIS 9495:1997. Furthermore, assessment methods for elastomeric materials for absorbers, connecting pipes and fittings are described in ISO 9808:1990 and methods for testing pre-formed rubber seals and sealing compounds are described in ISO 9553:1997. Information about durable collector materials, designs and references to appropriate test methods are given in EN 12975–1 (informative Annex B and Bibliography).

Today the customer no longer has to worry about the long-term properties of collectors. A number of testing institutes, especially in Europe, have tested most of the products on the market. The harmonization of the quality labels delivered by these institutes in Europe is underway. At the same time, a number of manufacturers can look back at more than 20 years of experience in collector manufacturing. Many products have demonstrated their long-term stability over 15–25 years.

Requirements on the other components of a solar heating system, such as piping, expansion vessels, insulation, etc., are compiled in ENV 12977–1:2001. Some of these deserve particular attention and are therefore specifically addressed in the following.

Amongst the most critical components are the connecting pipes between the collectors in the collector array. They must be able to withstand high stagnation temperatures and mechanical strain due to absorber thermal expansion, without leaking or ageing. Good products are available on the market.

Pipe insulation in the collector circuit should be resistant to stagnation temperatures (in some cases above 200°C) and, where installed outdoors, protected against solar radiation, weather and animal impact. Protection of the pipe insulation is fulfilled when the collector is mounted integrated in the roof, and integrated mounting is thus recommended in general. Furthermore, materials in the pipework connecting collector and heat storage should withstand stagnation conditions and thermal expansion. In Section 7.2 the issue of how to deal with the stagnation in collector and system construction is further developed. Good products are available on the market.

For heat exchangers in contact with potable water having a high concentration of calcium, special precautions have to be taken in order to prevent scaling because temperatures above 60°C often can occur in a solar heating system. More generally, guidelines on how to deal with heat exchanges at installation, operation and maintenance stages are found in EN 307:1998.

Another effect of the relatively high temperatures is that corrosion protection of freshwater tanks using organic or inorganic liners is generally not appropriate. The use of more durable materials such as copper or stainless steel in contact with fresh water has to be matched to the local water quality in the region where the system is to be installed. However, that is more of a conventional installation problem and not solar-specific.

The heat transfer media used in the collector loop of a solar combisystem should be chosen wisely from the durability point of view, where they have to match the materials used in pipes, absorbers, pumps, gaskets, etc. Improper combinations may result in internal corrosion and/or leaking systems. In case of doubt, one should consult ISO/TR 10217:1989, which is a guide to materials selection with regard to internal corrosion. The heat transfer media should also be considered from a reliability point of view in that some combinations of fluids, high-performing collectors and inappropriate system designs (see Section 7.2) can result in clogging of the entire circuit. In a thorough study on the high-temperature properties of a number of water/glycol mixtures, Wedel and Bezzel (2000) point out the most and least appropriate ones and offer some practical guidelines about 'stress-reducing' system layouts. The latter are all in agreement with the results presented in Section 7.2.

As floor heating is often used in conjunction with solar heating systems, it should also be pointed out that there are requirements specified for the materials used in these systems, for example in DIN 4726:2000.

The full names of the standards and the most relevant references from them are cited at the end of this chapter.

7.1.2 Reliable components and systems

In EN 12976–1:2001 (factory-made systems) and ENV 12977–1:2001 (custom-built systems) – see the Appendix for the definition of factory-made and custom-built systems – there are a number of requirements regarding reliability, imposed on the solar heating system as a whole and on its components. Some have to be observed by the system planner at design time, others by the installer when mounting the solar heating system. In addition, there are different national guidelines and regulations in force in the Task 26 participating countries, to be observed mainly by the installer at mounting, commissioning and maintenance time. To date, these guidelines have not been harmonized in an international document.

No component used in a conventional space heating technology (e.g. pump, valve, sensor, heat exchanger, etc.) may be used in a solar heating system *unless its ability to meet solar-specific requirements has been checked.* This is particularly true for solar combisystems because they encounter high temperatures in the summer more frequently than solar water heaters.

EN 12976–1 and ENV 12977–1 include solar-specific rules for:

- the dimensioning of the expansion vessel of the collector loop
- the dimensioning of the heat exchanger between the collector loop and the other parts of the system
- the dimensioning of the thermal insulation thickness of the storage device
- the safety components of the collector loop
- the venting components of the collector loop
- the temperature sensors in the collector loop
- the indicators (pressure, temperature) in the collector loop
- the control unit of the system.

EN 12976–1 and ENV 12977–1 also require comprehensive and easily understandable documentation describing system dimensioning, assembly and installation, as well as including all necessary instructions for operation and maintenance.

As solar combisystems are more complicated than solar water heaters, the requirement for easily understandable documentation is of particular significance, since some installers may not have the required skills. Frequently observed mounting errors include:

- interchanged flow and return pipes in a loop
- interchanged pipe connections to a three- or four-way valve
- check valves mounted in the wrong direction
- temperature sensors (e.g. collector sensor and storage sensor) mounted at the wrong location or without the required thermal contact to the measured object.

Proper design and installer education have been shown to reduce dramatically the risk of installation errors:

- As far as possible the system should be pre-assembled in the factory by the manufacturer's skilled staff. More and more manufacturers of combisystems are following this trend, which started more than a decade ago in the solar water heater market. Factory assembly is at the same time a cost reduction factor.
- The design should strive for a high level of system integration, e.g. boiler, heat exchangers and stratifiers integrated in the tank. Generic Systems #8 and #15 are good examples of this approach.
- A number of 'hardware' measures should be taken to prevent possible wrong installation: flow and return lines can be of different diameters or colours; three-way valves should be clearly marked; groups of hydraulic components (e.g. pump, valves, check valve, fill-in and drain valves in the collector loop, as

well as its pressure and temperature indicators and sensors) can be factory-mounted even though the remaining parts of the system are not; etc. If siphons are required by the manufacturer on the connecting lines to the storage tank to reduce stand-by heat losses from the store, these siphons should be pre-mounted in the factory.

- Installer training by the manufacturer, mostly as 'learning by doing', is recommended. Even the best drawings and documentation do not replace experience!

It is concluded that the risk of an incorrect installation cannot be assessed from the hydraulic scheme alone.

Solar heating systems require only low-level maintenance if they have been well designed and properly installed.

The most frequent failures in the system operation occur in the heat transfer fluid circulation: leakage, air locks (especially in one amongst several parallel collector rows), back flow during the night (cooling the storage tank) as well as all well known conventional failures such as a damaged pump, valve or expansion vessel and an altered temperature sensor or electronic control unit. The system should be constructed in such a way that failures are quickly noticed by the users.

Simple devices in the collector loop, such as a pressure indicator, two temperature indicators for the flow and the return temperature as well as a short transparent section in the pipework, are recommended features to monitor the heat transfer fluid circulation. In addition, advanced control units feature indications on a display or signal lamps for system supervision. These control units mostly use the control sensors themselves to compute the information needed for the supervision. For example, the temperature difference between two sensors may be checked and compared to a reference value. Another desirable feature of controllers is the integration of the controllers for the different sub-systems into one single controller unit. This integration improves the reliability of the system (in terms of stable optimum performance) as it makes it easier to minimize and match the use of auxiliary heat both to the instantaneous load and to the available solar heat. In addition, such a solution is likely to be more cost-effective than three or four separate controllers. A foolproof controller interface is another feature that will prevent unskilled 'optimization' of the system, and thus assure a more reliable system.

To accelerate the recognition of failures by the user, the system should be designed in such a way that some thermal comfort reduction is created by the failure. For example, a three-way valve mixing or switching between solar and auxiliary heat should remain in the solar heat supply position if its power supply breaks down. This is particularly important for the class of solar heating systems considered: they all are solar-plus-supplementary systems; a failure in the solar part does not necessarily result in a reduction of comfort because the auxiliary heat source can 'jump into the gap' and deliver more heat to compensate for the missing solar contribution. In such a case, the user may not notice the failure until he receives his next auxiliary bill for payment! Of course, the system failure shall not create, besides the comfort reduction, any dangerous or damaging condition in the system.

Following a quantitative assessment of system reliability in the next chapter, overheating protection aspects for solar combisystems are addressed in detail in Section 7.2.

7.1.3 Quantitative assessment of system reliability

An assessment of the reliability of a variety of solar combisystems was made during the course of IEA SH&C Task 26. The work (Johannesson and Persson, 2001) resulted in two different kinds of analyses, where one approach could be characterized as a relative comparison of system complexity between the generic systems of Task 26. The second approach, presented in a technical report (Kovács 2003), is a calculation model in which the component's lifetime, quality level and maintenance frequency are included. This is more of a 'design tool' that can be used in the assessment and development of a particular system. However, both approaches have their limitations because that they do not take into account the different criticality of each component to the system function or the effects of possible degradation with time. All components with the same estimated lifetime are thus considered to be equally critical to the system function and a component either works or it doesn't work. Where maintenance is considered, it is assumed that it will bring a component back to an 'as new' state. The system border in both approaches incorporates all storage units and the components directly related to the collector loop and the domestic hot water loop: sensors, controller, heat exchangers, etc. Neither the space heating loop nor the auxiliary heating equipment with their controller, sensors, heat exchangers, etc. are included.

The estimate of reliability according to the first approach is based on a generic list of main components used in the 21 generic systems. All components are treated on a general level, i.e. a pump is simply a pump with a certain lifetime, no matter whether it is part of a Swedish system or a Dutch system. An average lifetime of each component is assumed based on studies of the literature and contacts with different experts (see e.g. Kronvall and Ruud, 1997). See Table 7.1 for details.

From a component lifetime, the yearly component reliability is calculated according to:

$$\text{failure probability per year} = \frac{1}{\text{lifetime in years}}$$

and

$$\text{reliability per year} = 1 - \text{failure probability per year}$$

The system's yearly reliability is calculated by simply multiplying together the reliabilities of the system's individual components. The figure, called the characteristic reliability factor, expresses a mean value of the reliability of the system per year and is meant to be used as a base for comparison between the analysed

Table 7.1. Component lifetimes and reliabilities used in the comparison of 21 generic systems

Sub-system/component	Lifetime in years	Component reliability	Sub system/component	Lifetime in years	Component reliability
Space heating tank	20	0.95	*Control unit*		
Domestic hot water tank	12	0.92	Electronics	10	0.90
Drainback tank	20	0.95	Temperature sensor, domestic hot water tank	15	0.93
Heat store in floor	NRI*		Temperature sensor, solar collector	10	0.90
Safety valve	30	0.97	Temperature sensor, drainback tank	15	0.93
Expansion vessel, closed	20	0.95	Temperature sensor, floor	15	0.93
Solar collector	30	0.97	Temperature sensor, space heating tank	20	0.95
Collector loop			Temperature sensor, external heat exchanger	15	0.93
Pipes	85	0.99			
Filter	50	0.98	*Domestic hot water loop*		
Pump	20	0.95	Check valve	10	0.90
Pump, variable speed	20	0.95	Heat exchanger, internal (finned coil)	50	0.98
Check valve	15	0.93			
Safety valve	30	0.97	Heat exchanger, external (flat-plate)	30	0.97
Expansion vessel	20	0.95	Temperature sensor	15	0.93
Insulation	NRI		Pump, variable speed	20	0.95
Antifreeze	8	0.88			
Fittings	70	0.99			
Heat exchanger (finned coil)	50	0.98			
Heat exchanger external (flat-plate)	30	0.97			
Motorized 3-way valve	20	0.95			

* NRI: no reliable information about the lifetime could be found

system designs. From the component lists of the 21 generic systems the characteristic reliability factor is calculated, as shown in Table 7.2 for System #12.

In Johannesson and Persson (2001) the resulting characteristic reliability factor for each system is discussed and further differentiated in an attempt to overcome some of the limitations mentioned above. The resulting characteristic reliability factor for each system is shown in Figure 7.1. (System #3 was modified to #3a during the project and, as a result, the characteristic reliability factor was improved from 0.30 to 0.36 [not included in Figure 7.1]).

The characteristic reliability factor should be interpreted cautiously, bearing in mind that this is a rough estimate carried out on a general level. The figure is a measure of the complexity of the systems (increased complexity or number of components results in decreased reliability) and can be considered as a relative reliability indicator for system intercomparison only. Systems getting a high score (= high reliability) in this comparison are in general drainback systems and systems with internal-tube heat exchangers for domestic hot water preparation. Systems that use more than one store and/or rely on several pumps, valves and sensors to charge solar heat into the system generally score low. An example of a system getting a high reliability score is generic System #5, and of one getting a low score is generic System #18. See the respective hydraulic schemes in Chapter 4.

Table 7.2. An example of how the characteristic reliability factor is derived for one generic system.

System #12	Lifetime in years	Component reliability
Tank	20	0.95
Safety valve, tank	30	0.97
Expansion vessel, closed	20	0.95
Collector loop		
Solar collector	30	0.97
Pipes	85	0.99
Filter	50	0.98
Pump, variable speed	20	0.95
Motorized three-way valve	20	0.95
Safety valve	30	0.97
Check valve	15	0.93
Heat exchanger (finned coil, two pieces)	50	0.98
	50	0.98
Expansion vessel	20	0.95
Insulation	NRI★	
Antifreeze	8	0.88
Fittings	70	0.99
Control unit		
Electronics	10	0.90
Temperature sensor, solar collector (two pieces)	10	0.90
	10	0.90
Temperature sensor, domestic hot water tank (two pieces)	15	0.93
	15	0.93
Domestic hot water loop		
Heat exchanger (finned coil, two pieces)	50	0.98
	50	0.98
	Characteristic reliability factor	**0.32**

★NRI: no reliable information about the lifetime could be found

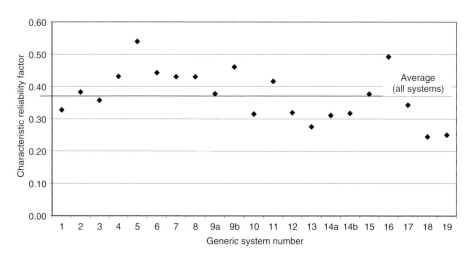

Figure 7.1. A comparison of 21 generic systems in terms of the characteristic reliability factor

The values given for the characteristic reliability factor are only valid for the part of the system that is within the border defined above. An issue of particular interest from a durability point of view, still left outside the border and not considered in the calculation, deserves mentioning. It is the case where high thermal power is input to a domestic hot water store either by an integrated burner or via an integrated heat exchanger fed by an external boiler. In particular, if the water contains high amounts of calcium, this will give deposits and corrosion on the hot parts in contact with fresh water and should thus be avoided.

Unfortunately, the characteristic reliability factor gives no guidance as to the absolute reliability of these systems. In order to assess absolute reliability, the analysis must be deepened and most of all, has to be applied to a specific product (system) instead of general considerations on a generic system, i.e. a class of systems. Detailed knowledge of the probability of failure of individual system components is necessary in order to determine the absolute reliability of a system. Such information is not available on innovative and new components as experience on their long-term behaviour is lacking.

From the investigation, some general conclusions about how to design a reliable system can be drawn:

- Minimize the number of components in general and in particular the number of tanks, sensors and valves.
- Minimize the number of fittings.
- Choose internal coil or external flat-plate heat exchangers for hot water preparation instead of an extra tank if the calcium content of the water is low.
- Use the drainback principle if possible. Water is a stable and reliable heat transfer medium (when it does not freeze) and the thermal stress on the components decreases. However, one should be aware that drainback also has its limitations and is not always possible to realize (see Section 7.2.2).

In addition, although Table 7.1 shows equal reliability for pumps and valves, practical experience indicates that choosing a pump should be preferred to choosing a control valve, when possible.

7.2 STAGNATION BEHAVIOUR

According to EN ISO 9488, stagnation is the status of a collector or system when no heat is being removed by a heat transfer fluid. Stagnation may occur both as the result of normal operation or following abnormal circumstances like a temporary interruption of the circulating-pump power supply.

7.2.1 Stagnation in solar combisystems

Solar heating systems have to be designed to withstand stagnation. More precisely, EN 12976–1 states that 'the system shall have been designed in such a way that prolonged high solar irradiation without heat consumption does not cause any situation in which special action by the user is required to bring the system back to normal operation.' (Clause 4.1.4). Furthermore, the same standard and the European pre-standard ENV 12977–1 stipulate that 'the system shall have been designed in such a way that the maximal allowed temperature of any material in the system is never exceeded. (Clauses 4.1.4.2 and 6.1.4.1, respectively), with the following note added in ENV 12977–1 only: 'Care should be taken in cases where under stagnation conditions steam or hot water can enter the collector pipes, pipe work, distribution network or heat exchanger.'

Manufacturers of solar heating systems have developed a number of different overheating protection schemes. To operate properly, some of them require power from the grid while others are able to protect the system even if power fails. The following is a partial list of examples:

- A magnetic valve is activated by the control unit if the bottom store temperature exceeds a certain threshold value, e.g. 90°C, and domestic hot water is run to waste until the alarm condition disappears as a result of store cooling by cold water from the mains. This scheme is mostly applicable to large solar water heaters; however, it may not be very reliable as the seldom-operated magnetic valve may be inoperative as a result of limestone deposits.
- The collector-loop pump is operated after the sun has set, cooling the bottom part of the store by means of heat rejection from the collectors (System #9a). This scheme requires the availability of power from the grid. The store fraction that may be cooled down is limited to the vertical extension of the immersed collector loop heat exchanger.
- In drainback systems, the heat transfer fluid is removed from the collector each time the collector pump stops. This scheme is also used as overheating protection. It is independent of the grid power. See Section 7.2.2.
- An inherently safe scheme to prevent boiling of the heat transfer fluid in the collector is to maintain sufficient pressure in the loop. This may be difficult to implement when the operating pressure of the whole loop (including the collectors) has to be increased up to, say, 10 bar. The constraint is much lower if the collector stagnation temperature does not exceed 150°C, as is the case with single-glazed, non-selective collectors; in such a case, a system pressure of 3 bar prevents 50% ethylene glycol/water mixtures from boiling.
- The most modern overheating protection scheme is the use of collectors designed in such a way that heat-transfer boiling expels all of the liquid from the collector to an expansion vessel in a short time. In this scheme, only a very limited quantity of heat transfer fluid is evaporated and the part of the loop subjected to high-temperature strain is restricted to the collector array itself. see Section 7.2.3.

Because of the large collector areas and small summertime loads, combisystems are more frequently exposed to an excess in solar heat production than are solar water heaters. Adequate protection against high temperatures in the system is therefore an important issue to make sure that these systems operate properly in the long term, with minimum maintenance. The behaviour of combisystems at stagnation has to be considered critically.

South-facing façade-integrated collectors have the interesting feature of behaviour that, as a result of an unfavourable angle of incidence in the summertime when there is no space heating load, their heat output is automatically reduced. Roof-mounted collectors do not have this advantage. Architects and engineers are advised to consider both possibilities and optimize the corresponding collector areas. Architectural aspects are treated in Section 5.2.

In Section 7.2.2 the stagnation problem in pressurized collector loops with expansion vessels is discussed, and in Section 7.2.3 the strategy using the drainback principle for solar combisystems is discussed.

7.2.2 Stagnation in pressurized collector loops with expansion vessels

In the summer, solar space heating systems often reach stagnation conditions, since on a clear day the storage tank easily reaches the maximum temperature (e.g. 95°C). In this case, the collector-loop pump is switched off by the controller. Then, the temperature of the absorber rises rapidly and reaches the so-called stagnation temperature, which is between 180° and 210°C for selective coated absorbers of flat-plate collectors and between 220° and 300°C for vacuum-tube collectors.

Evaporation of the collector fluid often occurs even with flat-plate collectors (selective-coated absorbers) and in collector loops with 6 bar maximum pressure. The usual design rules state that the volume of the membrane expansion vessel should exceed the volume of the expanded collector fluid plus the volume of the displaced fluid from the absorber. This design practice should prevent the activation of the collector loop safety valve and thus loss of fluid.

Nevertheless, there are sometimes problems with overheating of system components and loss of fluid during summertime:

• high-temperature exposure in parts of the collector loop including some sections in the heat storage room; malfunctions of system components and system leaks can result from this exposure
• opening of the collector loop safety valve even though the usual design guidelines have been followed with regard to size of the expansion vessel and pressure conditions
• condensation pressure shocks in the collector loop and in secondary circuits heated by this loop.

In the framework of a European Craft project and an Austrian national project (Fink *et al.*, 2001) the stagnation behaviour of combisystems was investigated. In the following, the results and recommendations of these projects are discussed.

7.2.2.1 Processes encountered during stagnation
The sequence of events during stagnation can be divided into five different phases on the basis of a simplified collector model (Hausner and Fink, 2000, 2002):

- **Phase 1 – expansion of liquid.** The collector temperatures rise until the evaporation process begins in the upper part of the collector array, somewhere in an absorber. The increase in the system pressure is small.
- **Phase 2 – pushing the liquid out of the collector.** Large amounts of liquid are pushed into the expansion vessel by the formation of saturated steam within the collector. As a result, the system pressure rises rapidly, as does the boiling point in the pipe sections filled with saturated steam. Liquid that is almost at the boiling temperature puts a high-temperature stress on the system components. This phase lasts for only a few minutes and ends when there is a continuous path for steam from the collector inlet to the outlet. Residual liquid remains in the collector.
- **Phase 3 – emptying of the collector by boiling.** The residual liquid in the collector evaporates and transports energy very effectively to other system components as steam. These other components are heated to the local boiling temperature by the condensing steam. The local temperature is determined by the system pressure and the local composition of the heat transfer medium. With the system pressures common in combisystems of around 1.5–3.5 bar, the boiling temperatures are between around 130°C up to a maximum of around 155°C. The energy transported out of the collector is released to components (connection lines and, for example, a heat exchanger) and ultimately to the environment via the formation of condensate. At the end of Phase 3, the steam volume and the system pressure reach their maximum values.
- **Phase 4 – emptying of the collector by superheated steam.** The collector becomes increasingly dry and the steam is superheated, resulting in a decrease in the effectiveness of energy removal. As a result, the steam volume can fall and draw liquid back until the lower connection of the collector is reached despite the fact that solar irradiation continues. The superheating phase can take a few hours on cloudless days, and ends when irradiance is on the decline. With collector designs where the fill lines are on top, slow saw tooth-like pressure fluctuations of moderate amplitude can occur.
- **Phase 5 – refilling of the collector.** The collector begins to refill when the collector temperature falls below the boiling temperature and condensation begins as a result of a reduction in the solar irradiation.

Slightly different system behaviour is observed if the arrangement of the check valve in the evaporation process does not allow the expansion vessel to be filled with liquid both from both the return and the flow line. The five phases are essentially the same, but with different quantitative aspects.

7.2.2.2 Critical phases

The hot liquid pushed out of the collector in the course of Phase 2 can put a critical temperature strain on components other than the collector. The most critical aspect is the heat transport by saturated steam produced in the collector and condensed at high temperatures at all 'cold' locations in the loop, with potential degradations of components even though they are located far away from the collector, for example the expansion vessel installed near the heat storage tank.

The course of Phases 2 and 3 determines the maximum system temperatures. The liquid remaining at the end of Phase 2 determines the length of Phase 3. The evaporation of the remaining liquid keeps most of the collector at the boiling temperature with a comparatively high efficiency of energy removal. This leads to a large steam flow rate, which reaches a maximum level at the end of Phase 3. Once the evaporation of the liquid has been completed, the whole collector reaches its maximum stagnation temperature and thus no longer transfers any energy to the remainder of the system (around the middle of Phase 4).

The emptying properties of the collector and the collector loop during Phase 2 are important in determining the stagnation behaviour of the plant. Figure 7.2 illustrates three different emptying behaviours, from poor to very good. The systems and collectors are the same – with the exception of the emptying behaviour. A high pressure also means that system components will have to bear the strain of the boiling. The stagnation phases are illustrated using a collector that has not been emptied effectively. In this example a pressure of around 3.2 bar corresponds to a steam volume that only encompasses the collector area. In the event of pressures higher than this, the steam also reaches more distant parts of the system.

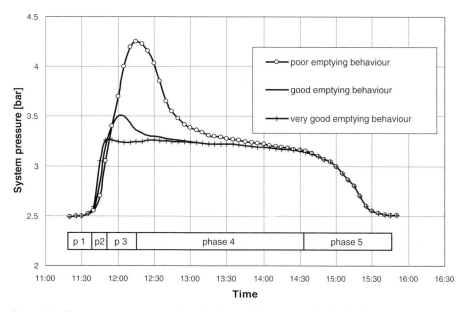

Figure 7.2. System pressure versus time for three different emptying behaviours

7.2.2.3 Emptying behaviour of collectors

The emptying behaviour of collectors determines the frequency, area, magnitude and duration of the maximum temperature of the system and of its components.

Collector piping networks should have a good emptying behaviour to avoid stagnation problems. Systems with good emptying behaviour minimize the amount of residual liquid and thus reduce the period of time and extent of the critical stagnation Phase 3.

Collector examples with poor emptying behaviour are shown schematically in Figure 7.3. Arrangements to be avoided are connection of the return and flow lines at the top of the collector with the absorber pipes laid 'down and upwards', horizontal absorber pipes and parallel U-tubes (e.g. vacuum-tube collectors). These configurations do not lead to good emptying behaviour as a result of the liquid trapped in parts of the collector (illustrated in the final schematic of Figure 7.3), which cannot be expelled in liquid form but rather has to evaporate to be removed. This trapped liquid leads to a large amount of energy that is transported via steam in the event of stagnation throughout the system. The pressure develops in the way shown in Figure 7.2, which is described as 'poor emptying behaviour'. In addition the probability of condensation pressure shocks increases (Streicher, 2000).

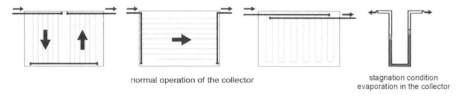

normal operation of the collector   stagnation condition
evaporation in the collector

Figure 7.3. Schematic examples of common collector circuits with poor emptying behaviour (the three schematics on the left illustrate the normal function of the collectors, while the right-hand schematic shows in simplified terms the condition of steam formation in the collector)

The collector circuits shown schematically in Figure 7.4 provide for a much more favourable emptying behaviour. The return line (and/or flow line) is located at the bottom of the collector. With this or similar arrangements, the liquid is driven out of the collector in Phase 2. Consequently the duration and extent of the critical stagnation Phase 3 is reduced so that the areas with saturated steam only reach to just below the bottom of the collector. These arrangements produce the pressure development described in Figure 7.2 as 'very good' or 'good emptying behaviour'.

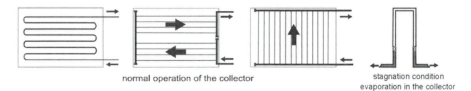

normal operation of the collector   stagnation condition
evaporation in the collector

Figure 7.4. Schematic examples of common collector circuitries with good emptying behaviour (the three schematics on the left illustrate the normal function of the collectors, while the right-hand schematic shows in simplified terms the condition of steam formation in the collector)

7.2.2.4 Emptying behaviour of collector fields

Good emptying behaviour in individual collectors does not guarantee good emptying behaviour of collector fields. The basic principles for individual collectors also have to be observed for collector fields. If the connecting lines of the collectors are not arranged in a favourable manner, good emptying behaviour for a collector can become poor emptying behaviour for a collector field.

In the example shown on the left-hand side of Figure 7.5, the return line connection is arranged in such a way as to trap liquid. At the end of Phase 2, this arrangement leads to one of the two collectors becoming filled with steam as a result of slight individual differences. The resulting steam–liquid circuit, which can last for a long time, supplies liquid to the not yet fully emptied collector by condensing the steam in the condensation stretch of pipe. This process also leads to a greater volume of steam in the remaining system. A simple solution to the problem is to ensure that the system will drain as shown on the right-hand side of Figure 7.5.

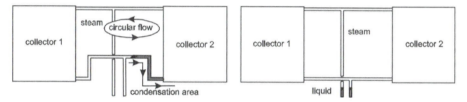

Figure 7.5. Examples of the interconnection of two collectors that empty well with poor emptying behaviour (left) and good emptying behaviour (right). The circular flow shown in the left-hand side of the Figure supplies liquid and continues for a long period of time, which leads to the further formation of steam in one of the collectors

7.2.2.5 Influence of system hydraulics on the emptying behaviour of collectors

The emptying behaviour of collectors is considerably influenced by the position of the check valve in relation to the expansion vessel. If the arrangement of the components in the return group is as shown in the right-hand side of Figure 7.6, then emptying during stagnation conditions can only be performed through the collector outlet line (flow line of the system). This arrangement results in a large amount of residual liquid in the collector. The resulting large volume of steam generated has only the flow line available for the release of heat, so steam can penetrate very far into the system. The collector inlet line (return line of the system) remains filled with liquid up to the entrance to the collector because of the position of the check valve.

The condition for good emptying behaviour of collectors in the event of stagnation can be achieved by the simple repositioning of the check valve in relation to the expansion vessel, as shown on the left-hand side of Figure 7.6. In this arrangement the contents of the collector in the event of stagnation can be driven into the expansion vessel via both the return and flow lines, whereby little residual

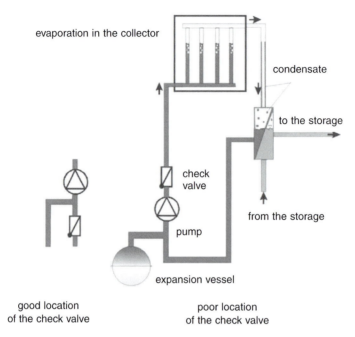

Figure 7.6. Good and poor arrangements of the components of the primary solar circuit

fluid remains in the collector. In addition, the volume of steam flow and the associated energy flow is divided between the two lines.

7.2.2.6 Measures to improve the stagnation behaviour given an unfavourable emptying behaviour

In the event that unfavourable conditions (e.g. an unfavourable pipe layout as a result of unusual geometric conditions in the building) do not provide an opportunity to obtain optimum emptying behaviour, different measures can bring about an improvement in the stagnation behaviour. Details are given in Fink and Hausner, 2000. These are as follows:

- avoidance of stagnation condition using night cooling
- active removal of energy transported via the steam in the event of stagnation with:
  - a small-volume heat sink with a large surface or
  - the controlled use of the external heat exchanger and the secondary circulating pump.

The second and third measures only protect system components from high-temperature loads, and the high-temperature loads on the heat-transfer medium are not reduced by this technique. With the first and third measures, additional parasitic energy has to be used to remove excess energy, thus reducing the overall efficiency of the solar plant.

Examples of the use of a simple small-volume heat sink with a large surface that operates automatically in the case of stagnation and does not use additional parasitic energy are shown in Figure 7.7. The heat sink has to be positioned about 2 metres or more above the level of the components to be protected (communicating vessels). A simple and inexpensive room heater (copper tube with aluminium fins) is a well tried solution. A commercially available heat exchanger (22 × 1 mm tubes with 70 × 60 × 0.5 mm aluminium sheets spaced at a distance of 5 mm) can dissipate about 750 W/m at the boiling temperature.

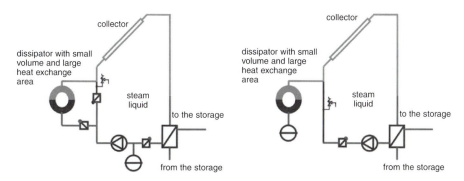

Figure 7.7. If the emptying behaviour of the collector cannot be improved, a simple automatically controlled air cooler in the primary solar circuit can limit the steam volume

7.2.2.7 Steam power
Measurements of the maximum steam power emerging from the collector at the end of Phase 3 quantified the different emptying behaviour of different collector types (Fink et al., 2001). Collectors of the type shown in Figure 7.4 (i.e. collectors with good emptying behaviour) exhibit short-lasting maximum steam power values of around 20 W for each square metre of collector area. Collectors of the type shown in Figure 7.3 (i.e. collectors with poor emptying behaviour) exhibit long-lasting maximum steam power values of up to 120 W for each m^2 of collector area.

The specific heat loss of common insulated return and flow lines at saturated steam temperature is around 25 W/m. Consequently, in small plants using collectors with good emptying behaviour, the steam does not penetrate more than a few metres into the system and thus does not represent a problem. In contrast, collectors with poor emptying behaviour, can enter the critical range even in small domestic hot water plants (e.g. 6 m^2 of collector area) since 20–30 m of pipe is necessary to dissipate the steam power. When steam reaches this far into the system, temperature-sensitive system components can be affected. In combisystems, which have very large collector areas, excess steam problems can be severe.

7.2.2.8 Dimensioning of membrane expansion vessel
The sizing of the membrane expansion vessel is important to ensure that heat-transfer fluid is not lost through the pressure-relief valve in the event of stagnation

conditions. The following suggests a way to calculate the minimum volume of the expansion vessel for safe operation.

Estimate the maximum steam power depending on the type of emptying behaviour of the collector and the system according to the discussion above. For good emptying collectors/systems, an estimate of the steam power is about 50 W/m², whilst for poor emptying collectors/systems an estimate of the steam power is about 120 W/m². These values are on the safe side and, with experience with specific systems, can be lowered; for example, increasing the system pressure can, depending on collector types, lower these values (Fink et al., 2001).

Calculate the energy removal capability of the return and flow lines. Often the horizontal parts of interconnections between collectors remain filled with liquid, so only the vertical sections have to be taken into account. For pipes where the insulation thickness equals the outer tube diameter the specific heat losses will be approximately 25 W/m for a low preset pressure in the expansion vessel (e.g. 1.5 bar) and up to 31 W/m with a high preset pressure (e.g. 3.5 bar) at the boiling point. If this length appears to be critical such that steam will reach temperature-sensitive components, then measures have to be taken to limit the steam volume (see Section 7.2.2.6)

On the basis of these calculations, calculate the volume of the pipes and components outside the collector that can be filled with steam. This volume, together with the collector volume, gives the maximum volume of steam V_S. The common procedure for calculating the nominal volume of the expansion vessel V_N (Terschuren, 1994) has to be modified to:

$$V_N \geq \frac{V_M * n + V_V + V_S}{N}$$

$$n = \frac{\rho_{cold}}{\rho_{hot}} - 1 \approx 0.09$$

$$N = \frac{P_m - P_{diff} + 1 - (P_0 + 1)/0.9}{P_m - P_{diff} + 1} \quad \leq 0.5$$

$$P_{diff} \approx H_{diff} \cdot \rho_{cold}/10,000$$

where pressures are above atmospheric (i.e. gauge pressure) and the variables have the following meanings:

V_N nominal volume of the expansion vessel (litres)
V_M entire volume of the heat transfer medium (litres)
V_V spare liquid in the expansion vessel (litres)
V_S maximum steam volume (litres)
n expansion factor (approximately 0.09° to ~120°C for 40% propylene glycol)
N maximum operational capacitance of the expansion vessel (–)
ρ density of the heat transfer medium (kg/m³)

P_m maximum allowable pressure = opening pressure of the safety valve − 20% (bar)

P_0 preset pressure in the expansion vessel (bar). The factor 0.9 in the term (P_0 + 1)/0.9 allows for temperature changes in the gas volume due to hot liquid (Hausner and Fink, 2002)

H_{diff} if the safety valve and the expansion vessel are mounted at very different heights, this should be corrected for. H_{diff} = altitude of expansion vessel − altitude of safety valve (metres)

P_{diff} pressure difference corresponding to H_{diff} (bar).

7.2.2.9 Thermal load on the heat transfer medium

The glycol component in the heat transfer medium and the inhibitor additives become unstable at high temperatures, and can degrade as a result of flocculation and the formation of solid residues. The normal function of the system represents no essential load for the heat transfer medium. However, long-lasting high temperatures, which may occur in the event of stagnation, are to be avoided as far as possible to prevent the premature ageing of the heat transfer medium (Hillerns, 2001; Wedel and Bezzel, 2000). Collectors with a good emptying behaviour largely comply with this requirement. With the system pressures common in solar plants, boiling temperatures from around 130°C to a maximum of around 155°C are reached, but only have a short-term influence on a small amount of the liquid heat-transfer content, given good emptying behaviour.

With poor emptying behaviour, the residual liquid can be exposed to boiling temperature for a long period of time. This boiling results in the preferred evaporation of water (fractional distillation) with corresponding increases in the concentration of glycol and inhibitor components in the residual liquid. This increased concentration leads to a local increase in the boiling temperature. The process continues until the highly concentrated residual liquid no longer evaporates, resulting in extremely long-lasting and high temperatures with significant corresponding ageing (for the pure glycol components the boiling point exceeds 210°C with the usual pressures at stagnation conditions).

The high temperatures of the steam phase within the collector at stagnation temperature should not represent any serious problem, since this steam mainly contains water (fractional distillation) and only affects very small amounts of glycol.

7.2.2.10 Condensation pressure shocks

The arrangement of the pipes inside and outside the collector has a great influence on the formation of condensation pressure shocks. Not all of the causes are known, but some known causes are long horizontal pipes or sags in horizontal pipes, where steam could be enclosed from liquid (condensate). As this trapped steam condenses, liquid columns collide with one another or with the walls of the pipes.

While collectors with good emptying behaviour do not have great potential to generate condensation pressure shocks, collectors with poor emptying behaviour have a much greater potential. Because of pressure fluctuations, residual liquid can be pushed to and fro and can enclose steam pockets.

All of these pressure shocks can give uncomfortable acoustic emissions. However, measured pressure peaks are moderate (~0.1 bar, and the safety valves do not usually react). On the other hand, at the point of origin the pressure peaks can be higher and failures cannot be completely excluded.

To avoid pressure shocks, good emptying behaviour for the whole system is recommended, and long horizontal lines, lines with sags or lines that slope towards the collector should be avoided.

7.2.3 Drainback technology

Drainback technology provides an interesting alternative for overheating protection of fluid in the solar collector loop, and also prevents the heat transfer fluid from freezing. Thanks to drainback of the collector fluid when the collector circuit is not running, the circulation can operate using plain water without (antifreeze) additives. This system concept is based on draining the water from the tilted collector and outdoor collector pipes using the gravitational force and replacing the liquid with air from the top. When water in the collector is replaced with air, ice cannot be formed and damage is therefore avoided. The water also drains back if the heat store is fully charged, thereby avoiding boiling of water and high pressures inside the system. When polymer materials are used in the collector circuit, both stopping the pump in time and a permanent opening in the collector loop to the atmosphere are needed to avoid overpressure.

7.2.3.1 Introduction

In comparison with the use of heat transfer fluids, drainback technology using water features has both advantages and disadvantages. Advantages are:

- Water does not face the ageing drawbacks exhibited by collector fluids with additives, such as a change in material properties and possible corrosion of the collector loop.
- The heat transfer properties of water, i.e. both heat capacity and viscosity, are better than those of other heat transfer fluids.
- Water is much cheaper than all other collector fluids and easily available.
- The collector circuit does not generally face high overpressures, possibly requiring additional guarantees for safety.
- The level of maintenance for drainback systems is lower.

Disadvantages are:

- There is less flexibility in the choice of the solar collector.
- Special attention must be given to the design and installation of the drainback collector loop.

In the Netherlands, drainback technology evolved from regulations in the 1980s concerning the quality of potable water. These regulations permitted additives in the collector fluid only if it was separated from the potable water by a double-wall heat exchanger. In order to maintain good heat transfer, a single-wall heat exchanger was combined with plain water in the collector circuit. Manufacturers such as Atag Verwarming and ZEN Solar have developed this idea over a number of years into foolproof drainback systems (Noij, 2001). Nowadays, regulations in the Netherlands on double separation are not as strict as they were in the 1980s. However, drainback systems are still used because of their advantages compared with the use of collector fluids with additives.

The application of polymer absorbers connected to rectangular heat stores, as in the SolarNor system, is another reason for applying the drainback concept (Meir *et al.*, 2000; Meir *et al*, 2002; Rekstad *et al.*, 1999). Significant overpressure must be avoided to protect the absorbers and the tank against mechanical stress that might harm the structure. This leads to a system that is permanently open to the atmosphere. Moreover, collector circuit, heat store and space heating distribution have been designed without any intermediate heat exchanger. Hence, the large volume of heat transfer and heat store fluid should be inexpensive and environmentally friendly.

7.2.3.2 Implementation of the drainback concept in solar heating systems

Although the drainback concept is simple and inexpensive, draining a solar collector requires special qualities in the hydraulic design. The major feature is that all of the water must run down to the level of the drainback storage part of the system when the pump stops. This requirement means that *every pipe* from the top of the solar collector loop to the drainback volume must slope downwards. When the collector loop is in operation, the drainback volume is filled with air. This volume can be part of the heat store, or integrated into the collector-side heat exchanger within the store, or designed as an external drainback tank. When the pump in the collector circuit stops, water drains from the collector to the drainback volume as a result of gravity. Simultaneously, air from the drainback volume flows upwards into the collector. This process stops when the water levels in the two pipes are equal or when the collector loop is empty. When the process is complete, the collector and all outdoor pipes must be fully filled with air.

Drainback collector circuits can be implemented as closed loops or be open to the environment. Closed loops are commonly used in collector circuits that can withstand pressures up to at least 3 bar, which usually requires metal absorbers and pipes. After some time, the metal absorbs the oxygen in the circuit and no further corrosion occurs. Open loops are applied in systems with plastic materials. Pressures higher than the hydrostatic level should be avoided, as the combination of high temperature and pressure may cause weeping and may damage the plastic materials.

Figure 7.8 shows four examples of the drainback concept where the drainback volume has been integrated into the heat store or into the heat exchangers in the store. Attention should be directed to the hydraulic design of the drainback loop as the space heating has been left out in order to simplify the figures. All collectors have the ability to drain fully when the pump in the collector circuit stops. Both serpentine absorbers and collectors with headers and risers (among others, channel plates) can successfully use the drainback concept.

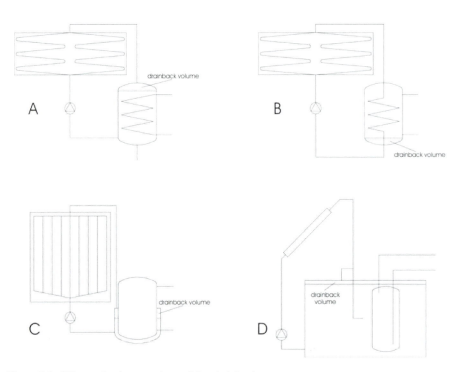

Figure 7.8. Different implementations of the drainback concept

The collector water may be stored directly in the heat store, as in systems A and D. Energy for domestic hot water is then withdrawn through a heat exchanger or an immersed domestic hot water tank. In systems B and C, a drainback volume located below the tank is combined with the heat exchanger in the collector loop (e.g. a coil heat exchanger with extra volume at the bottom as in B, or a mantle heat exchanger with relatively large volume as in C). These configurations minimize the required difference in the height between the collector and the heat store. The heat store can then be mounted on a wall in the attic, possibly next to the auxiliary heater.

In practice, systems B and C involve relatively small applications. For larger systems with collector loop heat exchangers, external drainback tanks are generally used. External drainback volume is also often applied if the distance between the collector and the heat store is relatively large, for instance, if the heat store is located in the basement. The drainback tank should be close to the collector, but with the drainback level lower than the lowest part of the outdoor collector circuit.

The drainback concept is even applicable if collector and heat store are on the same level, as shown in Figure 7.9. When the pump starts in system A, the three-way valve opens in the direction of the drainback tank. After a few minutes, when the collector loop has been filled, the three-way valve switches in the direction of the heat store. If the pump stops, the valve switches back again and air from the drainback volume replaces the water in the solar collector and outdoor piping. In

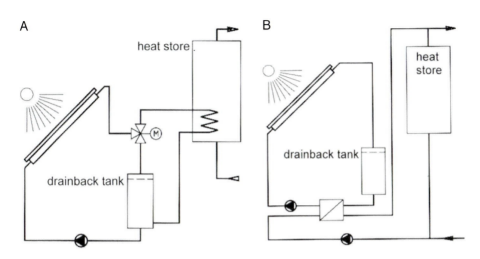

Figure 7.9. Implementation of drainback concept when the collector and the heat store are at the same level

system B, the problem of the collector and heat store being at the same level has been solved by an additional external heat exchanger in the collector loop.

The drainback concept has been applied to systems with collector areas ranging from a few square metres to a few hundred square metres. Recently, a drainback system with a few thousand square metres was successfully demonstrated (Bokhoven *et al.*, 2001).

7.2.3.3 Considerations for proper drainback system operation

A variety of aspects determine the quality of the collector circuit. Specific items for the drainback loop are as follows.

Pipes and fittings

All pipes must have sufficient fall, i.e. preferably 15–30 mm per metre of pipe, but at least 10 mm per metre. The fall should also be guaranteed at connections and must persist for the entire lifetime of the system, even if the pipes are deformed by accident or ageing. Figure 7.10 shows right and wrong pipe fittings and connections, indicating that collectors with flow (outlet) and return (inlet) pipes at the back of the collectors are inappropriate for series connection.

Special attention is needed to pipe fittings at the top of parallel-connected collector modules. Depending on the type of collector connections, flow pipes must be combined above the collectors (the joint is then the highest point, as shown in Figure 7.11a) or at the back of the collectors (the highest points are then in the individual collectors, as shown in Figure 7.11b). In the latter set-up, restrictions are built into the flow pipes of all individual collectors. Moreover, the lengths of the individual flow

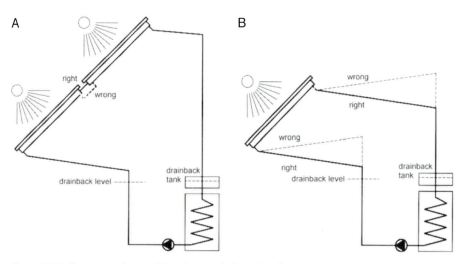

Figure 7.10. Examples of the fall for pipes in drainback collector loops

pipes connecting to the main flow pipe should be kept as short as possible. For collectors with internal headers, the upper header is generally the highest point, but this is not strictly necessary, as shown in Figure 7.11c. As for non-drainback systems, the so-called Tichelman scheme is used for parallel connection of the collectors, where pipe design is such that the summed length of the return pipe is equal to the summed length of the flow pipe, leading to identical flow-resistance conditions for each collector including the manifold, as in all three parts of Figure 7.11.

The hydraulic resistance of return and flow pipes must be low compared to that of the collector. A large diameter for the return pipe is not a problem, but the diameter of the flow pipe requires some attention. When collector operation begins, air from the collector has to be carried away with the water flow down to the drainback volume. Accordingly, the velocity of this air–water mixture must be sufficiently high. On the one hand, this restricts the diameter of the flow pipe, while, on the other hand, this diameter should not be too small. If it is too small, the pipe does not properly empty with an air flow in the opposite direction when the pump stops. In practice, the flow pipe is often one size smaller than the return pipe. The precise pipe diameters, of course, depend on the size of the system, just as for non-drainback systems.

Rather new is the closed drainback concept, where the downward pipes in the collector loop are not completely filled with water when the pump is in operation (Bokhoven *et al.*, 2001). The highest point or points in the collector circuit work(s) as overflow. Essential here for proper operation is the large flow resistance through the collector compared with the flow resistance of the connecting pipes.

Choice of materials

The presence of air in a drainback collector circuit must be considered. Oxygen in the air can cause corrosion of metal, especially steel parts. For a closed loop, the

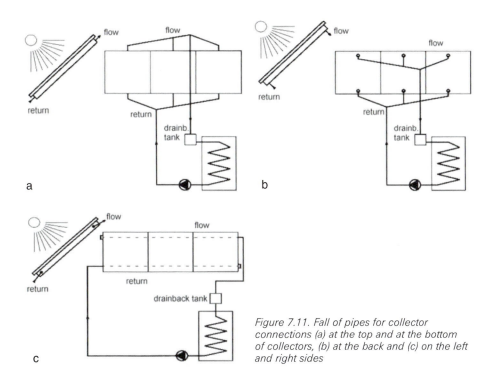

Figure 7.11. Fall of pipes for collector connections (a) at the top and at the bottom of collectors, (b) at the back and (c) on the left and right sides

process of corrosion will stop quite soon after the system comes into use. For large systems, the larger amount of corrosion products (such as magnetite, Fe_3O_4) can be removed with special filters, thus preventing collectors from clogging. In order to prevent corrosion, components in open loops are made of stainless steel, copper, brass or plastic materials.

Mounting of pipes

Sags in the hydraulic circuit must be prevented, as sagging may cause incomplete drainback, leading to frost damage during critical weather conditions. Sags may be caused by non-linear extension due to temperature differences. Plastic tubes may creep. Compensators and sufficient fixing material can be used to prevent sagging. The use of correct mounting materials and careful mounting guarantee the necessary fall of pipes in the long term. On flat roofs, precautions are sometimes needed to prevent people from stepping on the pipes.

Pump

Apart from the flow rate required to transport the hot water from the collector to the heat store, the pump in the drainback loop must be able to overcome the maximum height of the collector loop when filling. Moreover, the flow rate during filling should be high enough to dispel the air and prevent imbalanced flow through parallel-connected collectors. A common value is 10–20 ml/s (approx. 40–80 l/h) per m² collector area. After a few minutes, the flow rate may be reduced, resulting in lower electricity demand.

The pump must be installed in such a way that air is not trapped. For open loops, a sufficient hydrostatic head at the inlet of the pump is needed to prevent pump cavitation. Another requirement for open loops is that materials inside the pump should not be corrosive.

The pump has to be placed in a configuration that allows drainback of the collector water if the pump stops. If the pump does not permit the flow of water in the opposite direction or air flow from the drainback volume towards the collector through the pump (as in a positive displacement pump), then a bypass has to be added. This bypass will contain a check valve that opens automatically when the pump stops so that air can flow through the bypass into the collector circuit. Figure 7.8D shows an example of a bypass where a check valve is not needed.

Drainback tank or volume

The difference in the height between the lowest part of the outdoor collector loop and the drainback level should be as small as possible in order to limit the requirements for the pump. The content of the drainback volume is commonly twice the content of all collector pipes and collectors. If the content is too small, the pump may suck in air, resulting in incorrect operation. The air in the drainback volume also provides for expansion. After the pump is switched off, the pressure in the collector circuit will not commonly exceed 0.5 bar.

Depending on the amount of water stored inside the drainback tank, open loops may require a periodic check of the drainback level. Because of the large water volume of the space heating store, which simultaneously serves as a drainback tank, this is not necessary for the Norwegian system. Measures should be taken to keep the opening of open-loop systems free of dirt and to prevent dirt from dropping into the drainback (or heat store) volume.

7.2.3.4 The state of the art and future outlook

The potential of drainback technology is high because of its excellent thermal properties, inherent safety, low costs and easy maintenance. Over 80% of Dutch solar energy systems and virtually all Norwegian solar combisystems include the drainback concept. Other northern and central European manufacturers have experience with drainback systems and have started commercial production. Often, only minor modifications are needed to change from a circuit with collector fluid containing additives to a drainback loop.

A major barrier to drainback technology in Europe is a lack of skilled workers when it comes to proper installation. The disadvantage of complex drainback collector loop designs and installation can be overcome by the manufacturer combining as many drainback components as possible into a single, factory-assembled component. The manufacturer can also ensure proper installation by providing accurate guidelines for mounting, as well as directed training.

For open drainback systems, installers often exhibit scepticism with regard to corrosion problems, even though this is unwarranted. The open technology is seen as a step back to the past. Even though drainback systems are inherently safe, e.g. if the electricity supply or pump fails the system automatically drains and remains in a state where freezing or strong irradiance is not harmful, most installers cannot be convinced that drainback systems are safe and reliable. Today, education and training of installers focus on pressurized systems. Closed and pressurized systems filled with antifreeze determine the present state of the art in most countries.

An increased acceptance of drainback systems requires some investment in product development and in the education of installers. Although the installation of drainback systems is increasing in Europe, the advantages of drainback do not seem to be attractive enough to launch the technology to a wide market. In some countries, the existing infrastructure is an obstacle for the introduction of new technologies.

REFERENCES

Bokhoven T P, van Dam J and Kratz P, 2001, 'Recent experiences with large solar thermal systems in the Netherlands', in *Proceedings Industry Workshop, April 2001, Delft*, IEA-SHAC Programme Task 26.

DIN 4726:2000, 2000 *Warmwasser-Fußbodenheizungen und Heizkörperanbindungen – Rohrleitungen aus Kunststoffen*

EN 12975–1:2001, 2001, *Thermal solar systems and components – Collectors – Part 1: General requirements.*

ENV 12976–1:2001, 2001, *Thermal Solar Systems and Components – Factory Made Systems – Part 1: General Requirements.*

ENV 12977–1:2001, 2001, *Thermal solar systems and components – Custom-built systems – Part 1: General requirements.*

EN 307:1998, 1998, *Heat exchangers – Guidelines to prepare installation, operating and maintenance instructions required to maintain performance of each type of heat exchanger.*

Fink C and Hausner R, 2000, 'Strategien zur Vermeidung von unzulässigen Temperaturbelastungen an Anlagenkomponenten im Stagnationsfall', in *Proceedings of conference Materialien und Komponenten in Solaranlagen, Salzburg*, AEE INTEC, Gleisdolf, Austria.

Fink C, Hausner R, Wagner W and Riva R, 2001, 2. *Interim report to the project 'Entwicklung von thermischen Solarsystemen mit unproblematischem Stagnationsverhalten'*, program line 'Haus der Zukunft', Federal Ministry for Traffic, Innovation and Technology, Vienna, Austria.

Hausner R and Fink C, 2000, 'Stagnation behaviour of thermal solar systems', in *Proceedings of EUROSUN, 2000, Copenhagen, Denmark*, ISES-Europe, http: //www.ises.org

Hausner R and Fink C, 2002, 'Stagnation behaviour of thermal solar systems', in *Proceedings of EUROSUN, 2002, Bologna, Italy*, ISES-Europe, http: //www.ises.org

Hillerns F, 2001, 'Untersuchungen zur thermischen Dauerbelastbarkeit von Solarflüssigkeiten', in *Proceedings, Elftes Symposium Thermische Solarenergie, OTTI, Kloster Banz, Staffelstein, Germany*, OTTI, Regensburg, Germany.

ISO 9488:1999, 1999, *Solar Energy – Vocabulary – Energie Solaire – Vocabulaire – Sonnenenergie – Vocabular*, also available as EN ISO 9488:2000.

ISO 9808:1990, 1990, *Solar water heaters – Elastomeric materials for absorbers, connecting pipes and fittings – Method of assessment.*

ISO 9553: 1997, 1997, *Solar energy – Methods of testing preformed rubber seals and sealing compounds used in collectors.*

ISO/DIS 9495:1997, 1997, *Solar energy – Transparent covers for collectors – Ageing test under stagnation conditions.*

ISO/DIS 12592:1997, 1997, *Solar energy – Materials for flat plate collectors – Qualification test procedures for absorber surface durability.*

ISO TR 10217:1989, 1989, *Solar energy-water heating systems. Guide to materials selection with regard to internal corrosion.*

Johannesson K and Persson J, 2001, *Reliability Analysis of Solar Combisystems. A Method and a Model.* Swedish National Testing and Research Institute, Work Report SP AR 2001: 37.

Kovács P, 2003, *A calculation model for assessment of reliability in solar combisystems*, IEA SH&C Task 26, Technical report, http://www.iea-shc.org/task26.

Kronvall J and Ruud S, 1997, 'System safety analysis on the performance of mechanical ventilation systems – The quantitative approach,' in, *1997 18th Annual AIVC Conference, Athens, Greece.* http://www.aivc.org

Meir M, Rekstad J, Peter M, Henden L and Sandnes B, 2002, 'Determination of the performance of solar systems with the calorimetric method', in, *Solar Energy*, 73 (3), pp.195–207.

Meir M, Rekstad J and Sandnes B, 2000, 'Solar combisystems for a multi-apartment building – The Klosterenga residence in Oslo', in, *Proceedings Industry Workshop – October 2000 – Helsinki*, IEA-SHAC Programme Task 26, http://www.iea-shc.org/task26

Noij J, 2001, 'Drain back in small systems', in, *Proceedings Industry Workshop – April 2001 – Delft*, IEA-SHAC Programme Task 26, http://www.iea-shc.org

Rekstad J, Henden L, Imenes A G, Ingebretsen F, Meir M, Bjerke B and Peter M, 1999, 'Effective solar energy utilisation – more dependent on system design than on solar collector efficiency', in, *Proceedings ISES Solar World Congress – Jerusalem, Israel.*

Streicher W, 2000, 'Minimising the risk of water hammer and other problems at the beginning of stagnation of solar thermal plants – a theoretical approach', in *Proceedings of EUROSUN, 2000 Copenhagen, Denmark*, ISES-Europe.

Terschüren K-H, 1994, 'Anlagenkomponenten, Inbetriebnahme und Betriebssicherheit', seminar 'Thermische Solarenergienutzung an Gebäuden', FhG ISE, Freiburg, in, Marko M, Braun P (ed.), 1997, *Thermische Solarenergienutzung an Gebäuden*, Springer-Verlag, Berlin, Heidelberg.

Wedel S and Bezzel E, 2000, *Heat Transfer Fluids for Solar DHW Systems*, Technical report SEC-R-8, Danish Technological Institute

8 Dimensioning of solar Combisystems

Chris Bales, Wolfgang Streicher, Thomas Letz and Bengt Perers

Solar combisystems differ from purely solar domestic hot water systems in several key aspects, which means that the dimensioning of them differs in several ways. The main differences are the extra space heating load, resulting in a total heat demand that varies considerably during the year, and the fact that the thermal energy is not usually stored as hot water used for showers etc. Consequently, solar combisystems tend to be more complex and larger than solar domestic hot water systems and they have excess capacity during the summer. The first section in this chapter gives general guidelines on the dimensioning of solar combisystems. This gives some rules of thumb and important points to consider. Much of this is equally relevant for solar domestic hot water systems. No detailed dimensioning guidelines for pumps, pipes etc. is given, as the procedure for this is the same as for any heating system.

There are a number of terms used in this chapter that are defined elsewhere in this handbook; the most important are described briefly here.

- *Systems studied in Task 26.* Each system has been given a specific number and is described in detail in Section 4.3.
- *Fractional energy savings.* This is the fraction of energy saved by a solar combisystem compared to the Task 26 reference system without solar. Three different terms are defined: $f_{sav,therm}$ includes only thermal energy; $f_{sav,ext}$ includes parasitic energy use of pumps, controllers, etc., as well as thermal energy; and f_{si} is a version of $f_{sav,ext}$ with penalties added for periods when the solar combisystem does not meet the defined comfort requirements. See Section 6.2.
- *Reference houses.* Four different reference houses have been used in Task 26 (see Section 6.1) and have the following nomenclature: SFH 30, SFH 60 and SFH 100 for single-family houses with a 30, 60 and 100 kWh/m² per year specific heating load respectively for a 120 m² house located in Zurich; and MFH for a multi-family house with five apartments in a row.

The following sections give more information about the tools that are available for planning and designing solar combisystems, as well as those for doing more detailed simulation of the systems. In Section 8.2 there is an overview of planning tools, including a tool developed by Task 26. This may be of interest to a wide audience and gives advice as to what types of tools are suitable for various situations. Section 8.3 gives information on more detailed, time-dependent simulation of systems and the main assumptions used in the simulation of the Task 26 systems. These simulation tools are of more interest to those designing or developing systems as well as to researchers. Finally, a section is devoted to the simulation models used in the work of Task 26. This is given as background information and is mostly relevant to researchers and those wishing to simulate combisystems using TRNSYS.

Finally, it is worth noting that it is relatively easy to get a rough approximation of the performance of a solar combisystem, but it is very difficult to get close to the 'reality' because of the complex nature of combisystems. Details in the system design, especially for the store and how heat is transferred to and from it, do make a significant difference to the overall system performance. These differences can only be shown using detailed simulation tools or direct measurements (Drück and Hahne, 1998; Pauschinger *et al.*, 1998). System performance can be catastrophically reduced by bad design (Lorenz *et al.*, 1997), but the systems shown in this book are believed to be of good design. Creation of an accurate simulation model of a system requires detailed measurements as well as detailed modelling, both needing considerable effort.

A list of internet addresses for the simulation programs mentioned in this chapter can be found in a special section in the references at the end of the chapter.

8.1 DIMENSIONING GUIDELINES

In this section guidelines are provided for the most important components of a solar combisystem.

8.1.1 Collector slope and orientation

The dependency of the solar fraction on collector tilt angle and azimuth angle for System #19 is shown in Figure 8.1. The highest solar fraction is achieved with southward orientation (slightly westwards) and the optimum tilt angle is about 55°. Nevertheless, the decrease in performance between tilt angles from 30° to 75° and from azimuths from 30° east to 45° west is very small. Most of the solar collectors can therefore be installed in the roof of the building without expensive and aesthetically unattractive collector array racks. It should be noted that a collector mounted vertically on a south-facing wall has only 20% less fractional savings than an optimally mounted one and has much higher fractional savings than a horizontally mounted one. As the direct solar irradiance in summer at midday on a south-facing wall is only about 50% of the radiation on an optimally tilted surface, wall-mounted collectors do not have big problems with stagnation (see below). For higher fractional energy savings the optimum inclination of the collector increases because of the higher amount of winter sun being used (see Figure 2.3).

Collector orientation
Collector orientation can vary 30° from south and from 30° to 75° in slope with less than a 10% reduction in energy savings for a central European climate. Within this range it is generally easy to compensate with a slightly larger collector area.

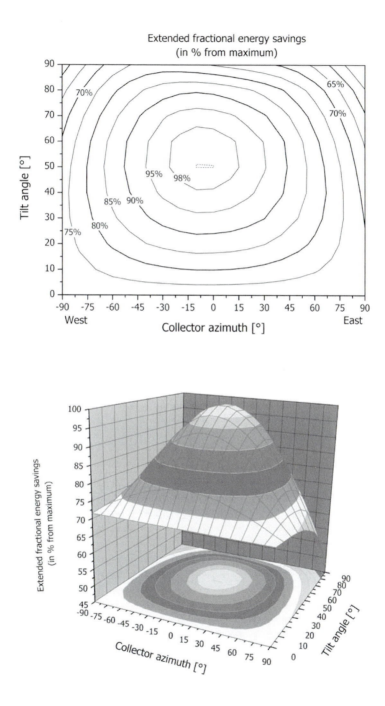

Figure 8.1. Dependency of the extended fractional energy savings on tilt angle and azimuth of the collector (climate: central Europe, 100% = 39% of f$_{sav,ext}$) (Heimrath, 2002). See also colour plate 20

8.1.2 Collector and store size

Figures 8.2 and 8.3 show the influence of collector size and store volume on the extended fractional energy savings ($f_{sav,ext}$) for System #19 and all climates. One important observation that can be made is that for solar combisystems with relatively small collector areas, a small water store is sufficient. Bigger stores do not

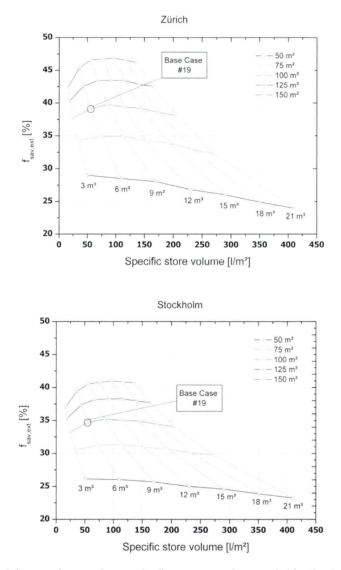

Figure 8.2. Influence of store volume and collector area on the extended fractional energy savings ($f_{sav,ext}$) for the Zurich and Stockholm climates (System #19, MFH). The solid lines are for different, fixed collector areas whereas the dotted (nearly vertical) lines are for different, fixed store volumes

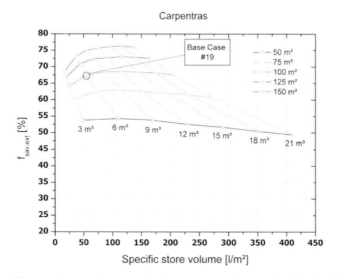

Figure 8.3. Influence of store volume and collector area on the extended fractional energy savings ($f_{sav,ext}$) for the Carpentras climate (System #19, MFH)

increase performance significantly and can even decrease the fractional energy savings as a result of the increasing heat losses of the store as the size increases. This is generally true for all climates and all combisystems investigated.

Increases in store volume

Increased **store volume** does not necessarily result in increased savings (see Figures 8.2 and 8.3). For all climates and system sizes for System #19, the savings decrease with a specific volume above 150 l/m² as a result of increased store losses. The results for many other systems are similar. A rough rule of thumb for the store volume is 50–100 litres for every square metre of flat-plate collector area.

Collector size

The **'best' collector size** is dependent on the user's priorities: energy savings, economy, or space requirements. No general guideline is possible. Small areas are common in the Netherlands while large areas are common in Austria. Both countries have many happy owners

Figure 8.4 shows the size of collector required to achieve a range of fractional energy savings for three different types of collector and two collector slopes. It can be readily seen that a higher slope is advantageous, especially at higher fractional savings. The evacuated-tube collector requires nearly two thirds the aperture area compared to the flat-plate collector in order to achieve 25% fractional energy savings, but only slightly more than half the area for 45% savings. The ratio between required areas for the evacuated-tube and Load Adapted (LA) collectors remains the same over the whole range of savings. The calculations were carried

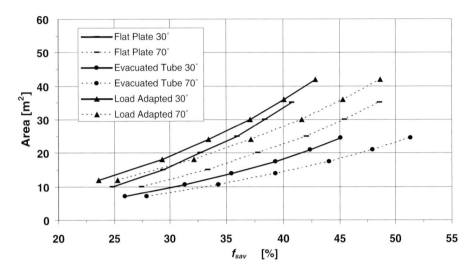

Figure 8.4. Comparison of collector aperture areas that are required for three collector types to achieve a range of fractional energy savings. The data are valid for a well-stratified system in Stockholm. The different types of collector are generic and are not specific commercial units. For each collector, two lines are shown: for slopes of 30° (solid line) and 70° (dashed line)

out for a Swedish solar combisystem with external heat exchangers for both collector circuit and domestic hot water preparation and are not for the specific conditions of Task 26 (Lorenz *et al.*, 2000). The LA collector (see Figure 8.5) uses reflectors inside the collector in order to reduce costs and to give it varying optical properties during the year. It is designed to work efficiently during most of the year apart from the summer, thus avoiding unnecessary overheating in the collector circuit when there is usually excess capacity (Nordlander and Rönnelid, 2001).

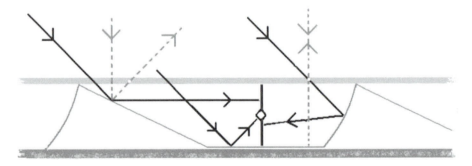

Figure 8.5. Simplified diagram of the principle of a LA collector. For low solar altitudes, all rays reach the absorber, whereas for high solar altitudes some are reflected out

8.1.3 Climate and load

In Figure 8.6, the three defined fractional energy savings for System #19 and all climates are shown. The Carpentras climate has much higher fractional energy savings than the climate in the other two locations. Results for Stockholm and Zurich are quite similar despite the large geographic separation in latitude. It can also be seen that there is a significant difference in values for the thermal ($f_{sav,th}$) and extended ($f_{sav,ext}$) fractional energy savings. This difference is due to differences in parasitic electrical energy usage of the solar and reference systems. It is, however, possible to have lower parasitic energy consumption in the solar heating system if low-energy pumps are used instead of the more conventional ones. Choice of low-energy pumps can make an important contribution to overall savings. This is, of course, also true for conventional heating systems.

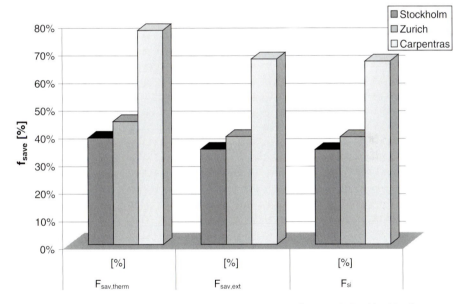

Figure 8.6. Variation of fractional energy savings with climate (System #19 with 100 m² collector and 5.5 m³ store)

Figure 8.7 shows the variation of thermal savings $Q_{sav,th}$ (kWh) and thermal fractional energy savings $f_{sav,th}$ (%) for one solar combisystem of a fixed collector area for three climates on three different buildings. Two observations can be made:

- For a chosen climate, an increase of the load due to a less well insulated house (SFH 100 compared to SFH 30) leads to higher energy savings, but to lower fractional energy savings. In other words, the higher the load, the more 'efficiently' the solar loop works, but also the higher the auxiliary energy needs are.

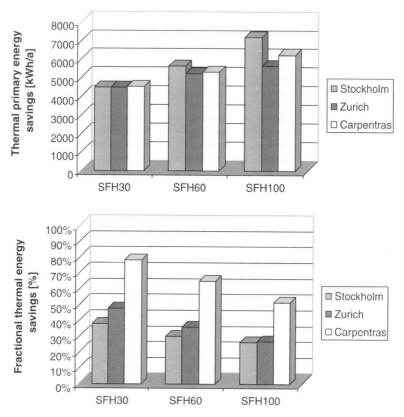

Figure 8.7. Influence of climate on the savings and the thermal fractional energy savings for System #9b with a 10 m² collector area

- For well insulated houses, energy savings do not change much with the climate, which is not the case for fractional energy savings. The same combisystem installed in an 'identical' well insulated house will provide more or less the same energy savings and consequently the same money savings. Differences between climates become greater for houses with greater heating loads. In other words, it is as profitable to install combisystems anywhere in Europe.

8.1.4 The boiler and the annual energy balance

The savings achieved by any solar heating system are very dependent on three other key parameters:

- the boiler efficiency
- the temperature of the auxiliary heated part of the store (thermostat setting for store charge)
- the volume heated by the auxiliary heater.

The boiler efficiency is an obvious factor, but one that is sometimes underestimated in solar heating systems. The other two are less obvious factors, but these are equally important. Figure 8.8 shows that the setting of the thermostat for the auxiliary heating of the store greatly affects the energy savings for a system, in this case System #11 with an oil boiler. High settings result in large heat losses as the collector must work at high temperatures before the use of the auxiliary heater is avoided (set temperature exceeded in the store). However, at low settings the desired thermal comfort may not be achieved. This low thermal comfort is seen here from the decrease in the indicator f_{si} (see Section 6.2) at a temperature of 60°C. At a setting of 60°C the hot water demand is not fully met on certain occasions during the year. Significant improvements in system performance can be achieved by reducing the requirements for thermal comfort, especially for hot water. This in practice means that on occasions one must have a slightly shorter shower, or a bath with less water in it. Similarly, the volume that is heated by the auxiliary also affects both thermal comfort and savings. A larger heated volume ensures greater thermal comfort but results in lower savings. *There is thus always a trade-off between the level of guaranteed thermal comfort and the energy savings.*

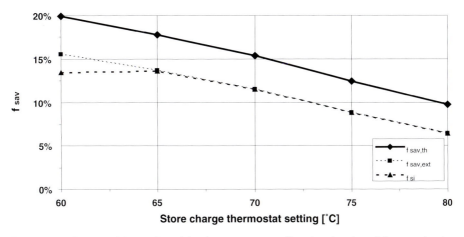

Figure 8.8. Influence of the setting of the thermostat controlling the charging of the store by the auxiliary heater, for System #11 using an oil boiler as auxiliary heater. This setting affects the temperature of the auxiliary heated part of the store

Low thermostat setting
Always set the thermostat controlling the auxiliary heating of the store to the lowest value that will give the thermal comfort and hygiene that the user desires. Too high a setting results in smaller energy savings without any extra benefit to the user. Note that if the domestic hot water is prepared in a separate store or in a tank-in-tank store, this setting is recommended in many countries to be 60°C or higher because of potential problems with bacterial growth. *A small volume heated by the auxiliary* also leads to improved savings but possibly to lower thermal comfort.

During summer, when there is often a nearly 100% coverage of the load by solar, the boiler does not supply much useful energy to the system. However, it still has significant losses to the environment. This is especially true for older boilers that do not turn off completely and automatically when not required, and in this case it can be advantageous to turn off the boiler manually during the summer. An electrical heater can be used instead, or alternatively the boiler can be turned on manually for the few times that it is required. Figure 8.23 shows that during summer both the gas and oil boiler have efficiencies much less than 40%.

Figure 8.9 shows the annual energy balance for System #11 for the Zurich climate and the SFH 60 house, resulting in a total load of 11,600 kWh. This annual energy use is approximately the same as the solar radiation on the 10 m² of collector during the year. 26% of the energy falling on the collector is delivered to the store and the remaining 74% is lost due to pipe and collector losses during operation,

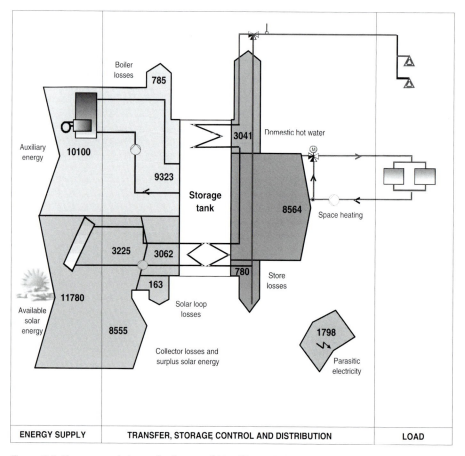

Figure 8.9. The energy balance for System #11 with gas boiler, 10 m² collector, Zurich climate and SFH 60 house. All values are in kWh. The value for parasitic electricity is given as primary energy and thus a factor of 2.5 greater than the electrical energy used

periods of insufficient radiation to make the collector hotter than the store and periods when the collector loop pump is switched off because the store is already fully charged. The boiler uses gas with a fuel energy content (final energy demand, E_{boiler}) of 10,100 kWh, of which 785 kWh is lost during operation and stand-by. This loss is nearly exactly the same as the losses from the well insulated store. Neither of these losses is treated as gains to the house in the simulations.

Of the primary energy E_{par}, 1798 kWh (720 kWh electrical, W_{par}) is required for parasitic usage for pumps, controllers and valves, and is nearly 20% of the final energy supplied to the boiler. For the reference, non-solar system, 1495 kWh of primary energy was required for parasitics ($E_{par,ref}$).

Electrical energy for pumps, controllers etc.
Electrical energy for pumps, controllers etc. can account for as much as 20% of the combined total energy use of the system. It is thus important to use low-energy pumps and to switch off pumps when they are not needed.

8.1.5 Design of the heat store

One of the key components of a solar combisystem is the heat store(s). Figure 8.10 shows schematically the different zones of a heat store using water as the storage medium, but without the necessary heat exchangers for heat transfer to/from the store. In the following sections some layout aspects of the tube connections to the different heat sources and heat sinks are described. The first section discusses the concept of stratification, which is the key to efficient storage and use of heat in a solar combisystem. Additional information on this can be found in Streicher (2002a).

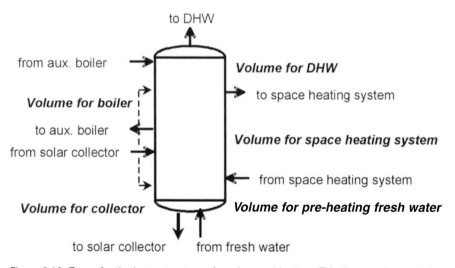

Figure 8.10. Zones for the hot water store of a solar combisystem. This diagram does not show the heat exchangers that are necessary for the heat transfer to/from the store

8.1.5.1 Stratification

The hotter the water, the lower the density of the water. Hot water thus naturally and stably finds its way above layers of cold water. This phenomenon makes it possible to have **stratification**, with **zones** of different temperature in one physical store. The zones indicated in Figure 8.10 can therefore be at different temperatures, and more specifically at the temperatures required of the loads for domestic hot water and space heating. Stratification allows an optimal use of the store with limited heat losses and, in addition, can be used to ensure that the collector inlet temperature is as low as possible. However, it is not obvious or easy to maintain good stratification in the store. In fact, the terms stratified and stratifying are used for slightly different phenomena and approaches. The following diagrams and descriptions show important differences in how the store can be charged. The same distinctions can be applied to discharging the store. To maintain stratification, all charging and discharging must be done in such a way as to improve or maintain the stratification. If only one heat source or sink causes significant mixing, it can destroy the benefit of the stratification created by other sources/sinks.

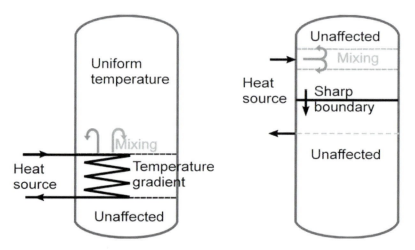

Figure 8.11. Charging using an internal heat exchanger (left) and with direct connections (right). The zone at the top of the tank with direct connections will be affected if the inlet temperature is higher than the temperature at the top of the tank

Figure 8.11 shows schematically what happens within the store when it is charged with an internal heat exchanger and with direct connections. The water heated by the internal heat exchanger starts to rise and mixes with the surrounding water. In this way the heat is transferred to a large volume of water, which is heated slowly. The net result is usually a zone of uniform temperature above the heat exchanger. This zone extends as far as another zone with higher temperature, if one exists. Once the temperature of this higher zone is reached, both zones will be heated uniformly at the same temperature. Below the heat exchanger, the store is unaffected. There is a small temperature gradient in the store at the same height as the heat exchanger. An electric element in the store acts in a similar way, but as a result of the relatively high power and small heat transfer area, the heated water does not mix fully with the surrounding store water, resulting in a small temperature gradient (stratification) above the heater.

With a direct connection there is some mixing in the store at the inlet. The degree of mixing is dependent on the inlet velocity and the difference in temperature between that of the incoming water and that of the store at the inlet. The zone above the inlet will be unaffected by the incoming water if the latter is colder. Beneath the inlet, the store water is pushed down and out through the outlet. There is usually a sharp boundary between the hot water, at nearly the same temperature as that entering through the inlet, and the original store water. This boundary moves downwards during the charge. However, if the incoming water is hotter than the upper zone, then heat will be transferred into that zone, causing mixing there, as well as into the volume below the inlet. A large volume is thus affected and the temperature below the inlet will be significantly lower than that of the water entering the store. The temperatures of the inlet water from both the collector and the space heating circuits vary in time, and there will be times when the incoming water is hotter than the water in the store at the inlet, and other times it will be colder.

Charging with direct connections thus tends to enhance stratification, with the volume of the zone increasing during charging. In contrast, charging with an internal heat exchanger tends to destroy stratification. In the store of a solar combisystem, there are several heat sources as well as sinks, and so the flows and stratification are complex.

Neither the internal heat exchanger nor the direct inlet is perfect for creating stratification, so different methods have been applied to improve stratification. The first, and simplest, is to increase the number of internal heat exchangers, as illustrated in the store on the left of Figure 8.12. This arrangement creates more

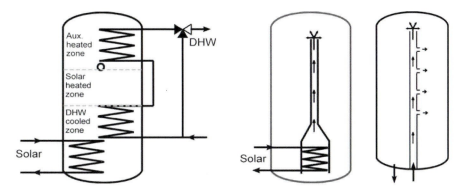

Figure 8.12. Three different methods of causing stratification with internal heat exchangers: several internal heat exchangers (left); stratifying tube (middle); and stratifying unit with multiple outlets (right). The stratifying unit can be used with an internal heat exchanger or for other inlets that vary in temperature

zones between the heat exchangers and thus a greater degree of stratification. However, the whole of each zone is heated/cooled by the heat exchangers, and the temperature in the zones does not change rapidly. In order to create a variable-volume zone that can be heated/cooled quickly, several manufacturers have added a **stratifying tube** to the internal heat exchanger, as illustrated in the middle store of Figure 8.12. This tube acts in a similar way to a direct inlet. However, the flow in the tube and thus the temperature at the outlet of the tube is dependent on the temperatures in the store as well as those of the heat source, as the flow is the result of natural convection. This flow can vary considerably depending on the conditions within the store. Thus, with this method, the water entering the store from the tube can be either hotter or colder than the surrounding water.

Another method is to use a **stratifying unit** with several outlets, as illustrated in the right-hand store of Figure 8.12. This arrangement allows water to exit the unit at the height that has approximately the same temperature in the store, thus maximizing stratification. This method is better than the other two, but requires careful attention. The flow in the tube should be within a limited range; otherwise the water comes out at an incorrect height. In addition, it is important to minimize drawing in of water through outlets into the passing flow in the tube, because this would lead to mixing on the way up, resulting in lower outlet temperatures. Such stratifying units have been successfully used with both internal and external heat exchangers in the solar circuit and for the return from the space heating loop.

Stratifying tubes and units with internal heat exchangers work with natural convection as mentioned above. It is important that the pressure drop through the tube/unit, the heat exchanger's effectiveness and the expected heat transfer rate are matched so that the flow in the tube is similar to that in the collector circuit, thus ensuring low temperatures to the collector and high outlet temperatures. Both stratifying tubes and units can be used advantageously in low-flow systems.

Figure 8.13 shows how a good stratification unit works when the temperature in the tube is between that at the top and at the bottom of the store – in fact, between that at the second and third outlets.

8.1.5.2 The collector

The collector circuit usually has an antifreeze/water mixture as the heat transfer fluid. A heat exchanger is therefore required for heat transfer to the store. An exception to this are systems that use the drainback principle, such as System #9b. The input to the collector should always be as cold as possible, in order to keep its efficiency high. Therefore, the connecting tube to the collector is mounted at the bottom of the store, where the coldest water is. The height of the input from the collector into the store varies with different applications.

For so-called **high-flow** systems, with flow in the collector circuit of approximately 50 l/h per m^2 of collector area, the temperature rise in the collector is of the order of 10°C. The input into the store for these high-flow systems should be near the bottom of the store, and the store is heated slowly from the bottom to the top. An exception to this rule is for stores with more than one heat exchanger in the collector loop, for example System #12.

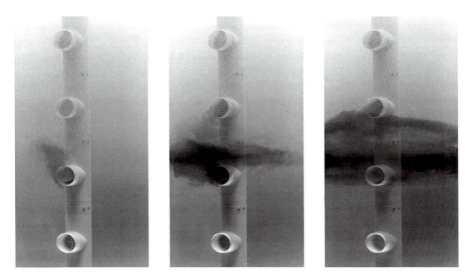

Figure 8.13. Stratifying unit for hot water stores showing outlet into the middle of the store (Source: Solvis, Germany). See also colour plate 21

For so-called **low-flow** systems with a specific collector flow of 10–15 l/h per m² of collector area, the temperature rise in the collector is of the order of 40–50°C. The input to the store in low-flow systems should be higher up than in the high-flow systems, the best height depending on the flow and system design. It can be advantageous to use a stratifying unit to make sure that the heat from the collector goes to the right level in the store. Low flow should not in general be used with internal heat exchangers, as these cannot fully utilize the high temperature built up in the collector, and the resulting temperature in the store is much lower because the water in the store is mixed rapidly. Moderate flows can be used, but in this case the internal heat exchanger should have a greater vertical extent than when high flows are used.

8.1.5.3 The auxiliary heater

The input tube from the auxiliary heater should be on the top of the tank. The outlet position to the auxiliary heater is determined by several factors:

- There should always be enough hot water in the store to fulfill the heat demands. The peak heat demand in single- or double-family houses occurs when a bath tub is filled (about 25 kW). Therefore, the recommended volume for the DHW can be calculated from this demand and the power of the auxiliary heater. Additionally it must be possible to deliver heat from the auxiliary heater to the space heating system as well. Therefore, the outlet position must be below the DHW and the space heating outlet.
- The auxiliary heater often needs a minimum running time (especially solid wood burners). The volume between auxiliary heater inlet and outlet must be sufficient to prevent overheating during this minimum running time.

- The outlet to the auxiliary heater should be as high as possible (limited by the above factors) in order to leave as large a volume as possible for the solar collector.

8.1.5.4 Domestic hot water (DHW)

The DHW outlet most often needs the highest temperature of the combisystem (50–60°C). Therefore, it is located at the top of the tank. The fresh water (or the water from a heat exchanger for DHW production) is always the coldest part and therefore located at the bottom. The volume heated by the auxiliary must be big enough to guarantee that all demand for DHW can be met (i.e. 200 litres at 40°C for a hot bath).

8.1.5.5 The space heating system

The temperatures in the space heating system range between the mains water temperature and that necessary for DHW. Consequently, the zone for the heating system is positioned in the middle of the tank. During the heating season, space heating is the dominant heat sink. Therefore, the volume for this is kept relatively large.

8.1.6 Design of the collector circuit

In most countries within Europe, the collector circuit needs to be such that it can tolerate periods of frost. The most common method of protection is use of an anti-freeze mixture of propylene glycol and water. In addition, the most common collector circuit layouts are also subject to periods of stagnation when the collector pump is switched off because the store is fully charged. This is more common in solar combisystems than in solar domestic hot water systems. Section 7.2 describes some of recent work carried out on what happens during stagnation. In many systems, the pressure in the collector circuit is kept below 3 bar. During stagnation the collector fluid evaporates and is forced down into the expansion vessel. Figure 8.14 shows two possible hydraulic schemes. In the top scheme (Case 1), the increasing vapour pressure forces all liquid out of the collector as the increased pressure pushes the liquid down equally on both sides. There is no vapour in the connecting tubes because only the liquid is transported through them during the emptying of the collector. In the lower scheme (Case 2), if the pressure is equal on both sides, all liquid in the 'U' has to be evaporated because it is 'trapped' in the collector. The steam is forced into the tubes and has to be condensed in the heat exchanger to the heat sink. Very high temperatures occur in the whole collector circuit. Additionally, there is an increased degradation of the propylene glycol and the corrosion inhibitors, because of the high temperature in the collector. Therefore Case 1 is recommended for the collector layout. The rest of the hydraulic flow scheme of the collector circuit must allow for the liquid to be drained from both sides of the collector to the expansion device. Figure 8.15 shows one possible hydraulic flow scheme.

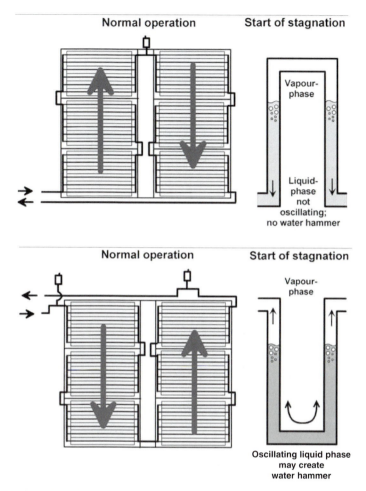

Figure 8.14. Hydraulic collector flow scheme forcing steam out of the collector during evaporation; top – Case 1; bottom – Case 2. (Source: Streicher, 2002b)

Drainback systems, where the collector is drained of fluid when it is not in operation, are common in the Netherlands, as described in Section 7.2. Even more details can be found in the proceedings of the fifth industry workshop of Task 26 (Weiss, 2001). This method is used for protection from both frost and overheating. The Dutch designs have shown that it is possible to design reliable collectors and stores for this method. However, it is still possible for the pipes to be installed in an incorrect way, leading to problems. In practice, however, this does not occur in the Netherlands. See Chapter 7 for more details.

Another method of overheating protection involves keeping the collector circuit pump in operation and dumping heat in the ground or some other heat sink. Some systems even cool the store at night so that the risk of overheating the next day is reduced. A system design that can withstand high pressures (up to 9 bar) in the

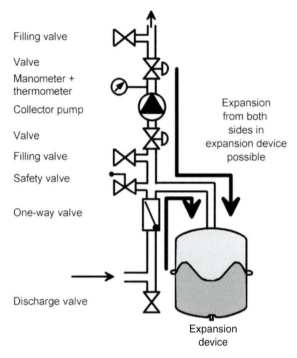

Figure 8.15. Hydraulic flow scheme of the pump, the one-way valve and the expansion device allowing the flow from both sides of the collector. (Source: Streicher, 2002b)

collector circuit enables the fluid to remain in the collector at all times. However, this approach can lead to rapid deterioration in the glycol and is not to be recommended for systems with stagnation temperatures over 140°C.

8.2 PLANNING AND DESIGN TOOLS

Planning or design tools can be split into *three categories*: **rules of thumb**, where the whole design is produced using simple rules of thumb based on pooled knowledge; **diagram–based tools**, where simple calculations are performed with the aid of diagrams and simple equations; and **computer-based tools** where detailed designs can be made using specially designed computer programs. The latter can be split into several sub-categories with varying degrees of detail and complexity. In addition there are *two levels of design*, from the **overall sizing** of the *entire system*, principally the collector and store, to **detailed sizing** of *smaller components* such as pumps and pipes. The detailed level is, in principle, the same as for other types of heating system and the methods for design and sizing of these small components are well known. There are, of course, a number of different tools or rules available, most of them being for specific countries or regions because of varying plumbing practices and traditions. These are not discussed here.

Rules of thumb are very simple for anyone to understand and can give a good first estimate for system design. They often do not cover the full range of possible applications, or are possibly not applicable for all countries. They may also vary from system to system. They are, however, very useful as overall guidelines and, where possible, rules of thumb have been included in the previous section. There are very few commonly used diagram-based tools for solar combisystems. A nomogram has been created within the work of Task 26 and is described in Section 8.2.1, but it is restricted to the systems simulated in Task 26. Another nomogram including both solar combisystems and hot water systems was created as part of a European project (Karlsson and Zinko, 1997). Task 26 has developed a new diagram tool using the FSC method developed within Task 26. It is essentially a diagram-based tool made into a computer program for flexibility. It is described in Section 8.2.2. A variation of diagram-based tools is form sheets, where one can go through the sheet and make simple calculations to arrive at sizes for components. This approach can even include more detailed sizing.

Rules of thumb, manufacturers' guidelines and diagram tools

Rules of thumb, manufacturers' guidelines and **diagram tools** are simple, and give a rough approximation of system performance and required size for a given location and user. They are good for preplanning and for determining the overall size of a factory-made system for single- or two-family houses. The methods are not always easy to apply to all locations and cases.

Computer-based tools vary greatly in complexity. The simplest programs make rough calculations using a mixture of rules of thumb and simple equations. These can be based on spreadsheets or on a calculation program that is part of the tool and are generally simple to use. The level of detail varies considerably from those that give only rough sizing information to those that give suggestions for the choice of components and an economic summary. These tools do not make detailed time-dependent simulations, although they do take into account the variation of the climate and load over the year. However, few of these cover solar combisystems. The results are usually in the form of annual and sometimes monthly values. They do not simulate the dynamic behaviour of the system and are therefore sometimes referred to as static calculation tools. An example of such a tool that can be used for solar combisystems is F-chart from the USA. It was the first of its kind, being developed in 1975. F-chart uses its own internal computational routines based on a special method of the same name (Duffie and Beckman, 1991) and is quite comprehensive with many input parameters and several different system types. The program, in increasingly more advanced forms, has been available for many years. The design program PSDMI, specific to Systems #1 and #3 with direct solar floor heating, is also available free of charge from the internet.

The simpler computer tools discussed above do not take into account the dynamic behaviour of the system; rather they make use of correlations that are often empirical. The more detailed simulation programs, however, can take into account the dynamic, or time-dependent, nature of systems to give more accurate results for time periods that are of the same order of magnitude as the time constants of the system components. These time constants range from seconds for temperature sensors to hours or days for the thermal storage. There are two generic types of **dynamic simulation tools: system-based** and **component-based** tools. System-based tools allow the user to choose between a number of alternative system configurations, and then the whole system is simulated. With component-based tools the user connects the components of the system together and then simulates the whole group or system. This latter type of tool is much more flexible than the system-based one as any configuration can, in principle, be simulated. The disadvantage is that the computation time is often quite long, as the tool has to be robust enough to solve any combination of components. The flexibility also brings with it administrative problems for the user. It is often more difficult to keep track of what exactly is part of the system and to make sure that all the values are as they should be. It is thus relatively easy to have errors, in the form of incorrect values for parts of the system. This can also be true for system-based tools that allow the user to change a large number of system parameters.

Computer tools

Simpler computer tools allow more detailed design of the system while still being relatively easy to use. A variety of systems and a large number of locations and loads can be simulated. Some more detailed studies can be carried out. They are generally suitable for dimensioning both single- and multi-family dwellings and as an aid in the design process.

There are a number of system-based dynamic simulation tools that can simulate solar combisystems. Examples of these are the commercial programs Polysun from Switzerland and T-sol from Germany, and the university-developed SHW-WIN from Austria. Polysun and T-sol are available in several languages, including English and German, and can simulate both solar domestic hot water systems and combisystems. They are both easy to use and have significant numbers of parameters that the user can vary. It is also easy to import weather data from a range of sources. As these programs use different models, it is not easy to compare results from the two programs with any great accuracy, even with the results from Task 26. SHW-WIN is only available in German, but is available free from the internet.

Simulation programs

Detailed simulation programs require detailed knowledge of both the program and the physics of the system to be simulated. They are thus generally only suitable for experts who wish to carry out detailed development work or research. Some programs can generate, based on the advanced models, a simpler tool that can be used by non-experts.

There is an even greater number of component- or equation- based dynamic simulation tools that allow simulation in great detail. All can in principle be used to simulate solar heating systems, but in practice there are only a few that are used because it takes time to build databases of the relevant components. Examples of programs that have been used to simulate solar heating systems are Colsim, Smile, IDA, Matlab Simulink and Dymola. They each have their own advantages and disadvantages with respect to simulating solar combisystems, but none of them was used within Task 26. Instead Task 26 used TRNSYS, a program that has been used for over 25 years and of which there is a great deal of experience in the solar heating community. With TRNSYS it is possible to take the very detailed system model and to create a simple computer application with fewer variables open to the user, a so-called TRNSED application. This can be used by a much wider group of people. More details of TRNSYS can be found in Section 8.3.1.

Summarizing, one can say that the tools that are simplest to use give the roughest estimates and also the least flexibility. At the other end of the scale, the tools offering the greatest accuracy are also far more flexible. However, they require expert knowledge and a great deal of effort. In between there is a wide range of possibilities allowing differing degrees of flexibility and ease of use.

8.2.1 The Task 26 nomogram

The Task 26 nomogram is based on the FSC method described in Section 6.3 and can be used for sizing a given system or comparing different systems. It is limited to the systems and climates used in Task 26, but the load can be chosen arbitrarily. The method is described below, together with a small version of the nomogram (Figure 8.17). A copy of the nomogram can be downloaded from the Task 26 website (http://www.iea-shc.org/task26). In Task 26, the FSC characteristics have been derived from the results of the detailed simulations using TRNSYS for a number of different systems. A list of the systems available in the nomogram is found in Table 8.4.

Table 8.1. List of axes for the four diagrams in the nomogram

	X axis	Unit	Y axis	Unit	Diagonal axis or parameter	Unit
1	Collector area	m²	Specific collector area	10^{-3} m²/ kWh	Annual reference consumption	kWh
2	Specific collector area	10^{-3} m²/ kWh	Fractional solar consumption	–	Climate	–
3	Fractional solar consumption	–	Fractional energy savings	%	System	–
4	Specific collector area	10^{-3} m²/ kWh	Specific annual energy savings	kWh/m² per year		

The FSC nomogram is designed for quick estimation of the energy savings, after four parameters have been chosen:

- a system
- a climate
- a collector area
- a reference consumption.

The nomogram is built with four diagrams (Figure 8.16), connected together by common axes, as listed in Table 8.1. The different diagrams and their functions are as follows:

- Diagram 1 calculates the specific collector area (A/E_{ref}), according to the chosen **collector area** and the chosen annual **reference consumption**.
- Diagram 2 calculates the Fractional Solar Consumption (FSC), according to the specific collector area and the chosen **climate**.
- Diagram 3 calculates the thermal fractional energy savings $(f_{sav,therm})$, according to the fractional solar consumption and the chosen **system**.
- Diagram 4 calculates the annual energy savings (E_{sav}), according to the specific collector area and the thermal fractional energy savings.

A list of the intersections used in the nomogram and their meanings is given in Table 8.2.

Table 8.2. List of intersections used in the nomogram and their meanings.

Letter	Unit	Meaning
a	kWh/a	Reference consumption
b	–	Origin of the specific collector area axis
c	m²	Collector area
d		
e		
f	10⁻³ m²/kWh per year	Specific collector area
g		
h	–	Fractional Solar Consumption
i		
j	%	Fractional energy savings
k		
l	kWh/m² per year	Annual energy savings

8.2.1.1 Using the nomogram

For each step the example values are given in brackets (see Figure 8.16 for the example nomogram and Figure 8.17 for an empty nomogram page).

1. Choose an annual **reference consumption** E_{ref} **(a = 22,000 kWh).**

   The reference consumption is calculated according to Task 26 reference conditions:

   $$E_{ref} = \frac{Q_{SH} + Q_{DHW} + Q_{loss,ref}}{\eta_{boiler,ref}}$$

   The efficiency of the reference boiler is **0.85**. The yearly heat losses of the store are calculated according to the daily hot water demand V_d (litres/day), in the same way as in ENV12977–2 (CEN, 1997) (Table 8.3):

   $$Q_{loss,ref} = (UA)_{store,ref} \cdot (\bar{T}_{store} - T_{store,amb}) \cdot 8760 \frac{hr}{a} \text{ in units of kWh/a}$$

   with $T_{store} = 52.5°C$ (hot water temperature) and $T_{store,amb} = 15°C$ (ambient temperature).

Table 8.3. Calculated yearly heat losses

Daily hot water demand V_d (litres/d)	Reference store losses $Q_{loss,ref}$ (kWh/a)
100	455
150	557
200	644
250	720
300	788

2. Draw a line from point **a** to the origin.
3. Choose a **collector area** (**c** = 28 m²).
4. Draw a horizontal line from point **c** until you meet the segment [**ab**] at **d**.
5. Draw a vertical line from point **d** until you meet the diagonal line at **e**.
6. Draw a horizontal line from point **e** until you meet the vertical axis at **f**; you get the *specific collector area* (1.3).
7. Draw a horizontal line from point **f** until you meet the **climate** curve (**g** on the curve for Zurich).
8. Draw a vertical line from point **g** until you meet the horizontal axis at **h**; you get the fractional solar *consumption* (FSC = 0.64).
9. Draw a vertical line from point **h** until you meet the **system** curve at **i**.
10. Draw a horizontal line from point **i** until you meet the vertical axis at **j**; you get the *fractional energy savings* ($f_{sav,therm}$ = 47%).
11. Draw a horizontal line from point **j** until you meet the vertical line coming from **e** at point **k**.
12. Draw a line from the origin **b** to point **k**, and extend it if required. Point **l** at the intersection of this line with the energy savings axis gives the *specific annual energy savings* (kWh/m² per year) compared to the reference system with annual boiler efficiency of 85% (350 kWh/m² per year).

Colour versions of both the example and the empty nomogram are included in the colour section.

8.2.2 The Task 26 design tool

The Task 26 design tool, called CombiSun, is based on the FSC method described in Section 6.3. The FSC value is dependent on the size of the collector, its orientation and the total load of the system. It is thus possible to estimate the savings of any system using the FSC characteristic if one knows the system load and climate as well as the size and orientation of the collector. In contrast to the nomogram, this tool is not restricted to the three climates used in Task 26, as it comes with a larger database of different climates. The tool can be downloaded free of charge from the Task 26 website (http://www.iea-shc.org/task26/). Some of the detailed TRNSYS simulation models are available from their creators as Trnsed applications, in which the user, via a simple interface, can vary a limited number of the many available parameters.

CombiSun is aimed at a wide range of users and is designed principally to enable users to make a choice of the overall size of the system for the given location and

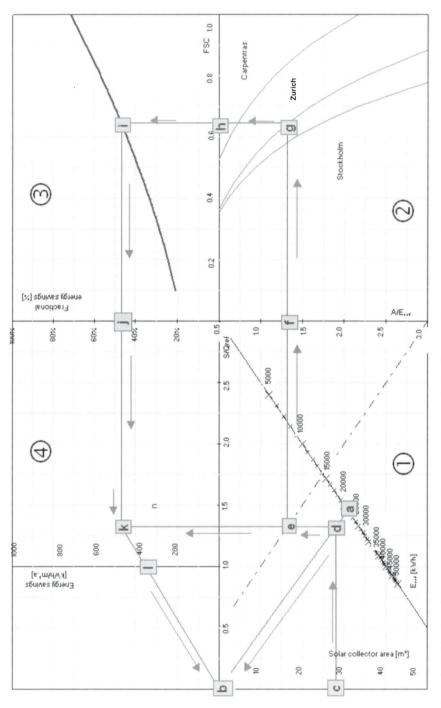

Figure 8.16. The four diagrams of the FSC nomogram and an example of its use. See also colour plate 23

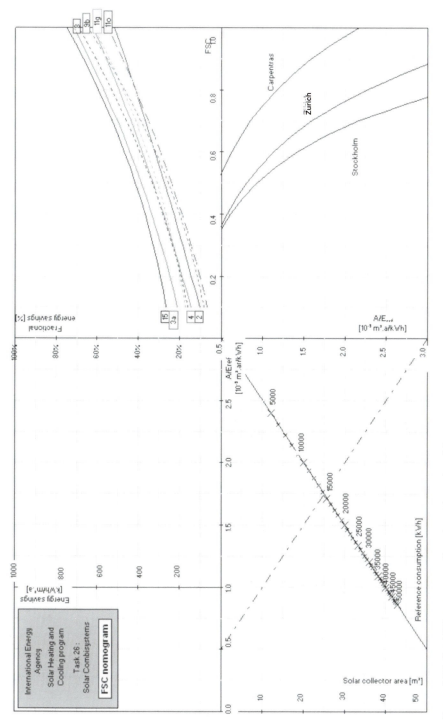

Figure 8.17. The FSC nomogram. See also colour plate 24

building size. It is really a computerized diagram-based tool and is not proposed as a detailed design tool. It can, however, be used to compare different system types for the same conditions. Several of the systems included in the tool are not sold with a specific boiler; rather, this is chosen by the buyer or installer. This choice greatly affects the overall savings of the system. The boilers used for the simulation of these systems, and thus the basis of the FSC characteristic, were the standard Task 26 boilers (see Section 6.1.1 for more details). It is possible to estimate the savings of these systems using another boiler, if so desired. The systems included in CombiSun are those listed in Table 8.4. It is possible to add new systems to the program database as long as there is an FSC characteristic for the system, relating FSC and fractional savings, as defined by Task 26. This characteristic can, in principle, be calculated using results from any simulation tool. Theoretically, it is also possible to derive a characteristic based on monitored data, but this data is unlikely to span a wide enough range of FSC values.

Table 8.4. Generic systems that are included in the design tool CombiSun. These are the same as are available in the Task 26 nomogram

System	Name
#2	Heat exchanger between collector loop and space heating loop (Denmark)
#3a	Advanced direct solar floor (France)
#4	DHW tank as a space heating storage device (Denmark)
#8	Space heating store with double load-side heat exchanger for DHW (Switzerland)
#9b	Small DHW tank in space heating tank (Norway)
#11	Space heating store with DHW load-side heat exchanger(s) and external auxiliary boiler (Sweden, Finland)
#15	Two stratifiers in a space heating storage tank with an external load-side heat exchanger for DHW (Germany)

Table 8.5 shows the user inputs to the program while Figure 8.18 shows the interaction of CombiSun with the user. *TRNSYS is used to simulate the building on*

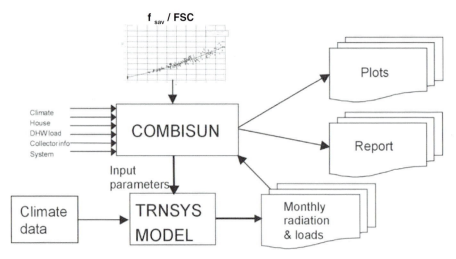

Figure 8.18. Information flow in the design tool CombiSun.

an hourly basis and to calculate the irradiation on the chosen collector orientation. The output from this TRNSYS simulation is then used by CombiSun to calculate the FSC values for a range of collector sizes. The corresponding energy savings are then calculated for these collector areas and the chosen system, based on the system FSC characteristic. These results are then written out in table form and can be plotted on a diagram such as Figure 8.19. Several different plots can be made on the same diagram, for different systems or other variations in user input. The diagram can be scaled and exported as a separate file so that it can be incorporated into reports. A standard report can also be created and printed out. It is possible to add additional climates to the database.

Table 8.5. The user inputs to CombiSun.

Input	Description
Climate	The climate for the calculation – from a database of climates.
Type of building	The user can choose from the three Task 26 single-family house constructions (insulation thickness)
Size of building	Floor area of the building
Azimuth	The azimuth of the collector field
Slope	The slope of the collector field
DHW load	The DHW load for the calculation

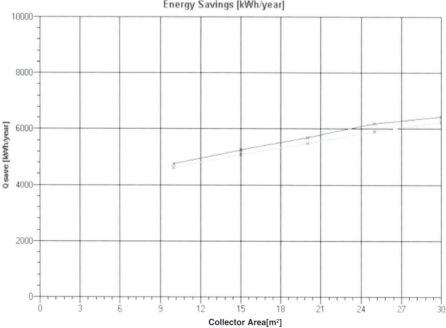

Figure 8.19. Example output diagram from CombiSun for the same system with 10 m² of collector, but two different azimuths (south-east and south)

As CombiSun is based on the FSC method, some major assumptions, and the results of Task 26, there are several limitations to the tool. These are summarized in Table 8.6.

Table 8.6. Limitations/assumptions of CombiSun and their implications.

Limitation/assumption	Implication
Selected systems	Only systems with a defined FSC characteristic can be calculated. These must be part of the program database
Limited range	The FSC method is not accurate for all variations of the input variables. See Section 6.3.1. The program does not allow values for which the method is not validated
FSC validity	The FSC method has been validated for a few systems and a wide range of input variables. It is not certain that it is valid over the same range for any systems that are added to the program
Fixed system parameters	The FSC characteristic was calculated based on fixed parameter values with, for example, a defined relationship between collector size and store volume. Alterations of individual parameters concerning operation, heat losses etc. cannot be made. There is thus limited flexibility
Savings relative to Task 26 reference system	The calculated savings are relative to the Task 26 reference system, which has a gas burner with 85% efficiency throughout the year, independent of load. Savings relative to other boilers or reference systems would need to be calculated separately using the monthly values of loads calculated by TRNSYS for the building in question

The results calculated by the tool are savings with respect to the Task 26 reference system. These reference conditions are useful in order to compare systems on an equal basis. However, users are likely to want to estimate savings compared to a specific system − their own or their clients' system. In order to do this, the consumption of the user-specified system needs to be estimated by dividing the monthly loads by the monthly boiler efficiency of that system, and then summing these monthly consumptions. In a similar way, the savings can be estimated for a different boiler in the solar heating system.

8.3 SIMULATION OF SYSTEM PERFORMANCE

Task 26 has used TRNSYS (Klein *et al.*, 1998) as the tool for simulation of system performance. It is just one of several possible tools, as discussed in the previous section. It is a modular program with each module representing a particular component or group of components in the system. These are programmed in Fortran and the source code is available to the user. TRNSYS has been used for over 25 years for the simulation of solar heating systems, and there is wide range of component models that have been validated over the years. Details of the component models that were used in Task 26 can be found in Section 8.4.

In more modern simulation programs such as IDA, Smile and Matlab Simulink, the process of calculation is different to that in TRNSYS. In these programs the equations used to define the behaviour of the individual components are all grouped, and solved all together. This type of program is sometimes referred to as **equation-based**, as opposed to TRNSYS, which is a **component-based** program. In TRNSYS, the components are solved separately and sequentially, as described in detail in Section 8.3.1. TRNSYS distinguishes between inputs, which are time-dependent, and parameters, which have fixed values for the whole simulation. All inputs and parameters have to have a given value, either constant throughout the simulation, or given to them from another component. Outputs are the results of the internal calculations in the component model, and are used as inputs to other components. Equation-based programs generally do not distinguish between inputs and parameters, as all can be time-dependent. The solvers can also calculate the required input to give a certain output value, if the output is fixed. TRNSYS cannot easily do this, making it less flexible.

8.3.1 TRNSYS simulations

In TRNSYS the components are calculated sequentially, i.e. they are calculated one after the other. The results, or outputs, from a component are given to succeeding components. If an input has not been calculated as the output from another component for the current time step, then the value from the previous time step is used. If components form a loop with feedback, where at least one of the inputs into one of the components is dependent on its own output, then an iteration process is performed. Here, calculations in the loop proceed from component to component with outputs from one being given to the next, as in Figure 8.20. When all components in the loop have been calculated, then the new input values (In_i) to the first component are compared to those for the previous iteration (In_{i-1}). If they are all within the convergence tolerance limit set for the simulation, then the program can go on to the next loop or process. The convergence tolerance thus affects how consistent the results are within a loop and therefore also the energy balance for the loop. A tight tolerance leads to consistent results with low energy-balance errors, but at the same time can require more iterations and therefore greater computational time. There is thus always a compromise between computational time and the accuracy of the results. This is true for all dynamic simulation programs, not just TRNSYS.

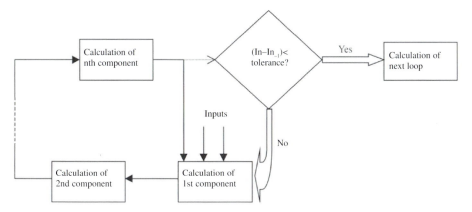

Figure 8.20. The iteration process for loops in TRNSYS

This process of calculating all components proceeds until all loops and all components have been completed successfully. Occasionally, a particular loop will not converge within the desired tolerance limit. In this case, the last values are used and a warning is generated. If too many such warnings occur in a simulation, then the simulation is terminated and considered to have failed.

In order to check that the simulation is working properly, the creator of the system model must be able to check the simulation outputs and to compare them with how the real system performs under the same conditions. This is generally done in two ways. The first is to check the total energies and the energy balances for sub-systems. The second is to look at the detailed dynamic behaviour of the system. In TRNSYS this is done with the so-called on-line plotter, an example of which is shown in Figure 8.21. Here, the simulation of System #11 can be seen over one day. Only a few of the possible outputs of the simulation model are shown. The dynamic behaviour of the collector model is clearly shown by the peak in the heating rate when the collector-loop pump is turned on.

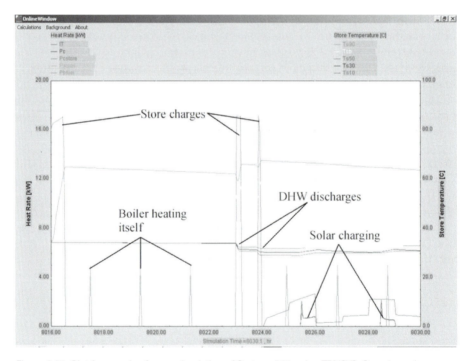

Figure 8.21. Plot for one day from a simulation of System #11 using TRNSYS. See also colour plate 22

8.3.2 Simulation of Task 26 systems

In order to be able to compare the performance of very different systems, a simulation methodology has to be created, as well as a set of reference conditions. This ensures that the results are as consistent as possible and thus are the best possible basis for comparative purposes. The reference conditions used in Task 26, including climate and load, are described in detail in Section 6.1. The models used for the different components are detailed in Section 8.4, as well as the values used for the standard boilers. However, despite these common grounds, there are still possible pitfalls, such as the use of old versions of component definitions. Several of the components used are very complex and have different versions. Other components have had to be created for specific systems, as they did not previously exist. It should be noted that Task 26 used TRNSYS version 14.2 for all of the work.

A specific methodology was used in Task 26 to ensure consistency of the different system simulation models. Each user created his/her own version of the calculation program, the so-called DLL. The DLL contained all the component definitions necessary for the simulation of the system. These individual DLLs were then used to simulate a reference system to check that it gave the same results as for other users. In the second step of the methodology, a sensitivity analysis on the main simulation parameters was performed. These are convergence tolerance, time-step and the number of nodes in the store model. These three parameters strongly influence the computation time, and thus it is good to have a set of these values that gives consistent results with the minimum possible running time. Each system was simulated so that the results were within 1% of those with very tight error tolerances. The maximum possible time step in Task 26 is 0.1 hour, as this is the resolution of the hot water load file. Most systems were simulated at time steps of 0.05 or 0.025 hour and with convergence tolerances of 0.001–0.01.

Solar combisystems vary considerably in size, and the energy in the store can be relatively large. If the conditions in the store are not the same at the start and end of the year, then there can be a significant inconsistency. To avoid this, all systems in Task 26 are simulated for 13 months, from 1 December one year to 31 December the year after. Only the results for the calendar year are considered.

There are a number of major assumptions and simplifications that are common to all the Task 26 system models. These are listed in Table 8.7. The major one, and one that causes much discussion, is the fact that the heat losses from both the store and the boiler have *not* been considered as heat input into the building. This is a simplification and is valid as a first approximation for certain types of houses, but it is certainly not valid for many other types of houses. The influence of this uncontrolled heat input varies considerably, depending on the exact placement of the store and boiler and how this room is used and ventilated. This requires the modelling of the house in several nodes, requiring a significant increase in computational time, and so this option was discarded. The other assumptions and simplifications affect how accurate the results are, compared to a system under real operating conditions. The main purpose of simulating in Task 26 has been first to lead to improvements in the system performance and second to be able to compare the different systems. In both these cases simulation results are compared with other simulation results, and most of the assumptions and simplifications affect the different system variations in more or less the same way. They therefore have a relatively limited effect on the results of the Task.

Table 8.7. Major simplifications and assumptions used in the simulations of Task 26 together with their implications

Simplifications/assumption	Implication
Heat losses from the store *and* boiler are *not* treated as heat gains within the building	The losses neither help in the heating of the building during winter nor add to overheating problems in the summer
Generated hourly weather data from Meteonorm	The data are based on average monthly data and have no variation within the hour. Short-timescale dynamic effects in the collector loop caused by clouds are therefore neglected
Hot water load with fixed time step of 0.1 hour	Really short discharges with low flow rates are neglected. High flow rates of up to 20 l/min are included
Collector treated independently from building	The collector does not affect heat transport through the roof

Assumptions that are system-specific can be found in the detailed technical documentation for each system, which is available from the Task 26 website. A list of the systems can be found in Table 8.4.

Of the many systems that were catalogued at the start of the work of Task 26, only nine have been modelled and simulated in detail, although several versions of some systems have been made. This reflects the amount of time and effort needed to accurately model a system and to ensure that the model works like the real system. This aspect of checking for the correct behaviour of the model is often called parameter identification and verification, and is discussed in more detail in Section 8.4. Table 8.8 lists the systems that were simulated in Task 26.

Table 8.8. List of systems that were simulated within the work of Task 26, together with the person who created the system model

System	Creator of system model
#2	K. Ellehauge
#3	P. Papillon
#4	L. Shah
#8	J. Bony
#9b	M. Peter
#11	C. Bales
#12	C. Bales
#15	D. Jaehnig
#19	R. Heimrath

8.4 NUMERICAL MODELS FOR SOLAR COMBISYSTEMS

Numerical models are the basis of all simulation programs. They consist of a number of equations that describe mathematically the operation of the component or group of components. There are often logical constraints on these equation sets.

The model can either be a **physical model** or an **empirical model**. In a physical model the equations describe well known and verified physical phenomena based on fundamental properties and dimensions. In an empirical model, the processes are described with sets of equations whose parameters need to be identified using experiments. The empirical models are obviously more difficult to apply for the average user, as they require either a database of components with previously identified parameter values, or a new experiment in which new values can be identified. However, in certain components the processes are so complex that the investment in time is too great to develop a working physical model that is validated. In other cases it can be judged that the computational time required for a physical model is too great and that a simpler empirical model is better. It is also possible to have combinations of empirical and physical models, and these are often called **grey box models**. Empirical models are sometimes referred to as **black box models**, and physical models as **white box models**. It should be noted that it is, in general, best to have components of the same level of detail. If one component is modelled in great detail while other important components are much simpler, much of the worth of the detail is lost.

In TRNSYS there are all three types of model. Many of the simpler models are physical ones, whereas the more complex ones are generally grey box models. All are written as Fortran subroutines, or in other languages in the latest version. Each unique model is called a **Type** and given a type number. Each component or subroutine is called in turn and the solver controls the iteration process. As the model is written in Fortran, very complex components can be created with internal solvers, etc., and new models are relatively easy to create and add to the database. In the so-called equation-based simulation programs, the models are built up as a set of equations and constraints on these equations. The solver then takes all the equations from all of the models in the system and solves them in the most efficient way it can. The resulting set of equations that is solved is thus for the whole system at one time, as compared to TRNSYS, which solves parts at a time. For similar levels of mathematical detail the two methods will lead to identical results.

8.4.1 Models used in Task 26

Solar combisystems consist of a relatively large number of different components, most of which are modelled as separate components in the simulations. This approach requires many different component models or Types. Most of these are the same as used for simulating solar hot water systems, but several have not been used frequently before. The Types used on a common basis in Task 26 are listed in Table 8.9. The majority of them are standard components, i.e. they are delivered with TRNSYS. Ten of them are, however, non-standard components and have been created by a variety of different users. Of these, many are available from Transsolar Energietechnik GmbH (http://transsolar.de/ts/english/maineng.htm), who donated them for use in Task 26.

Table 8.9. The TRNSYS component types that were used as standard in Task 26. Components that do not come as part of the standard database have references to the source of the component in parentheses. The Unit number refers to the sequential number of the component in the example system in Figure 8.22

Type	Unit	Description
Type 2	14, 20	Differential controller
Type 3	15, 22	Pump
Type 4	–	Stratified storage tank
Type 5	–	Sensible heat exchanger
Type 9	1, 3	Data reader
Type 11	12, 13, 24, 25	Flow diverter
Type 14	19	Time-dependent forcing function
Type 15	–	Algebraic operations
Type 16	4, 5	Radiation processor
Type 24	–	Quantity integrator
Type 25	–	Printer
Type 28	–	Simulation summary
Type 31	16, 18	Pipe or duct
Type 34	7	Overhang and wingwall shading
Type 44	–	Convergence promoter
Type 56	8	Building type
Type 60	–	Stratified storage tank
Type 65	–	On-line plotter
Type 69	6	Fictive sky temperature
Type 98	–	External hot water unit incl. controller (Drück, ITW, Universität Stuttgart)
Type 100	–	Floor heating (Papillon, Clipsol, Trevignan)
Type 120	9	PID controller (Transsolar Energietechnik GmbH, Stuttgart)
Type 123	–	Controller for Type 170 (Transsolar Energietechnik GmbH, Stuttgart)
Type 132	17	QDT collector (Perers, SERC, Högskolan Dalarna)
Type 135	34	Calculation of the heating season (Papillon, Clipsol, Trevignan)
Type 140	11	Multiport store model (Drück, ITW, Universität Stuttgart)
Type 147	–	Multiport store model with integrated gas burner (Drück, ITW, Universität Stuttgart)
Type 162	10	Dynamic radiator (Transsolar Energietechnik GmbH, Stuttgart)
Type 170	23	Biomass/gas/oil Boiler (Transsolar Energietechnik GmbH, Stuttgart)

8.4.1.1 Example system model

As a typical example of the system models from Task 26, Figure 8.22 shows the model for System #11 in the graphic pre-processor to TRNSYS, Presim. The black number next to each component is the so-called unit number, the sequential number for the calculation. For simplicity, the multitude of output components is not shown. The three most important non-standard components are described briefly in separate sections, whilst the other important components are described below.

The data reader is used to read data from files for climate (Unit 1) and hot water load (Unit 3). The radiation processors (Units 4 and 5) are used to calculate the radiation on the six different surfaces of the house walls as well as the collector. This component receives hourly radiation data for a horizontal surface and calculates the position of the sun in the sky dependent on time and location before calculating the radiation on the relevant surface. No interpolation of data is carried out within the hour, but because the sun's position varies over an hour, the calculated radiation on a surface also varies somewhat over that time. At the end of an hour it changes

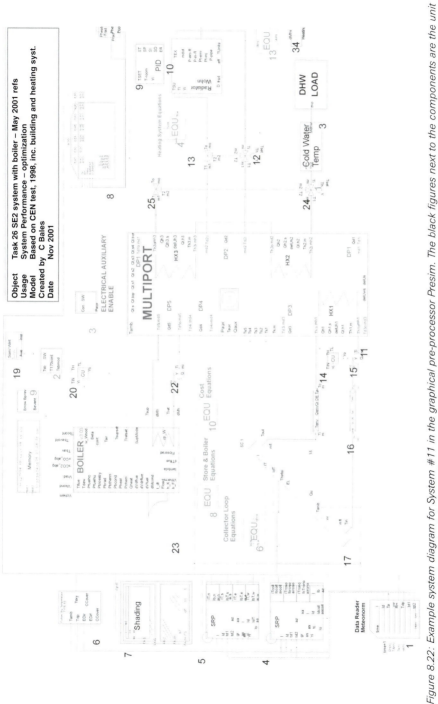

Figure 8.22: Example system diagram for System #11 in the graphical pre-processor Presim. The black figures next to the components are the unit number (sequential number) and the lighter number next to some of the boxes is the number of the relevant equation set. See colour plate 25.

in a step fashion. This step is seen clearly in Figure 8.23. For the building model a further calculation is required to take into account the effects of overhangs and shading (Unit 7) for the windows. Another model is used to estimate the sky temperature so that the radiation balance for the building can be calculated accurately, especially at night.

The multizone building model (Unit 8) is a very complex model, capable of calculating many separate thermal zones in a building. In Task 26 only one zone was used, so that simulation times could be kept reasonably short. This model is used extensively for building simulations, especially in Germany. It has amongst other things:

- detailed radiation balances for the walls
- a detailed window model with multiple reflections allowing accurate calculation of solar input
- transmission and ventilation losses
- a humidity calculation and thermal capacitance
- the possibility of input from heat sources such as a radiator (both radiative and convective heat)
- internal heat gains from machines, lighting and people.

The model calculates the resulting air temperature in the building dependent on the climate data, a schedule of internal gains, ventilation and the input from the dynamic radiator model (Unit 10). The model also calculates the radiative and convective heat transfer dependent on the room temperature, the flow temperature and the flow to the radiator. A PID controller (Unit 9) is used to model the thermostatic valve that modulates the flow to the radiator in order to maintain a room temperature of 20°C. Two valves (Units 12 and 13) are used to adjust the flow through the store in order to feed the radiator with the flow temperature calculated by a set of equations (EQU 4 in lighter type in Figure 8.22) and the outside air temperature.

The heat for the radiator loop, and thus the building, comes from the Multiport store model (Unit 11), which is described in mode detail in Section 8.4.1.2. This thermal store is provided with heat by both the collector and boiler loops. The collector (Unit 17) feeds heat to the store via a pipe (Unit 18) that has thermal mass and heat losses to the surroundings. From the internal heat exchanger in the store, the pump (Unit 15) supplies fluid to the collector via another pipe (Unit 16). This pump is controlled by an on/off controller with hysteresis (Unit 14), which has as its inputs the collector temperature and relevant store temperature. Overheating cut-off is included in the controller. The oil boiler (Unit 23) is fed by another pump (Unit 22), which is controlled by an on/off controller with hysteresis (unit 20) based only on the relevant store temperature. The boiler model has an internal controller for modulating the burner.

A peculiarity of System #11 is that it uses electrical back-up heating during the summer and the oil boiler during the winter. This is due to the low efficiency of the oil boiler during the summer (see Figure 8.23) when it is not heavily loaded.

This switching of heat source is controlled by a time-dependent forcing function (Unit 19) and sets of equations (equations 2 and 3 in lighter type near Units 19 and 20).

The hot water mass flow is read from a data file (Unit 3) and the temperature of the mains water is calculated by equations (equation 1) based on the location and time of year. As with the radiator loop, two valves (Units 24 and 25) are used to adjust the flow through the store, in this case through two serially connected internal heat exchangers, in order to maintain the desired domestic hot water delivery temperature of 45°C.

8.4.1.2 The multiport store model

This model has five double ports for direct connection to other components and circuits as well as three internal heat exchangers. These internal heat exchangers can be used to model tubular heat exchangers inside the store, mantle heat exchangers or tanks inside the main store. The heat transfer coefficient can be defined with temperature, flow and time dependency. Different heat loss coefficients can be defined for different parts of the store. There is also an electrical heating element with its own thermostat controller. The double ports can simulate perfectly stratified inlet of fluid, as can the heat exchanger if configured as a mantle heat exchanger. The possible stratification in the model is dependent on the number of nodes, the model allowing a maximum of 198. Most systems were simulated with between 50 and 100 nodes.

The model is a grey box model and has been validated for several very differently configured stores. It is used by many research groups. The heat exchanger's heat transfer parameter values are not easy to estimate without detailed measurements and parameter identification.

A newer beta version of the multiport store model was also used within the Task for the systems requiring four heat exchangers. This version can also calculate natural convection flows in encapsulated heat exchangers and stratifiers. A further extension to the model has been made in order to simulate an integrated gas burner.

8.4.1.3 The QDT collector model

This model has been created so that results from the new Quasi Dynamic collector Test method (Perers, 1993) can be used directly as parameter values, and has been validated for this use. It has a single thermal capacitance node and terms for wind and long-wave radiation losses as well as incident-angle modifier values that can vary in two dimensions. It is thus suitable for unglazed as well as glazed collectors and collectors with reflectors. The model has been validated against measured data for several collectors. Most system calculations were performed with the Task 26 standard flat-plate parameter values. These parameters are given in Section 6.1.2.

8.4.1.4 The biomass/gas/oil boiler model

The boiler model was originally developed for large-scale boilers with relatively little volume in relation to the flow and heating rate. It was modified within the

Task to be applicable to smaller systems such as domestic solar combisystems. It has not been validated in detail for this size and type of boiler and the standard values shown below are not for any specific boiler. The model is relatively detailed and calculates fuel usage and heat transfer dependent on the temperature of the exhaust gas, incomplete combustion, condensation and excess airflow, as well as stand-by losses. No detailed modelling of start and stop fuel usage and emissions is calculated, which is one important simplification of the model. Three fuel types are available: biomass, gas (two variations) and oil. The model has two main modes: a single-node heat exchanger model and a multinode heat exchanger model. The single-node model was used in Task 26.

Table 8.10 shows the parameter values that were chosen for the standard boilers to be used within Task 26. These were to be used for systems that are not supplied with a specific boiler. These parameters are for a moderately good condensing gas boiler and for a good non-condensing oil boiler. Figure 8.23 shows how the simulated overall efficiency of these Task 26 boilers varies over the year, both in the reference system and in System #11. In all cases the efficiency is significantly lower during summer, as less heat is supplied and the boiler stand-by heat losses are more significant. This is especially true when connected to a solar combisystem that has nearly 100% solar coverage over the summer, the case for most systems with an annual fractional energy saving of above 15%. In this case the efficiency during the middle of summer is near zero and it may make economic sense to turn off the boiler during these periods.

Table 8.10. The parameter values for the boiler model Type 170, for the standard gas boiler and an oil boiler

Parameter	Oil	Gas
Overall annual efficiency for the Task 26 reference system without solar heating for the Zurich climate and 60 kWh/m² per year house	80%	90%
Boiler water volume	37 kg	7.5 kg
Fuel type	oil (5)	gas (2)
Desired outlet temperature (parameter 1)	75°C	70°C
Internal controller on/off	70°/75°C	30°/70°C
Ambient temperature in boiler room	15°C	15°C
Temperature for loss data (parameter 6)	62°C	90°C
Rated heating power	15 kW	15 kW
Lowest modulation level	100%	25%
Mode (parameter 14)	10	10
Beta – fraction of CO in exhaust gas (input 9 – constant)	0.02	0.02
Lambda (input 11 – constant)	1.12	1.2
Temperature difference between inlet water and exhaust gas (input 12 – constant)	100	10
Radiative losses, fraction of rated power (input 13 – constant)	4.90%	3.5%
Stand-by losses, fraction of rated power (parameter 13)	0.70%	1.5%

8.4.1.5 System-specific models

Several of the systems simulated within the Task have special components that are not used in other systems. New component models have been developed for these and have been implemented in the relevant systems. Examples of such models are the floor heating model for Systems #1 and #3, the advanced controller for System

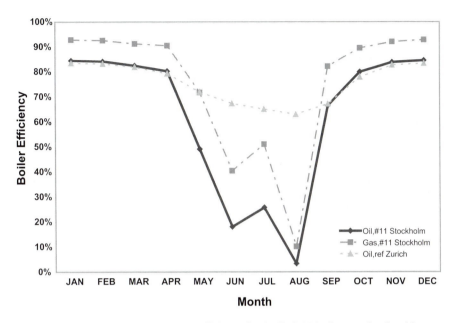

Figure 8.23. Variation of average monthly efficiency for the Task 26 boilers as simulated in System #11 with 10 m² collector in Stockholm and for the reference system in Zurich. All simulations are for the 60 kWh/m² per year house

#12 and the flow controller for domestic hot water preparation in System #15. These models are not described here, but are described in the technical reports for the relevant systems. These technical reports are available from the Task 26 website.

8.4.2 Parameter identification and verification

For really detailed simulation of systems it is necessary to have both a good model and the correct parameter values in the model for the specific system. For physical models, the fundamentals of the physics are well known and so the models are also accurate, although in some cases there are simplifications that cause inaccuracies. The standard models within TRNSYS have been validated against real components over several years. This is also true for the non-standard models, with the exception of the boiler model, which has only been validated for larger boilers.

For the grey box models and the purely physical modes the parameter values for the different systems have been identified using measurement data. Several of the systems have been tested according to strict test methods such as the Component Test and System Simulation method (CEN, 1997), while others have used available measured data to identify the parameter values. Once the parameter values have been identified, the model should then be checked, or verified, against other measured data, to ensure that the model can correctly simulate the real behaviour of the component or system. This is an important process, and is necessary if one is to rely on the results.

REFERENCES

CEN, 1997, *ENV 12977–2, Thermal Solar Systems and Components – Custom Built Systems – Part 2: Test Methods*, European Committee for Standardization Brussels, Belgium.

Duffie J and Beckman W, 1991, *Solar Engineering of Thermal Processes*, 2nd edn, John Wiley & Sons, Chichester, UK.

Drück H and Hahne E, 1998, 'Test and comparison of hot water stores for solar combisystems'. *Proceedings Eurosun '98, Portoroz, Slovenia*, pp. 3.3.1–7.

Heimrath R, 2002, 'Report on solar combisystems modelled in Task 26 (system description, modelling, sensitivity, optimization).', Appendix 9: System #19, *A technical report of subtask C*, IEA-SHC Task 26 Solar combisystems, http://www.iea-shc.org/task26

Karlsson B and Zinko H (eds), 1997, *CEC-Thermie B – Contract SME/0055/95-SV. Solar Heating in Northern and Central Europe*. Final report. ZW Teknik, Sweden.

Klein S A, Beckman W A., Mitchell JW, Duffie JA, Duffie NA, Freeman TL, Mitchell JC, Braun JE, Evans BL, Kummer JP, Urban RE, Fiksel A, Thornton JW, Blair NJ, 1998, *TRNSYS, A Transient System Simulation Program – Version 14.2* (as used in this project), Solar Energy Laboratory, University of Wisconsin-Madison, USA.

Lorenz K, Bales C and Broman L, 1997, 'Performance comparision of combitanks using a six-day-test', in, *Proceedings North Sun '97, Espoo, Finland*, pp. 119–128.

Lorenz K, Bales C and Persson T, 2000, 'Evaluation of solar thermal combisystems for the Swedish climate', in, *Proceedings Eurosun 2000, Copenhagen, Denmark*.

Nordlander S and Rönnelid M, 2001, 'Load adapted collectors for high solar fractions', in, *Proceedings North Sun 2001, Leiden, the Netherlands*.

Pauschinger T, Drück H and Hahne E, 1998, 'Comparison test of solar heating systems for domestic hot water and space heating', in, *Proceedings Eurosun '98, Portoroz, Slovenia*, pp. III.2.37.1–8.

Perers B, 1993, 'Dynamic method for solar collector array testing and evaluation with standard database and simulation programs', in, *Solar Energy* 50(6), 517–526.

Streicher W, 2002a, *Sonnenenergienutzung*, lecture book, Graz University of Technology.

Streicher W, 2002b, 'Minimizing the risk of water hammer and other problems at the beginning of stagnation of solar thermal plants – a theoretical approach', in, *Solar Energy*, 69(Suppl. 1–6), 187–196.

Weiss W (ed.), 2001, *Proceedings IEA-SHC Task 26 Industry Workshop V*, Delft, the Netherlands.

SIMULATION PROGRAMS

Colsim: http://www.ise.fhg.de
Dymola: http://www.dynasim.se/
F-chart: http://www.fchart.com/
IDA: http://www.equa.se
Matlab Simulink: http://www.mathworks.com/products/simulink
Polysun: http://www.solarenergy.ch
PSD-MI: http://evl.cstb.fr/soft/present.asp?context=PSD&langue=us&imprimer=&m=lpr
SHW-WIN: http://wt.tu-graz.ac.at/swdownload/shwindl.html
Smile: http://www.first.gmd.de/smile/, http://www.smilenet.de/
T-sol: http://www.tsol.de
TRNSYS: http://sel.me.wisc.edu/trnsys/

9 Built examples

9.1 SINGLE-FAMILY HOUSE, WILDON, AUSTRIA

Figure 9.1. General view. The house belongs to the Jaunegg family

Location

Town or village (country)	Wildon (Austria)
Latitude	47.07°
Altitude	350 metres

Building

Living area	175 m²
Heat load (at −14°C)	6.6 kW
Year built	2001

Solar heating system

Generic system	Variant of System #15
Collector area	24 m² roof-integrated flat-plate collector
Orientation/tilt angle	25° west of south/45°
Space heating storage volume	2400 litres
Domestic hot water preparation	External flat-plate heat exchanger
Design pressure (collector loop)	1.5 bar
Maximum system pressure	3 bar
Size of expansion vessel (collector loop)	105 litres
Fractional energy savings	35%
Overheating protection	Collector hydraulic with good emptying behaviour and appropriate expansion vessel
Auxiliary heater	Wood pellet boiler
Nominal power (auxiliary heater)	10 kW

System description

The single-family home was constructed in a low-energy mode typical for Austria. The outer walls are made of wooden frame structures with 26 cm insulation to obtain a U-value of 0.18 W/m²K. Since the roof is also well insulated with a U-value of 0.18 W/m²K, the heat load of the building at the design temperature of −14°C is only 6.6 kW. This is an ideal basis for a solar combisystem.

The building heat supply is 100% from renewable energy sources – solar energy and biomass.

The solar combisystem comprises a collector array of 24 m² and a space heating storage tank with a volume of 2400 litres. The space heating storage tank is located in the cellar of the building and has a diameter of 2.0 metres including the thermal insulation and is 2.4 metres high. Around 10 m² are required to accommodate the storage tank, the expansion vessels, pumps and all the hydraulic components required.

An external flat-plate heat exchanger connected to a self-regulating stratifying tube transfers the heat from the collector to the storage tank at the height at which the temperature corresponds to that of the heat exchanger's outlet.

Domestic hot water is prepared using a variable-speed pump and an external flat-plate heat exchanger. This concept for the preparation of domestic hot water offers the advantage that no intermediate storage is needed; this helps prevent the growth of legionella.

When the solar collector array cannot deliver all the energy required, the upper part of the heat storage tank is automatically heated by the pellet boiler.

Pellet boilers represent an ideal auxiliary heater for solar heating systems, since they are ignited in a similar way to oil or gas boilers, and the fuel is automatically fed by means of a feed screw or fan. Thus these biomass boilers offer a very high level of comfort. In the case depicted here the pellet boiler is located in the living room. About 20% of the energy is delivered in the form of radiant heat or by convection directly into the living area; the remaining 80% is fed into the space heating storage tank. With this arrangement the boiler losses are reduced to the energy of the exhaust gases alone. The stand-by losses of the pellet boiler go into the living space.

In the individual rooms, heat is provided by a wall and floor heating system.

Figure 9.2. The pellet boiler in the living room

Figure 9.3. Combustion with low emissions is guaranteed thanks to the standardized grain size and moisture content of the wood pellets

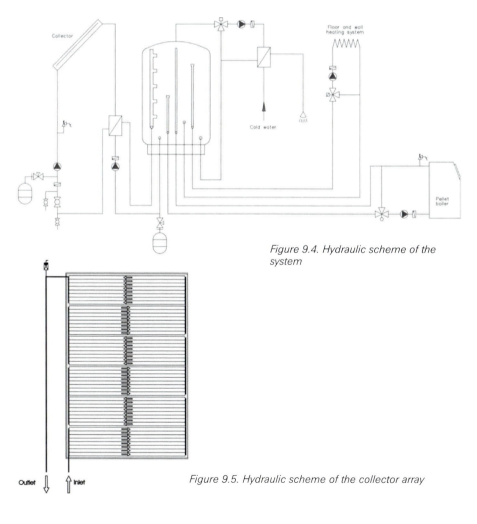

Figure 9.4. Hydraulic scheme of the system

Figure 9.5. Hydraulic scheme of the collector array

9.2 THE GNEIS-MOOS HOUSING ESTATE, SALZBURG, AUSTRIA

Fig. 9.6: General view

Location

Town or village (country)	Salzburg (Austria)
Latitude	47.48°
Altitude	425 metres

Building

Living area	4696 m²
Heat load (at −15 °C)	200 kW
Year built	1999

Solar heating system

Generic system	System #19
Collector area	410 m² roof-integrated flat-plate collector
Orientation/tilt angle	0° (south)/35°
Space heating storage volume	100 m³
Domestic hot water preparation	External flat-plate heat exchanger
Design pressure (collector loop)	1.5 bar
Maximum system pressure	3 bar
Size of expansion vessel (collector loop)	400 litres
Fractional energy savings	35%
Overheating protection	Night cooling via the collector array if the temperature in the storage tank exceeds 90°C
Auxiliary heater	Condensing gas boiler
Nominal power (auxiliary heater)	250 kW

System description

The Gneis–Moos housing estate was constructed with an overall floor area of 4696 m² on the outskirts of Salzburg.

Apart from innovative architecture – a low-energy mode of construction with a heating energy demand of 50 kWh per m² of residential area per year, the comprehensive passive solar energy utilization by means of conservatories directed towards the south – the planning team took particular care to ensure an ecological and efficient supply of energy.

The occupants of the 61 residential units, which are each divided into six individual houses, moved in in December 1999 and January 2000.

An area of 410 m² of roof-integrated collectors was installed on one house to supply the housing estate with heat. An energy storage tank with a capacity of 100 m³ was installed as a part of the solar heating system. A gas condensing boiler connected to the energy storage tank provides the auxiliary energy.

The energy is distributed to the six houses via a two-pipe network with decentralized heat transmission stations in the individual houses. The design of the heat transmission stations and the radiators demands a constant network supply temperature of 65°C throughout the year. The heat transmission stations contain both the external heat exchanger, to heat the DHW on the basis of the flow-through principle, and all the control elements, such as differential pressure control units and return-temperature limiting devices. The low network return temperatures of 30°C throughout the year that can be achieved with these heat transmission stations form the basis of a good collector efficiency and thus of corresponding solar yields.

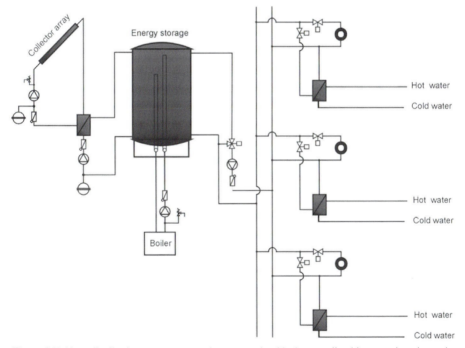

Figure 9.7. Heat distribution system: two-pipe network with decentralized heat stations in each residential unit

The average fractional energy savings of 34.5% for the two years 2000 and 2001 correspond almost exactly with the predicted fractional energy savings of 35%.

The solar yields were higher than predicted. The design values were 350 kWh/m² per year. The measured values are 378 kWh/m² for 2000 and 380 kWh/m² for 2001.

Environmental impact

The CO_2 reduction of the solar thermal installation – compared to a conventional oil boiler – is 67.7 *tonnes* per year or 1557 tonnes over the lifetime of the system.

Figure 9.8. Prefabricated heat transmission station with external heat exchanger to heat the domestic hot water and all the components for space heating operation including energy quantity counters

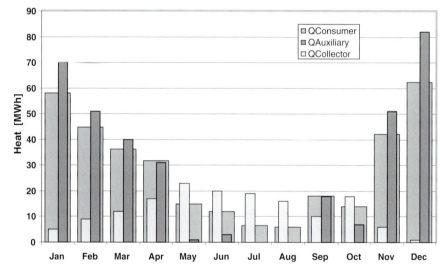

Figure 9.9. Heat balance 2001 for the Gneis-Moos project, Salzburg, Austria

Figure 9.10. A view of one of the six buildings on the housing estate

9.3 SINGLE-FAMILY HOUSE, KOEGE, DENMARK

Figure 9.11. General view

Location

Town or village (country)	Koege (Denmark)
Latitude	55.4°
Altitude	3 metres

Building

Living area	280 m²
Heat load (at −12 °C)	8.8 kW
Year built	1950 (renovated 2002)

Solar heating system

Generic system	System #2
Collector area	9 m² flat-plate collector
Orientation/tilt angle	0° (south)/45°
Space heating storage volume	280 litres (hot water storage)
Domestic hot water preparation	In solar hot water store and in boiler unit in winter
Design pressure (collector loop)	2 bar
Maximum system pressure	6 bar
Size of expansion vessel (collector loop)	8 litres
Fractional energy savings	18%
Overheating protection	Excess heat delivered to space heating loop
Auxiliary heater	Oil boiler
Nominal power (auxiliary heater)	20 kW

System description

The single-family house was erected in the 1950s and was completely renovated in 2002. The outer walls are made of bricks with an insulated cavity. Calculations of the heat demand have not been made, but it is expected that the annual heat demand will be around 70 kWh/m².

The lower floor, which has 177 m² of living area is heated via a floor heating system. On the upper floor, radiators are used to heat the rooms.

The storage tank for the solar heating system is placed in a boiler room in the middle of the house together with the oil-fired boiler, which acts as the auxiliary heater for the solar heating system.

The solar combisystem comprises a collector array of 9 m² and a domestic hot water storage tank with a volume of 280 litres. Heat is delivered directly from the solar–collector loop to the central-heating loop via a heat exchanger. The storage tank is integrated in a white casing together with all other components of the system, i.e. the expansion vessel, safety valve, pump, heat exchanger, etc. The dimensions of the tank are the same as other standard household modules, that is 60 × 60 cm.

In winter, the hot water is pre-heated by the solar collectors and heated up to the set-point temperature in a 110 litre hot water tank in the oil boiler unit. In summer the hot water is, if necessary, after-heated in the solar hot water tank by an electric immersion heater.

It is normally recommended that in winter the after-heating also takes place in the hot water store, which is charged by the boiler via a coil heat exchanger in the top of the tank, since this reduces the heat losses. However, in practice all heat losses from the hot water tank in the boiler unit will benefit the house and cause no extra energy use.

Experience has shown that the system benefits from the floor heating system as the temperature in the central-heating loop is reduced. Furthermore, the concrete floor acts as a heat store in the summer, for the heat delivered by the solar collectors, thus increasing the performance of the system.

Figure 9.12. The solar hot water store. The main hydraulic components are located beneath the store

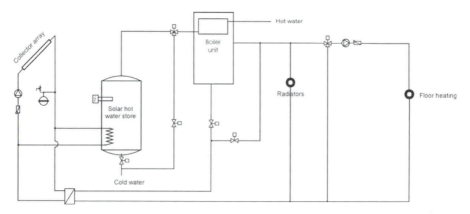

Figure 9.13. Hydraulic scheme of the system

9.4 MULTI-FAMILY HOUSE, EVESSEN, GERMANY

Figure 9.14. General view – the collectors are on top of the roof

Location

Town or village (country)	Evessen (Germany)
Latitude	52.3°
Altitude	81 metres

Building

Living area	386 m²
People	10 persons/four families
Heat load (at −14 °C)	15 kW/19,500 kWh in 2000–2001
Yearly specific heat load	50 kWh/m² floor area
Year built	1990

Solar heating system

Generic system	System #15
Collector area	10 m² flat-plate collector
Orientation/tilt angle	South/35°
Space heating storage volume	750 litres
Domestic hot water preparation	External flat-plate heat exchanger
Design pressure (collector loop)	1.5 bar
Maximum system pressure	3 bar
Size of expansion vessel (collector loop)	18 litre
Yearly solar gain	410 kWh/m² collector area
Fractional energy savings	15.5%
Overheating protection	Collector hydraulic with good emptying behaviour and appropriate expansion vessel
Auxiliary heater	Internal condensing gas burner using liquid gas
Nominal power	15 kW

System description

The four-family home with an office part was constructed for low-energy use as is typical in Germany. The outer walls are made with a well insulated wooden frame structure. The heat load of the building at the design temperature of −14 °C corresponds to 15 kW, and the specific energy demand is about 50 kWh per square metre per year. This is an ideal basis for a solar combisystem and shows that a system originally designed for single-family houses can also be used in well insulated multi-family houses.

Normally, the limiting factor of this kind of system is the hot water comfort. A low-energy house has a nominal heating power of about 7 kW, but for the hot water comfort the auxiliary burner should have at least 12 kW, otherwise it will sometimes take too much time to heat up the store so that more domestic hot water can be prepared (e.g. for a second person taking a bath).

There are 10 m² of flat-plate collectors flush-mounted on the floor so they are hidden in Figure 9.14.

Main features

This system consists of a compact unit, in which all components are integrated. Therefore, the space requirements as well as the installation time are reduced because of the reduction in the number of separate components and connections needed. Possible mistakes while installing the system are excluded, because everything is prefabricated.

The solar storage tank, with 11.5 cm thick insulation, works as an optimized energy manager for all types of incoming (solar energy, gas burner, etc.) energy and outgoing (domestic hot water, space heating water) energy.

Heat management philosophy

- The **collector loop** is completely designed as a low-flow loop. The collector is connected to the storage tank by a 'life-line' comprising two copper tubes with 10 mm outside diameter, insulation and collector sensor cable, which are combined in a tube and delivered to the plumber in 25 metre rolls. The speed of the **solar loop pump** is controlled so that it reaches an optimal temperature delivered to the storage tank and a minimum flow rate in the collector to ensure good heat transfer. The input of solar energy into the storage tank is carried out by an internal low-flow heat exchanger together with a stratifying unit (low-flow technology, see Figure 8.13).

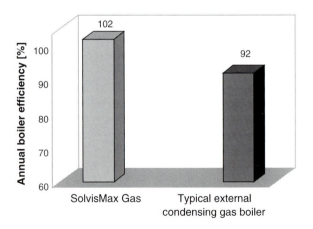

Figure 9.15. Yearly efficiency of the auxiliary condensing gas boiler in a single-family house for a total load comprising 30% for domestic hot water and 70% for space heating

- **Domestic hot water** is prepared via a variable-speed pump and an external flat-plate heat exchanger. This concept for the preparation of domestic hot water offers the advantage that no intermediate storage is needed; this helps prevent the proliferation of legionella. The hot water temperature is adjusted to the chosen set-point temperature by controlling the speed of the pump located in the primary loop of the heat exchanger.
- Heat delivered to the **space heating loop** is adjusted by a variable-flow-rate pump controlled by the valve position of the radiators (to save pump energy and ensure quiet operation of the radiator valves).
- In the event that the solar collector array cannot deliver all the energy required, the upper part of the space heating store is automatically heated by a **condensing gas burner** modulating between 5 and 15 kW, depending on the temperature in the tank and the requested temperature of the space heating loop (calculated from the ambient temperature, the room temperature and the time of the day).

This system design leads, on the one hand, to a very good solar performance and, on the other hand, to an efficiency of the auxiliary heater that is much better than in standard systems with an external boiler (see Figure 9.15). Both values in that figure include all standstill and store losses (Jaehnig *et al.*, 2002). The system was monitored by the University of Braunschweig, Institut für Gebäude- und Solartechnik (IGS) during the years 2000–2001.

The measured yearly gain from the collector in this system was 410 kWh/m² and the fractional energy savings were 15.5%, which is quite good considering the small collector size of 10 m² for this application (multi-family house with 386 m² of living space).

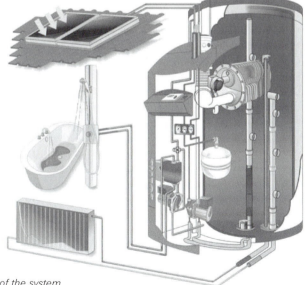

Figure 9.16. A cross-section of the system

The hydraulic scheme of the collector array shows that in each collector all tubes are in series, in a serpentine fashion. This is necessary to increase the performance, as it is designed for a low–flow system. In addition, the design allows the collector to empty as quickly as possible during the stagnation process, so that temperature stress in the heat transfer fluid and other components is reduced.

Figure 9.17. Installed system with additional energy counter and fully integrated pump station for the space heating circuit with a three-way mixing valve

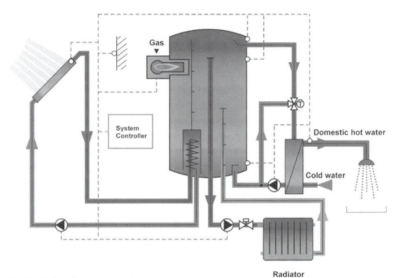

Figure 9.18. Hydraulic scheme of the system

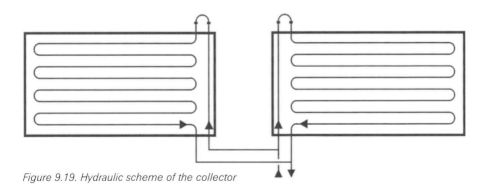

Figure 9.19. Hydraulic scheme of the collector

9.5 MULTI-FAMILY HOUSE WITH OFFICE, FRANKFURT/MAIN, GERMANY

Figure 9.20. General view

Location

Town or village (country)	Frankfurt/Main (Germany)
Latitude	50.20°
Altitude	250 metres

Building

Living area	1040 m²
Heat load (at −10°C)	40 kW
Year built	1957

Solar heating system

Generic system	Variant of System #17
Collector area	20 m² roof-mounted evacuated tube CPC collector
Orientation/tilt angle	0° (south)/60°
Space heating storage volume	2 x 800 litres
Domestic hot water preparation	Internal heat exchanger with stratifier using natural convection
Design pressure (collector loop)	2.5 bar
Maximum system pressure	4 bar
Size of expansion vessel (collector loop)	25 litres
Fractional energy savings	8–15%
Overheating protection	Small collector area, large tilt angle
Auxiliary heater	Modulating condensing gas boiler
Nominal power (auxiliary heater)	40 kW

System description

The house is located in the northern part of Frankfurt/Main. In 1998 it was renovated and the roof was raised. An insulation of 10 cm polystyrene foam was added to the walls and 20 cm to the roof. There are five flats and one office in the building.

The two oil boilers, located in the cellar of the building, were replaced with one modulating condensing gas boiler. Two identical combistores for domestic hot water preparation and space heating, connected in parallel, are located close to the boiler.

The stores incorporate two heat exchangers with attached stratifying tubes, one for solar and the other for preparation of hot water. The storage tanks are connected directly to the boiler and the floor heating circuit. The flow line of the boiler passes through a thermostatic three-way valve that can direct the water to the top (temperature < 53°C) for domestic hot water, or to the middle (temperature < 53°C) to store heat for space heating. Hot water is prepared via the internal flow through a heat exchanger at the top of the store. Solar charging is performed by the immersed solar heat-exchanger spiral situated at the bottom of the store. Both heat

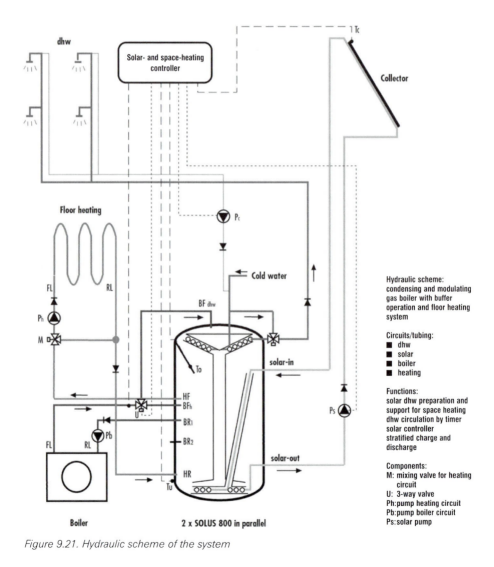

Figure 9.21. Hydraulic scheme of the system

exchangers are operating in counter-flow mode and have stratifier tubes connected to them to avoid mixing of water with different temperatures.

The controller for charging the store uses two sensors. The flow line of the space heating circuit is connected to the store at the same height as the lower of the two charging connections from the boiler. The return line of the space heating loop enters the stores at the bottom to secure maximal solar gains.

The 20 m² solar collector, connected in four arrays, is inclined at 60° and oriented directly to the south. It consists of evacuated–tube collectors using the so-called Sydney principle, and a parabolic reflector. Because of the relatively small collector size and the high inclination of the collectors, there are no stagnation problems during summer.

The floor heating system has controllers for each room to stop the flow of fluid in the circuit when the desired room temperature is reached.

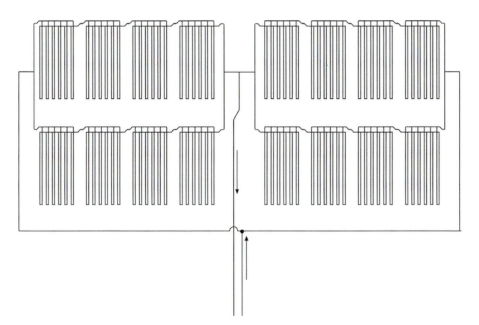

Figure 9.22. Hydraulic scheme of the collector array

9.6 SINGLE-FAMILY HOUSE, CÖLBE, GERMANY

Figure 9.23. General view. The house belongs to the Altmann/Tent family

Location

Town or village (country)	Cölbe (Germany)
Latitude	50.83°
Altitude	210 metres

Building

Living area	140 m²
Heat load (at −12°C)	4.2 kW
Year built	2001

Solar heating system

Generic system	Variant of System #15
Collector area	27.5 m² roof-integrated flat-plate collector
Orientation/tilt angle	0° (south)/35°
Space heating storage volume	3000 litres
Domestic hot water preparation	'Ratio fresh' external hot water unit
Design pressure (collector loop)	1.5 bar
Maximum system pressure	3 bar
Size of expansion vessel (collector loop)	35 litres
Fractional energy savings	40%
Overheating protection	Collector hydraulic with good emptying behaviour and an appropriate expansion vessel
Auxiliary heater	Wood pellet boiler
Nominal power (auxiliary heater)	8 kW water and 2 kW air

Photovoltaic system

System size DC	3.4 kW BP Saturn technology
AC-connected load	2.5 kW

Water supply system

Storage tank for rainwater	5500 litres
Rainwater collecting area	100 m²
Rainwater consumption	Toilet flushing, garden irrigation, washing machine

System description

This single-family house was designed for very low energy consumption. The outer walls are built with a wooden framework and are filled with 26 cm thick cellulose insulation. The roof insulation also has cellulose insulation, with a thickness of 38 cm. The windows are double-glazed and have a U-value of $0.9\,W/m^2K$. In order to reduce the ventilation heat losses, a mechanical ventilation system with heat recovery is installed. A soil-to-air heat exchanger provides frost-protected air in winter and pleasantly cool air in summer.

The heat distribution takes place via radiators that are designed to operate at flow/return temperatures of 55°/45°C for an outside air temperature of −12°C.

Heat and electricity to the building are supplied 100% by renewable energy sources, that is, solar energy and biomass. 100% of the water requirement for the toilets is also met by rainwater.

The solar heating system consists of a collector array of 27.5 m² (aperture area) and two storage tanks with a volume of 1500 litres each, located in the basement of the building. The heat from the collectors is transported into the storage tanks at two different levels by two three-way valves, via an external flat-plate heat exchanger.

Domestic hot water is prepared by an external 'ratio fresh' hot water unit containing a variable-speed pump and an external flat-plate heat exchanger. There is thus no intermediate storage with risk of legionella contamination. Another advantage is the low return temperature, which is only five degrees above the cold water temperature.

If the solar heating system cannot deliver all the energy required in the upper part of one of the storage tanks, this part is heated up by the pellet boiler. 20% of the heat produced by the boiler is directly radiated to the living room, thus the stand-by losses of the boiler are minimized.

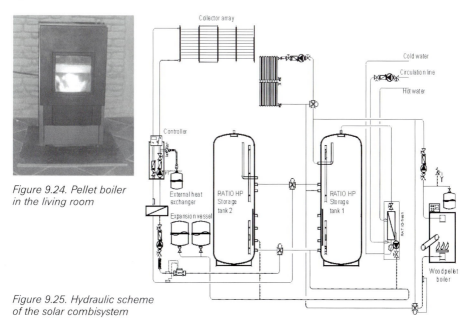

Figure 9.24. Pellet boiler in the living room

Figure 9.25. Hydraulic scheme of the solar combisystem

9.7 FACTORY-MADE SYSTEMS, DORDRECHT, THE NETHERLANDS

Figure 9.26. Row of houses with solar combisystems in Dordrecht

Location

Town or village (country)	Dordrecht (The Netherlands)
Latitude	52.6°
Altitude	0 metres

Building

Living area	100–200 m²
Heat load (at –10°C)	4–12 kW

Solar heating system

Generic system	Systems #5 and #6
Collector area	4–5 m²
Orientation/tilt angle	South, 45°/varied
Space heating storage volume	–
Domestic hot water preparation	DHW storage, 180–380 litres
Design pressure (collector loop)	1.5 bar
Maximum system pressure	8 bar
Size of expansion vessel (collector loop)	–
Overheating protection	Drainback
Auxiliary heater	Integrated condensing gas heater

System description

The largest application areas for solar combisystems in the Netherlands are detached houses and rows of single-family houses. Typical building materials for these houses are concrete for construction, combined with brick and gypsum for the other walls. The outer walls are double, with about 10 cm of insulation material. The roof is also insulated and can be flat or pitched. Windows are double-glazed. The typical design heat load of a house with 100 m² living area is 4.3 kW at a design temperature of –10°C. At the present time, there is a tendency towards more variation in house designs.

Average Dutch solar combisystems are standard, factory-made products from two main manufacturers. The collector circuit works according to the drainback concept with a typical collector area of 4–5 m². Filled water/glycol loops are less common. The heat store and auxiliary condensing gas heater have been combined into one compact unit, normally installed in the attic of the house. Less than 1 m² of floor area is needed to accommodate the complete indoor equipment. The heat store and auxiliary heater are easy to handle and install because of the two-part system, i.e. the upper part with the condensing gas heater and the (lower) heat store with the other components. All necessary components are included, i.e. controls, drainback facilities, mixing valve for space heating, filter, water safety valves and controls, etc. The solar combisystems work best in combination with low-temperature heat distribution.

Specific layouts are different for the various products; see Figures 9.27 and 9.28. One of the manufacturers also delivers a 380 litre heat store combined with a larger collector area. Hot water comfort determines the power of the modulating burner, which is available in different heating rates from 15 kW up to 35 kW.

The system is easy for the installer to understand because of the already well known condensing boiler. The highest Dutch space heating performance label is

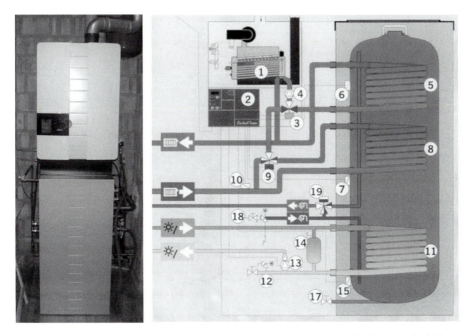

Figure 9.27. Solar combisystem with 'click-on' auxiliary (manufacturer: ATAG Verwarming). The auxiliary heater comprises (1) stainless steel heat exchanger, (2) control management system including solar module, (3) three-way valve and (4) system pump. The heat store contains (5) hot water heat exchanger, (6) hot water sensor, (7) sensor for control of the 'space heating/solar' three-way valve, (8) space heating heat exchanger, (11) collector-loop heat exchanger and (15) store sensor for collector loop control. Inside the system case, there are also (9) 'space heating/solar' three-way motor valve, (10) 'space heating/solar' return sensor, (12) a filling and draining point for the collector loop, (13) collector pump with flow restriction, (14) drainback tank with level tap, (17) tap for heat store drainage, (18) cold water inlet combination with safety valve and (19) thermostatic mixing device. Not shown in the Figure is (16), the collector sensor for collector loop control

applicable for auxiliary heaters from both manufacturers. The same applies to the label for low CO and NOx emissions. The relatively low cost–specification ratio is achieved by the use of standard products and/or standard machines for making these products. The manufacturers provide the guarantee.

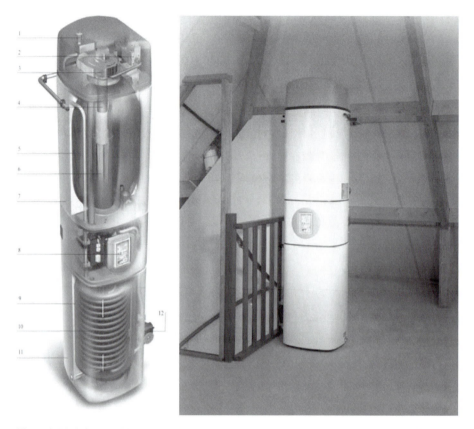

Figure 9.28. Solar combisystem with solar heat mainly stored in the bottom module and auxiliary heater in the top module (manufacturer: Daalderop). The top module (7) is a high-efficiency gas-fired combisystem and includes (1) automatic bleeding valve, (2) modulating gas unit, (3) continuously variable blower, (4) burner, (5) 80 litre domestic hot water heat store and (6) double-wall heat exchanger. The bottom module (11) is for solar and includes (8) control panel, (9) 100 litre solar heat store, (10) domestic hot water heat exchanger and (12) collector loop pump

9.8 SINGLE-FAMILY HOUSE, SAINT BALDOPH, FRANCE

Figure 9.29. General view. The house belongs to the Lambert family

Location

Town or village (country)	Saint Baldoph (France)
Latitude	45.39°
Altitude	291 metres

Building

Living area	132 m²
Heat load (at −10°C)	8.9 kW
Year built	1997

Solar heating system

Generic system	System #3
Collector area	15 m² roof-integrated flat-plate collector
Orientation/tilt angle	0° (south)/40°
Space heating storage device	Heating floor
Domestic hot water preparation	Two, 250 litre DHW tanks
Design pressure (collector loop)	1.5 bar
Maximum system pressure	3 bar
Size of expansion vessel (collector loop)	24 litres
Fractional energy savings	35%
Overheating protection	Additional pipes in the ground
Auxiliary heater	Gas boiler and wood stove
Nominal power (auxiliary heater)	24 kW

System description

This single-family house uses the main concepts of a solar and ecological house:

- The passive gains on the south face are optimized thanks to a large window area, with low-emissivity glass.
- Protection against the wind on the north side of the building is provided by small windows and service rooms (shed, boiler room).
- The wall construction consisting of a wooden frame with an insulation thickness of 15 cm reduces the thermal losses.

- A solar combisystem assisted by a gas boiler and a wood stove provide space heating and domestic hot water.
- In order to limit the use of drinking water, rainwater is recovered in a 6000 litre tank and is used for the toilets and the washing machines.

The solar combisystem, manufactured by CLIPSOL, comprises a roof-integrated collector area of 15 m², two, 250 litre domestic hot water tanks, and a heating floor, which serves as storage and as a heat emission device. The hydraulic equipment (expansion vessel, valves, pumps, DHW tanks, etc.) and the controller are integrated in a technical unit, which is located in the boiler room. This component requires only 2 m² of floor area.

The heat from the collector flows directly to the heating floor. Solar energy in excess of the space heating requirement is used, according to the season, for pre-heating or heating the first DHW tank.

When solar energy is not available, the gas boiler takes over both the space heating and the preparation of the domestic hot water in the second tank. In summer, the two domestic hot water tanks are heated up by solar energy.

A single controller, with telemonitoring capabilities and optimization strategies for the use of solar and auxiliary energy, manages the complete system.

This solar combisystem has been monitored (among 40 other combisystems) in a European project (Letz and Papillon, 2000), which has proved that these systems function well. From September 1999 to August 2000, the collectors produced 5137 kWh and the auxiliary boiler provided 8303 kWh.

This house was the winner of the seventh competition *Habitat solaire, habitat d'aujourd'hui* in 2001.

Figure 9.30. The solar combisystem with the auxiliary boiler

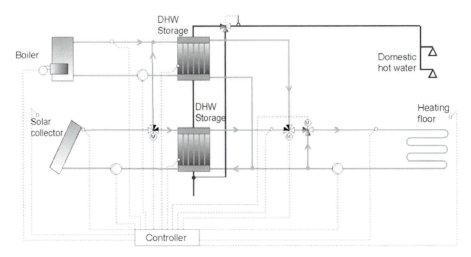

Figure 9.31. Hydraulic scheme of the system

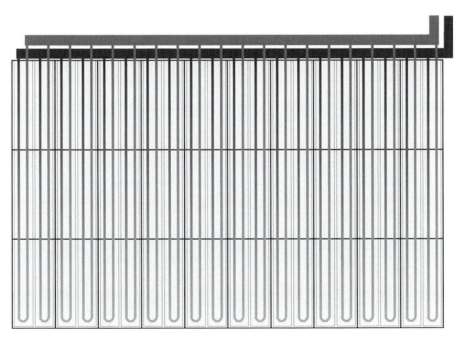

Figure 9.32. Hydraulic scheme of the collector array

9.9 SINGLE-FAMILY HOUSE, SAINT ALBAN LEYSSE, FRANCE

Figure 9.33. General view. The house belongs to the Courtois family

Location

Town or village (country)	Saint Alban Leysse (France)
Latitude	45.39°
Altitude	400 metres

Building

Living area	190 m²
Heat load (at −10°C)	11 kW
Year built	2000

Solar heating system

Generic system	System #3 (direct solar floor with integrated auxiliary)
Collector area	18 m² roof-integrated flat-plate collector
Orientation/tilt angle	0° (south)/30°
Space heating storage device	Heating floor
Domestic hot water preparation	330 litre DHW tanks
Design pressure (collector loop)	1.5 bar
Maximum system pressure	3 bar
Size of expansion vessel (collector loop)	24 litres
Fractional energy savings	35%
Overheating protection	Additional pipes in the ground
Auxiliary heater	Oil boiler
Nominal power (auxiliary heater)	24 kW

System description

This house is a typical large single–family house in France, in the suburb of a town. The structure and the insulation are typical and fulfil the thermal requirements of the French building regulations:

- 100 mm wall insulation
- 200 mm roof insulation
- prefabricated concrete block walls.

The architect paid special attention to:

- the site integration; this house is in a conservation area with an ancient monument
- the passive gains through the large windows on the south-facing side, which give very nice views of the mountains
- shading of the facade in summer
- the architectural integration of the 18 m² of collectors, which look like a small border at the top of the roof.

The house is heated by heating floors and the energy is provided both by an oil boiler and the solar collectors (System #3, an older version of system #3a).

When the sun is shining, the energy gained in the solar collectors flows directly to the heating floors without extra storage or a heat exchanger. In winter, when there is not enough solar energy available, the oil boiler takes over the heat production.

A 330 litre tank stores the domestic hot water. The lower part of this tank, (250 litres), is heated by the collectors, and the boiler provides the additional energy in the upper part in order to reach the set-point temperature.

A single controller manages all the components of the system. This controller also has a function that detects faults in the system and sends a fax to the installer. A prefabricated technical unit includes all the hydraulic equipment and the controller. This technical unit, called BLOCSOL, allows easier installation, limits the risks of mistakes by the installer and only needs 2 m² of floor area for the installation.

This solar combisystem is manufactured by CLIPSOL, in France, which is also the manufacturer of the roof-integrated solar collector.

This solar combisystem was the winner of the eighth competition *Habitat solaire, habitat d'aujourd'hui* in 2002.

Figure 9.34. The solar combisystem with the auxiliary boiler

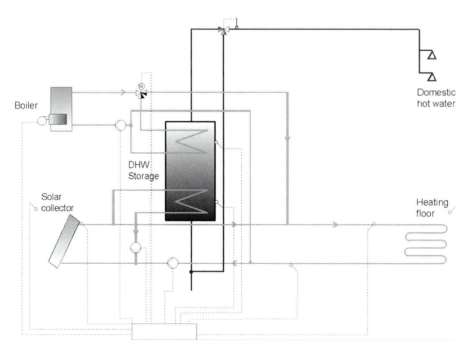

Boiler

DHW
Storage

Solar
collector

Domestic
hot water

Heating
floor

Figure 9.35. Hydraulic scheme of the system

Figure 9.36. Hydraulic scheme of the collector array

9.10 SINGLE-FAMILY HOUSE, FALUN, SWEDEN

Figure 9.37. Installation of the roof-integrated collectors on two roof surfaces on an old wooden building in Falun, Sweden

Location

Town or village (country)	Falun (Sweden)
Latitude	60.6°
Altitude	120 metres

Building

Living area	166 m²
Heat load (at –22°C)	9 kW (estimated)
Year built	1850–1950

Solar heating system

Generic system	Variant of System #11
Collector area	3.2 m² + 4.8 m² roof-integrated flat-plate collector
Orientation/tilt angle	26° west of south/27°
	54° east of south/27°
Space heating storage volume	640 litres
Domestic hot water preparation	Two internal finned-tube heat exchangers
Design pressure (collector loop)	1.5 bar
Maximum system pressure	9 bar (see text)
Size of expansion vessel (collector loop)	2 litres
Fractional energy savings	Unknown
Overheating protection	High maximum design pressure in collector loop to prevent boiling at stagnation in the collector
Auxiliary heater	Wood pellet burner integrated in store, in winter; electrical heater in summer
Nominal power (auxiliary heater)	25 kW (pellet burner) and 6 kW (electrical heater)

System description

The system has been installed in an old house of 166 m² that was built in stages from the 1850s to the 1950s. The outer walls are made of logs together with straw plastered with clay as insulation. The roof has modern cellulose fibre insulation. The house has a suspended floor with a crawl space below and no cellar. The overall insulation standard is thus significantly worse than modern standards, but this construction is common in Sweden, because adding insulation to old buildings is considered aesthetically unacceptable

The heating system consists of a heating floor in the kitchen and hall, while the rest of the building has standard radiators.

The majority of solar heating systems in Sweden are retrofits, that is, they are installed in existing buildings, and thus have to be adapted to the existing space heating system and boiler. In this case an oil boiler was replaced when the solar heating system was installed. In addition to the solar heating system, there is also a tiled stove in the living room using wood in the form of logs. Thus all energy comes from renewable sources, the small amount of electricity used in the summer being so-called 'green' electricity.

The solar combisystem comprises a collector array of 8 m^2 split into two sections that are located on two roofs at right angles to one another, as there was not sufficient space on one roof. The flow to these is controlled separately using separate controllers and pumps. The store has a volume of 640 litres and includes an integrated pellet burner, one finned-tube heat exchanger at the bottom for the collector circuit and two similar heat exchangers at the bottom and top for preparation of hot water. This is the first store-integrated pellet burner on the market. It is connected to a screw feeding the pellets automatically from a large store. The boiler room has an area of around 8 m^2 and accommodates the storage tank, pumps and all the hydraulic components required as well as working space around them, showing that the system including the boiler is very compact. The pellets store is located elsewhere and is not shown in Figure 9.38.

Figure 9.38. The boiler room off the dining room (left) and a close-up of the store (right) showing the integrated pellet burner and connections; this picture was taken during installation of the system

As with nearly all Swedish solar combisystems, the collector circuit is allowed to go up to a high pressure to avoid boiling, in this case 9 bar, before a pressure-release valve opens. This means that the collector remains filled during stagnation when the pump is stopped.

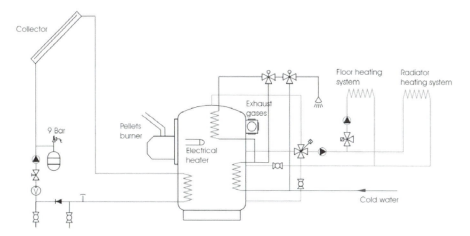

Figure 9.39. Hydraulic scheme of the system. There are in fact two separate collector arrays, each with its own pump and controller. The second was not included in the drawing to make it simpler to understand

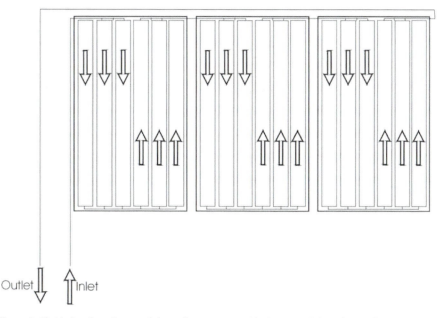

Figure 9.40. Hydraulic scheme of the collector array with three modules of 1.6 m² connected in series. A second group of two modules, connected in series, is located on the other roof. This second group is connected in parallel with the first one

9.11 SINGLE-FAMILY HOUSE, ÖREBRO, SWEDEN

Figure 9.41. 17 m² of roof-integrated collector retrofitted on a house from 1920 in Örebro, Sweden

Location

Town or village (country)	Örebro (Sweden)
Latitude	59°
Altitude	60 metres

Building

Living area	120 m² + partially heated basement
Heat load (at −14°C)	8.5 kW
Year built	1920 (renovated 1993)

Solar heating system

Generic system	Variant of System #11
Collector area	17 m² roof-integrated flat-plate collectors
Orientation/tilt angle	45° east of south/60°
Space heating storage volume	1500 litres
Domestic hot water preparation	Two internal finned-tube heat exchangers + one separate 50 litre store
Design pressure (collector loop)	1.5 bar
Maximum system pressure	9 bar
Size of expansion vessel (collector loop)	4 litres
Fractional energy savings	Unknown
Overheating protection	High maximum design pressure in collector loop to prevent boiling at stagnation in the collector
Auxiliary heaters	Two electrical heaters in the main space heating store and one in the hot water store. Wood stove (direct air heating) in the living room.
Nominal power (auxiliary heater)	6 + 6 kW main store, 2 kW DHW store

System description

The single-family home is a two-storey building plus basement. It is an old house renovated to a modern standard internally. The solar heating system, with auxiliary energy from electrical heaters in the main store, replaced an old oil boiler. Electrical heating is still common in Sweden, where half the electricity comes from hydropower and half from nuclear.

The solar combisystem comprises a collector array of 17 m^2 and two storage tanks for space heating connected in parallel, with a total volume of 1500 litres. The second store, with no heat exchanger in it, is disconnected manually from the other one during winter to minimize heat losses. An area of around 5 m^2 is required to accommodate the storage tank, the expansion vessels, pumps and all the hydraulic components required. This includes the auxiliary heater, which comprises two electrical immersion heaters in the main store. These ensure that the upper part of the store(s) is hot enough to supply the load. The heat from the collector is transferred to the bottom of the store via an internal finned-tube heat exchanger. Hot water is preheated by two other finned-tube heat exchangers in the main store and is topped up in a separate 50 litre hot water store, which is also electrically heated. This is similar to the method used in System #9b.

The collector area comprises two collectors of 8.6 m^2 each, which were lifted onto the roof on delivery by a crane on the lorry, enabling quick and efficient installation. Each collector has two halves with each half having all absorber strips connected in series. As in nearly all Swedish solar combisystems, the collector circuit is allowed to go to up to a high pressure to avoid boiling, in this case 9 bar, before a pressure-release valve opens. This means that the collector remains filled during stagnation when the pump is stopped. However, when there is overproduction of solar heat in the summer, the family uses a small pool for the children filled with hot water from the system.

Figure 9.42. The family solves the overheating problem in the summer by using hot water for pool heating for the children when the weather is nice. The picture on the left shows the two main stores connected in parallel and the smaller hot water store mounted on the wall. Below it is the expansion vessel for the stores

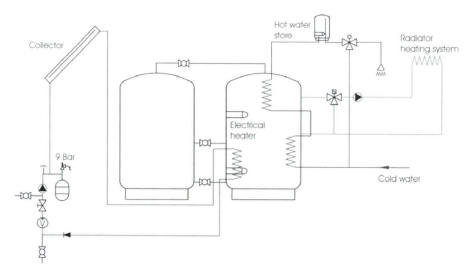

Figure 9.43. Hydraulic scheme of the system. The second space heating store is manually disconnected from the main store during winter to reduce heat losses. All stores and equipment are located in the basement

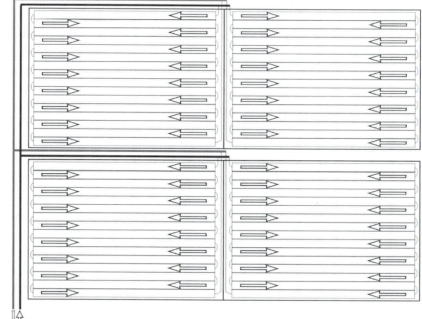

Figure 9.44. Hydraulic layout of the collectors. Two collectors are connected in parallel. In each collector there are two halves also connected in parallel. Each section (half) consists of 16 absorber strips connected in series

9.12 SINGLE-FAMILY HOUSE, DOMBRESSON, SWITZERLAND

Figure 9.45. General view. The house belongs to the Rahm-Matthey family

Location

Town or village (country)	Dombresson (Switzerland)
Latitude	47.07°
Altitude	745 metres

Building

Living area	160 m²
Heat load (at −10°C)	7 kW
Year built	1980 (renovated 1998)

Solar heating system

Generic system	System #8
Collector area	12 m² roof-integrated flat-plate collectors
Orientation/tilt angle	45° west of south/35°
Space heating storage volume	830 litres
Domestic hot water preparation	Internal heat exchanger
Design pressure (collector loop)	1.2 bar
Maximum system pressure	2.5 bar
Size of expansion vessel (collector loop)	80 litres
Fractional energy savings	25%
Overheating protection	Maximum storage temperature and appropriate expansion vessel, night-time cooling
Auxiliary heater	Condensing oil boiler
Nominal power (auxiliary heater)	21 kW

System description

The single-family house was built in 1980, but completely renovated in 1998. In the process of renovation, the insulation was improved and a solar combisystem was added. The outer walls and the roof are fitted with 20 cm of insulation material. The average specific heat loss rate is 0.3 W/m²K. The windows have a U-value of 1.4 W/m²K.

All rooms are on one floor. The heated area consists of one living room, four bedrooms, a kitchen and corridor. These rooms are heated by radiators. There is a moderately glazed attached sunspace. There are no radiators in the sunspace, but there is no wall separating the sunspace from the living room. The house is built of light materials. The effective storage mass divided by the heated surface is about 170 kg/m^2.

Measurements by means of CO_2 (used as a tracer gas), without wind and with the house unoccupied, showed that the infiltration air change rate is as low as 0.1 h^{-1}. Thus the occupants periodically need to open the windows for ventilation. The mean air change rate is estimated at 0.3 h^{-1}. The house has a small wood stove in the living room, which may be used as an alternative source for space heating.

'Arpège', manufactured by Agena SA (see Figure 9.46), is a storage tank with a volume of 830 litres and an integrated condensing boiler. In this case the boiler is oil-fired and the system includes 12 m^2 of flat-plate solar collectors. Internal heat exchangers are used for charging via the collector loop as well as for domestic hot water preparation. The controller is attached to the storage tank. A large number of parameters can be adjusted. There is optional auto-adaptation of the so-called 'heating curve', and the controller may take into account both the ambient outdoor temperature and the room temperature to determine the flow temperature in the space heating loop. The operation of the space heating loop may be made dependent on the solar input and the energy stored.

To avoid overheating of the tank, the collector loop is used actively to cool the tank when it has a high temperature, typically at night. After the nightly cooling, the tank should be ready to absorb the energy provided by the collectors during the next day. This night-time operation is often applied in Swiss solar combisystems.

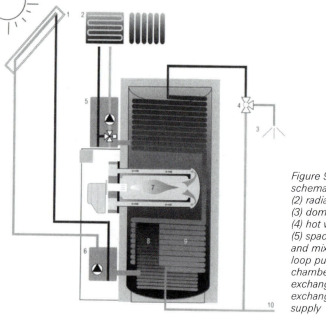

Figure 9.46. System schematics: (1) solar collectors; (2) radiators or heating floor; (3) domestic hot water (DHW); (4) hot water mixing valve; (5) space heating-loop pump and mixing valve; (6) collector-loop pump; (7) combustion chamber; (8) solar heat exchanger; (9) DHW heat exchanger; (10) cold water supply

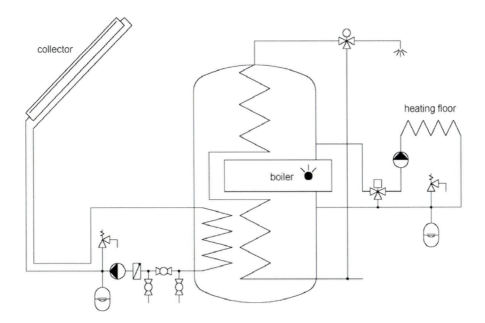

Figure 9.47. Detailed hydraulic scheme of the system

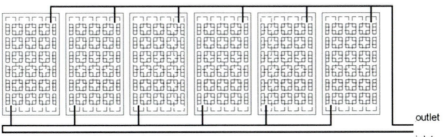

Figure 9.48. Hydraulic scheme of the collector array

9.13 SINGLE-FAMILY HOUSE, BUUS, SWITZERLAND

Figure 9.49. General view. The house belongs to the Bichsel family

Location

Town or village (country)	Buus (Switzerland)
Latitude	47.51°
Altitude	445 metres

Building

Living area	207 m²
Heat load (at −10°C)	5.5 kW
Year built	2000

Solar heating system

Generic system	Variant of System #10
Collector area	8 m² flat-plate collectors
Orientation/tilt angle	0° (south)/34°
Space heating storage volume	900 litres
Domestic hot water preparation	Internal tank, 225 litres
Design pressure (collector loop)	1.5 bar
Maximum system pressure	3 bar
Size of expansion vessel (collector loop)	50 litres
Fractional energy savings	25%
Overheating protection	Night-time circulation in collector loop, maximum storage temperature, collector hydraulics with good emptying behaviour and an appropriately sized expansion vessel
Auxiliary heater	Wood stove with heat exchanger
Nominal power (auxiliary heater)	12 kW/35 kg capacity

System description

The solar combisystem was installed when the house was built. The tank, and all controllers and pumps are located in the basement of the house (see Figure 9.52). The collector array with 8 m² of flat-plate solar collectors is integrated into the roof. The house is a wooden-frame construction filled with insulation material. It is heated by generously dimensioned radiators. The design supply temperature is low (45°C at −10°C) to optimize the heat storage management and the collector efficiency.

Figure 9.50. The wood stove in the living room. This model, made by Chiquet Energietechnik, combines the large heat storage capacity of an old-fashioned tiled stove with advanced controlled combustion for high efficiency and low emissions

The auxiliary heat source is a manually operated wood stove located in the living room. The temperature of combustion is measured and passed on to a fuzzy logic controller, which acts on a variable speed fan. The combustion occurs in two phases. To minimize emissions, the second phase uses pre-heated combustion air and takes place at about 800°C. Independent control of the primary and secondary combustion air-flow rates results in very low emissions and an efficiency above 80%. Also, it enables batch sizes of up to 35 kg. The stove is made of firebricks and heat-resistant concrete. With a mass of more than 1000 kg, the heating rate is moderate but long lasting to match the space heating demand. Even 24 hours after starting a combustion cycle, the direct heating power is still about 0.5 kW. On a typical winter day the stove only needs to be fired once. It includes a water heat exchanger, which absorbs about 60% of the total heat produced.

There is a heat management unit (see Figure 9.51), which includes three electronically controlled valves. The valve in the piping to the radiators and the

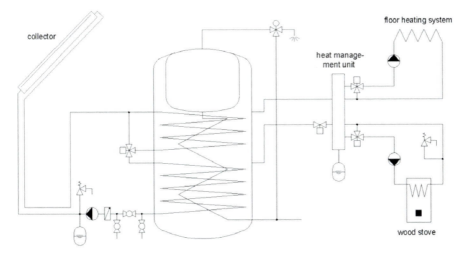

Figure 9.51. Hydraulic scheme of the system

valve in the piping to the stove are both mixing valves. In the piping to the tank there is a shut-off valve. There is one single controller for all three valves. Even after the fire has gone out, heat stored in the stove's thermal mass is still removed via the heat exchanger. This may take place at a supply temperature as low as 40°C. However, once the temperature level is insufficient for charging the tank, the heat management unit diverts residual heat from the stove directly to the radiators.

Hot water is prepared and stored in an inner tank made of stainless steel (tank-in-tank design). This method of hot-water preparation is widespread in Swiss solar combisystems.

The solar loop is controlled independently. If the temperature of the tank is high, the collector loop is operated during the night to achieve moderate temperatures and effectively avoid overheating. However, if the collector loop operation ceases as a result of an excessive storage temperature, steam will build up in the collectors and force the remaining collector fluid out of the array through the return (inlet) line (see Figure 9.53).

Figure 9.52. Components of the combisystem that are installed in the basement

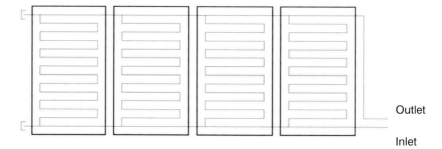

Outlet

Inlet

Figure 9.53. Hydraulic scheme of the collector array

9.14 SINGLE-FAMILY HOUSE, OSLO, NORWAY

Figure 9.54. General view

Location

Town or village (country)	Oslo (Norway)
Latitude	59°
Altitude	150 metres

Building

Living area	250 m²
Heat load (at 0°C)	4.2 kW
Year built	1999

Solar heating system

Generic system	System #9b
Collector area	30 m² roof-integrated flat-plate collector
Orientation/tilt angle	13° west of south/44°
Space heating storage volume	3000 litres
Domestic hot water preparation	200 litre immersed DHW tank for pre-heating; 200 litre external hot water tank with 3 kW electric heater
Design pressure (collector loop)	Unpressurized
Maximum system pressure	Unpressurized
Size of expansion vessel (collector loop)	–
Fractional energy savings	Approximately 30%
Overheating protection	Drainback system
Auxiliary heater	Electric heater
Nominal power (auxiliary heater)	12 kW

System description

The architect of the single-family house has given special attention to the building integration of the solar collectors. It can be seen that a large collector roof is not restricted to a flat rectangular form and can contribute significantly to the building design. The asymmetric elements in the front façade of the single-family house are repeated in the solar roof. Architectural integration can be achieved by covering a complete roof surface with collectors. In many cases this is also the most cost-effective approach.

The solar collector is a modular building element, which is available in various lengths and replaces the standard roof or façade *covers*. The collector consists of a polycarbonate twin-wall sheet as collector cover and a structured polyphenylene-based absorber (Figure 9.56).

The solar combisystem consists of 30 m² collector roof, a 3000 litre space heating storage tank, an immersed pre-heating tank for domestic hot water (DHW) and a heating floor as heat-emission system. The heated area is 250 m² and the annual heating demand is approximately 31,000 kWh. The fractional energy savings are in the range of 30%. The largest fraction of the building's total energy supply is covered by renewable energy resources. In Norway, electricity is generated by hydroelectric power plants, although a small fraction, in the range of 1–8%, has been imported in recent years.

The solar heating system is a drainback system. The heat storage tank and the solar and the heating-floor loops are non pressurized/open to atmospheric pressure

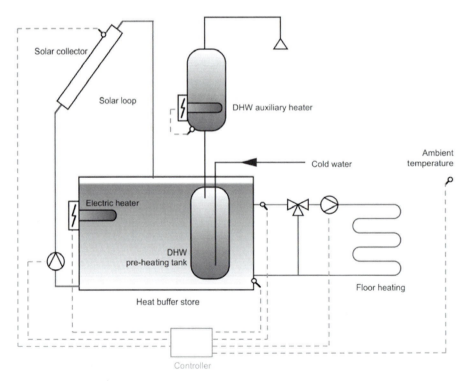

Figure 9.55. Hydraulic scheme of the system

and are connected without intermediate heat exchangers in order to keep the collector temperature as low as possible. The storage tank is located in an equipment room in the basement of the building. The square storage tank with a volume of 3000 litres includes an immersed 200 litre tank for pre-heating of DHW. The auxiliary heat is supplied by a 12 kW electric heater in the storage tank, maintaining a minimum temperature of 30°C for the heating floor system. The DHW is heated to the set-point temperature by an external 3 kW electric heater.

The single-family house includes a small flat. The comfort temperature levels of the heated floors in both living sections can be adjusted individually by the controller. A special control strategy allows separate energy metering in the flat. Hence, the tenant can be charged according to the heating demand.

Figure 9.56. Drainback collector with cover and absorber made of polymer materials

9.15 KLOSTERENGA ECOLOGICAL DWELLINGS: MULTI-FAMILY HOUSE, OSLO, NORWAY

Figure 9.57: General view

Location

Town or village (country)	Oslo (Norway)
Latitude	59.6°
Altitude	21 metres

Building

Living area	3500 m² (2901 m² heating floor area)
Heat load (at −20°C)	150 kW
Year built	1999

Solar heating system

Generic system	System #9b
Collector area	218 m² roof-integrated flat-plate collectors
Orientation/tilt angle	10.5° east of south/37°
Space heating storage volume	12,500 litres (6000 l + 6500 l)
Domestic hot water preparation	Six immersed DHW tanks, each 200 litres; 2 × 550 litre external DHW tanks with 15 kW electric auxiliary heater
Design pressure (collector loop)	Unpressurized
Maximum system pressure	Unpressurized
Size of expansion vessel (collector loop)	–
Fractional energy savings	Approximately 20%
Overheating protection	Drainback system
Auxiliary heater	Electric heaters
Nominal power (auxiliary heater)	Max. 150 kW (3 × 30 kW, 1 × 60 kW)

System description

The Klosterenga residence is a free-standing six-floor building complex with 35 flats and 2901 m² of heating floor area. The project aims at implementing and demonstrating innovative solar-based technology for new urban housing in the older parts of Oslo.

The highlights of the Klosterenga residence are the utilization of active and passive solar energy, installed energy and water-saving devices, and individual energy meters in each flat. The largest fraction of the building's total energy supply is covered by renewable energy resources. In Norway, electricity is generated by hydroelectric power plants, although a small fraction, in the range of 1–8%, has been imported in recent years.

The solar combisystem is a drainback system and consists of 80 collector modules of 218 m². The circulation of the water in the absorber is shown in Figure 9.59: In the absorber end-cup, the water is distributed over the width of the panel, moved upwards in the channel structure by pump power, and collected in the upper end-cup of the absorber. The water leaves the absorber through the central channel and a pipe-in-pipe connection in the lower end-cup. The technical room is located on the top of the building, just below the solar roof. The advantage is that it occupies a low-value space, which is not applicable for other purposes, and minimizes the piping between collector roof and heat storage. An important aspect of this system type is that the heat storage tanks, the solar and the floor-heating loops are unpressurized/open to atmospheric pressure and are connected without intermediate heat exchangers in order to keep the system temperature at a minimum level. Only the domestic hot water loop is pressurized.

For practical reasons, the total heat store volume is divided into two sections. The heat from the collector is passed to section 1 of the heat storage, a square tank with a volume of 6000 litres. This store includes six immersed tanks for domestic hot water (DHW) pre-heating with a total volume of 1200 litres. The auxiliary heat for DHW preparation is supplied by external electric heaters. Section 2 of the heat storage, a square-shaped tank of 6500 litres, provides heat to the floor system. A thermostat-controlled circulation pump transfers heat from storage section 1 to section 2. The auxiliary heat for space heating is supplied by electric heaters in section 2, with a maximum power of 150 kW. The supply is governed by the controller's outdoor-temperature-compensated dynamic thermostat function. The heat storage and the system controller are prepared for low-cost night-tariff electricity, which is expected to be introduced in the near future.

The heat-emission system in the Klosterenga dwellings is a heating floor system. As for the house in Section 9.14, the controller in each apartment allows individual adjustment of the temperature level and energy metering so that the owners of the apartments are charged according to their individual heating demands.

As well as the energy-related aspects, the demonstration project has focused on other aspects of urban ecology such as optimization of materials, indoor climate, simplified building details, water-saving and water-cleaning installations, reuse of ecologically treated water, garbage sorting and greening of outdoor areas.

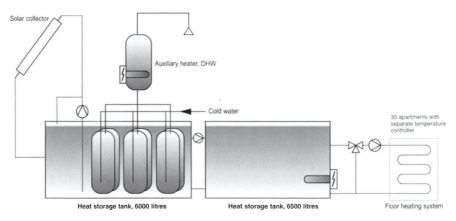

Figure 9.58. Hydraulic scheme of the system

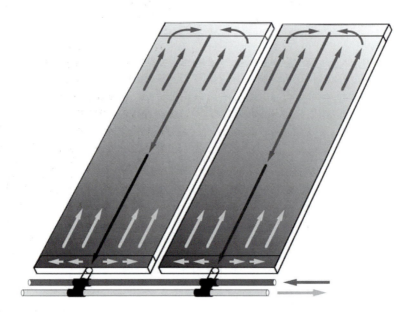

Figure 9.59. Hydraulic scheme of the collector array for the solar combisystem presented in this section and the single-family house shown in Section 9.14

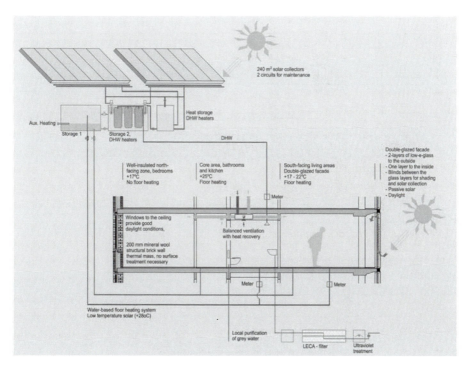

Figure 9.60. Klosterenga Ecological Dwellings: integrated technical systems

Figure 9.61. Interior with double façade

Figure 9.62. General floor plan with zoning: bedrooms to the north (top), bathrooms/kitchen in the centre, living areas to the south (bottom)

REFERENCES

Jaehnig D, Krause T and Hesse K, 2002, 'Vergleich der Jahresnutzungsgrade von solaroptimierten und herkömmlichen Heizungsanlagen', in *Proceedings of 12. Symposium Thermische Solarenergie, Staffelstein, 2002*, OTTI, Regensburg, Germany.

Letz T and Papillon P, 2000, 'An original French combisystem: Principles and in-situ monitored results', in *Proceedings of Eurosun 2000, Copenhagen, Denmark*, ISES-Europe.

10 Testing and certification of solar combisystems

Harald Drück and Huib Visser

During recent decades, considerable changes have been realized in the design and construction of solar heating systems. At the beginning, motivated builders usually designed their own 'alternative' systems to gain solar energy. In these cases, it was not uncommon to compensate for insufficient expertise with a lot of enthusiasm. Nowadays, components as well as whole systems are planned by experts and produced industrially. In Europe, the annual turnover for solar heating systems in the year 2000 amounted to approximately €1.5 billion, with an estimated annual increase of 20%. For the establishment of this market and its further development, the existence of uniform standards is quite important.

Hence, in 1994 the European Committee for Standardisation CEN/TC 312 (CEN: Comité Européen de Normalisation; TC: Technical Committee) was established, following the proposal of the European manufacturers' association ESIF (European Solar Industry Federation, nowadays abbreviated as ESTIF) and supported by the European Altener Programme. CEN/TC 312 is divided into three working groups, in which experts from industry as well as from research and test institutions set up standards for solar collectors, 'factory-made' systems and 'custom-built' systems. In these standards, basic requirements for products, as well as test methods for verification of these requirements, are specified. Furthermore, test methods for determination of the thermal performance are standardized. Target groups for the standards are manufacturers, testing institutions and interested large consumer parties.

Currently, the standards are mainly focused on solar domestic hot water systems. Solar combisystems comprise a quite new segment of the market. During revision of the standards, which is already in progress, it is also intended to include solar combisystems.

Whereas standards work in the field of proper product description, certification, which refers to the corresponding standards, contributes to marketing and sales. At present, a certificate for solar thermal products, called Solar Keymark, is being established, again with support from the EU Altener Programme. A product with Solar Keymark will fulfil all requirements in the relevant European standard, ensuring quality of products and user confidence.

10.1 EUROPEAN STANDARDS

The three current standards for solar heating systems and components consist of seven parts (see Table 10.1) and consider most types of collectors, heat stores and solar heating systems commonly available on the European market. In addition, there is a trilingual standard (English, German and French) standard that explains terminology used in solar engineering.

Table 10.1. Titles of the CEN/TC 312 standards

Working Group	Number	Title: *Thermal solar systems and components – ...*
1	EN 12975–1	*Collectors – Part 1: General requirements*
	EN 12975–2	*Collectors – Part 2: Test methods*
2	EN 12976–1	*Factory-made systems – Part 1: General requirements*
	EN 12976–2	*Factory-made systems – Part 2: Test methods*
3	ENV 12977–1	*Custom-built systems – Part 1: General requirements*
	ENV 12977–2	*Custom-built systems – Part 2: Test methods*
	ENV 12977–3	*Custom-built systems – Part 3: Performance characterisation of stores for solar heating systems*
–	EN ISO 9488	*Solar energy – Vocabulary*

The European standards are available from the national standardization bodies

10.1.1 Classification of solar heating systems

As can be seen from the titles of the standards, solar heating systems have been divided into two groups, **factory-made** and **custom-built** systems. This division was necessary in order to be able to include the whole spectrum of solar heating systems available on the European market, which ranges from small compact systems (thermosiphon and integral collector–storage systems) to very large systems individually designed by engineers. Classification of a system as factory-made or custom-built is a choice of the final supplier in accordance with the following definitions:

- **Factory-made solar heating systems** are batch products with one trade name, sold as complete and ready-to-install kits, with fixed configuration. Systems in this class are considered as a single product and assessed as a whole. For the determination of its thermal performance, such a system is tested as one complete unit. If a factory-made solar heating system is modified by changing its configuration or by changing one or more of its components, the modified system is considered as a new system for which a new test report is necessary.
- **Custom-built solar heating systems** are either uniquely built or assembled by choosing from an assortment of components. Systems in this category are regarded as a set of components. The components are separately tested and test results are integrated into an assessment of the whole system. Custom-built solar heating systems are subdivided into two categories:
  - **Large custom-built systems** are uniquely designed for a specific situation. In general, HVAC engineers, manufacturers or other experts design them (HVAC: Heating, Ventilation, Air Conditioning).
  - **Small custom-built systems** offered by a company are described in a so-called **assortment file**, in which all components and possible system configurations marketed by the company are specified. Each possible combination of a system configuration with components from the assortment is considered as *one* custom-built system.

The different types of solar heating systems have been summarized in Table 10.2. As a consequence of this way of classification, forced circulation systems can be considered either as factory-made or as custom-built, depending on the market approach chosen by the final supplier. Hence, it is essential that performance of these systems is determined for the same set of reference conditions, i.e. as specified in Annex B of EN 12976–2 and Annex A of ENV 12977–2.

Note that the division in Table 10.2 does not yet account for **factory-made** solar combisystems, i.e. for hot water preparation *and* space heating.

Table 10.2. Division for factory-made and custom-built solar heating systems

Factory-made solar heating systems EN 12976–1, -2	Custom-built solar heating systems ENV 12977–1, -2, -3
Integral collector–storage systems for domestic hot water preparation	Forced-circulation systems for hot water preparation and/or space heating, assembled using components and configurations described in an assortment file (mostly small systems)
Thermosiphon systems for domestic hot water preparation Forced-circulation systems as batch product with fixed configuration for domestic hot water preparation	Uniquely designed and assembled systems for hot water preparation and/or space heating (mostly large systems)

10.1.2 Current status of the European standards

Results of the work carried out by the Working Groups are prENs or prENVs (pr: preliminary; V: pre-standard). These proposed standards are put to a formal vote in the EU/EFTA countries, i.e. for approval of the proposal, to become a regular standard called EN or a pre-standard called ENV. Within three months, these countries can accept or reject the documents. When approved, EN standards have to be published within six months by each CEN member country. At the same time, any national standard or part of a standard in conflict with the new EN has to be withdrawn and not used. In this way, uniform standards are being progressively introduced in all CEN member countries. CEN documents are available from each national standardization institute and are not published centrally by CEN in Brussels.

In principle, an EN standard has unlimited validity. However, it is necessary to check a standard at regular time intervals, usually every five years, in order to update or adapt it to new developments. An ENV is a pre-standard and is valid for three years. After that, it can be replaced by a regular standard, or its validity as a pre-standard can be prolonged. Generally, regulations remain pre-standards as long as the included test procedures are still in the testing phase, or if it is necessary to gain more experience with these procedures.

At present (at the end of 2002), the formal voting on the standard series EN 12975, EN 12976 and ENV 12977 has been completely finished, with positive results. The standards have been published as EN or ENV respectively. In order to update and revise the standards, CEN/TC 312 and also its three Working Groups are still active.

10.2 TESTING OF SOLAR THERMAL COMPONENTS

10.2.1 Collectors

In the European standards, requirements for solar collectors regarding safety, reliability and durability have been specified in EN 12975–1. The scope of this standard includes both glazed and unglazed collectors operating with a fluid as the heat transfer medium. Test procedures described in EN 12975–2 for reliability and durability testing, as well as for determination of the thermal performance, are mainly based on the international collector test standard ISO 9806. The aim of performance testing for solar collectors is the determination of characteristic parameters describing their thermal behaviour. Knowledge of these parameters is essential for prediction of the annual energy output of the collector as well as of the whole system with the collector as a component.

Up to now, determination of the thermal performance of collectors according to ISO 9806–1, ISO 9806–3 or DIN V 4757–4 has been carried out under steady-state conditions. The required measuring data have been gathered either in outdoor tests or by using a solar simulator; see Figure 10.1.

Figure 10.1. Solar simulator at ITW, University of Stuttgart

As well as the well known test method under steady-state conditions, EN 12975–2 permits a quasi-dynamic test method for characterization of the thermal performance of solar collectors. This means that EN 12975–2 now contains two test methods, the 'classical' steady-state method and the 'new' quasi-dynamic test method. Several research projects indicate that the two test methods provide comparable results. The advantage of the quasi-dynamic method is that it allows for a much wider range of test conditions. This leads to easier and cheaper tests, especially for places with varying climate conditions such as in northern and central

Europe. Furthermore, the quasi-dynamic test method offers a much more complete characterization of the collector and a much wider range of collectors can be tested (Fischer, 2001).

10.2.2 Testing of hot water stores

Requirements on solar domestic hot water stores regarding safety, corrosion protection and drinking water quality are standardized among others in prEN 12897. In addition to these aspects, it is necessary, especially with regard to stores for solar heating systems, to have knowledge about their thermal behaviour. This information is quite important in order to be able:

- to determine the thermal performance of solar heating systems if component-based test procedures are used
- to compare and assess stores with regard to their intended application, i.e. selection of a suitable store.

With regard to the main aspect of the standard, i.e. determination of parameters for description of the thermal performance of stores, two completely different test and evaluation procedures have been described in ENV 12977–3. They can be called the 'classical' and the 'advanced' procedures; see Figure 10.2.

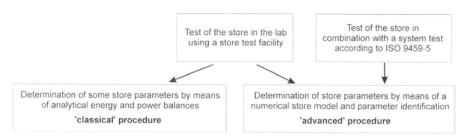

Figure 10.2. Scheme of the test and evaluation methods of ENV 12977–3

With the classical test and evaluation procedure, the most elementary store parameters can be determined. The method for determination of thermal capacity and heat loss rate is based on the work carried out by the European Solar Storage Testing Group (SSTG) at the end of the 1980s (Visser and van Dijk, 1991). The method for determination of heat transfer rate of immersed heat exchangers was developed in Switzerland (Suter and Brack, 1987).

The advanced procedure allows a more detailed characterization of the thermal behaviour of the store by using a numerical store model. Parameters of this model are determined through parameter identification using measured data from several test sequences.

The two procedures differ both in the test sequences to be performed and in the evaluation method. Both procedures use the so-called black box approach, where test sequences are applied to the store and all measurements are made outside the physical store. Data required for the classical procedure are obtained from measurements using a store test facility. Data for evaluation with the advanced procedure can either be from tests carried out in a store test facility or gained during a system test according to ISO 9459–5 (dynamic system test, DST) with additional sensors in the collector loop.

With regard to evaluation, the main advantage of the classical method is the transparent evaluation procedure, based on analytical energy and power balances. This method reveals the thermal capacity and heat loss rate of the store as well as the heat transfer rate of immersed heat exchangers. The classical method enables the determination of store parameters without any numerical model. However, since dynamic behaviour and thermal stratification effects cannot be assessed with this method, it is not possible to characterize the store in great detail.

As mentioned above, the main purpose of ENV 12977–3 is determination of parameters for calculation of the annual thermal performance by means of numerical simulations. Therefore, numerical models for detailed description of the dynamic behaviour of the components are required. With the advanced procedure, the thermal behaviour of the store can be characterized in detail by using a numerical model such as the MULTIPORT store model for TRNSYS (Drück, 2000). Parameters of this model are determined by means of parameter identification using measuring data from several test sequences. This advanced test procedure was mainly developed by ITW within several research projects, such as Task 14 of the IEA Solar Heating and Cooling Programme (Drück and Hahne, 1997). The advanced procedure is more flexible and even cheaper than the classical one and delivers a more detailed description of the store. It is thus the most suitable and promising method.

10.3 TESTING OF SOLAR HEATING SYSTEMS

In European standards EN 12976–1 and ENV 12977–1, many requirements are defined regarding safety, reliability and durability of solar heating systems. Their objective is to ensure that systems operate reliably, even under extreme conditions such as heavy snow or wind loads or extended stagnation periods during the summer. In addition, the documentation of the system, as well as the installation and operation manuals, has to fulfil certain requirements in order to ensure correct installation and operation by the installer and owner respectively.

The thermal performance of **factory-made solar domestic hot water systems** (for classification, see Section 10.1.1) is determined according to EN 12976–2 either by applying the CSTG method (CSTG: Collector and System Testing Group; see ISO 9459–2) or by using the DST method. For both test procedures, the *whole* solar heating system is installed at a test facility and operated under real climate conditions. Domestic hot water draw-off is varied so that at the end of the test, measuring data fulfil well defined test conditions. The aim of both test procedures is to determine the annual system performance for specified reference conditions based on short-term tests.

For **custom-built solar domestic hot water systems and combisystems**, the CTSS method (Component Testing – System Simulation) is used to determine the annual system performance. The most important components are tested separately in this method, and test results are used in a numerical model for calculation of the annual thermal performance of the whole system.

Factory-made solar combisystems are lacking in the classification in Section 10.1.1. A new approach has been developed for these systems including whole-system testing under well defined yearly average operating conditions. The approach includes two methods: the DC and the CCT methods (DC: Direct Characterization; CCT: Concise Cycle Test). At the time of publication, neither of these methods has the status of a preliminary standard.

10.3.1 The CSTG test method

The CSTG test method is based on a simple 'input/output' correlation and can only be applied for **solar domestic hot water systems without auxiliary heating devices in the store**. This method is standardized in ISO 9459–2. Since solar heating systems of this type are rare in northern and central Europe, the CSTG test procedure is predominantly applied in test laboratories in South Europe.

10.3.2 The DST method

The DST method can be applied for **solar domestic hot water systems with and without auxiliary heating**. It is therefore the most relevant test method for 'typical' factory-made solar heating systems used in northern and central Europe. The aim of the DST test is to determine a set of parameters, giving a detailed description of the thermal system behaviour in combination with a numerical system model. These parameters are determined by means of parameter identification using measurements recorded during operation of the system at a test facility. Annual performance of the system can be predicted by using the numerical system model and the parameters determined from the system test.

The DST test method is standardized in ISO/DIS 9459–5 (a formal ISO/CEN joint procedure, aiming at publishing the DST test method as an official standard, is underway) and has been developed mainly within the German research project VELS I (VELS: Verfahren zur Ermittlung der Leistungsfähigkeit von Solaranlagen). Its comprehensive validation was principally carried out within the work of the International Energy Agency (Solar Heating and Cooling Programmes Task 14) and in a project supported by the EU (Bridging the Gap). It was shown that the DST method is able to give reproducible results for a wide range of various types of solar domestic hot water systems and different climate conditions and locations. Furthermore, it was shown that results determined with the CSTG and DST methods for solar domestic hot water systems without an integrated auxiliary heater are comparable.

10.3.3 The CTSS method

For determination of the thermal performance of small custom-built systems according to ENV 12977–2, the CTSS (Component Testing – System Simulation) method has to be used. The CTSS method is based on separate tests of the most important components (see Figure 10.3). The test for the collector is carried out according to EN 12975–2. The store is tested according to ENV 12977–3. The controller is checked according to ENV 12977–2, Annex B. Based on the parameters determined for the different components, the thermal performance of the complete system is predicted by using a component-based system simulation program such as TRNSYS.

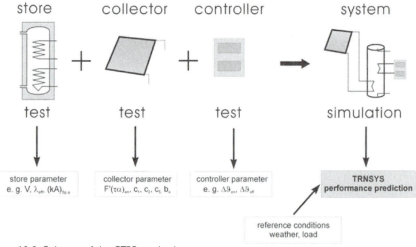

Figure 10.3. Scheme of the CTSS method

The application range of the CTSS method is very flexible because of its component-oriented approach. Hence, it is possible to apply the CTSS method on nearly every system configuration, including solar combisystems.

10.3.4 The DC and the CCT methods

The DC (Direct Characterization) test method offers a second way of characterizing solar combisystems, especially **factory-made** systems. DC tests are carried out at an indoor test facility. Solar input is generated by means of a solar simulator and the actual collector or by a heater simulating the solar collector. In the latter case, collector parameters determined according to EN 12975–2 should be available. The space heating load is emulated following specified climate conditions and is based on a specific low-temperature heat distribution system. The core phase of the test method consists of six days, with two days simulating winter, two days summer and two days spring/autumn. Both the climate and the domestic hot water draw-offs are arranged so that evaluation of the measuring data to derive annual system performance is relatively simple. No numerical system model is needed for this.

The major performance indicator of the solar combisystem given by the DC test is the final energy used by the auxiliary heater. This implies that the solar combisystem is always tested in combination with the auxiliary heater. This feature is considered to be favourable, because many problems in system operation appear to be due to improper control strategy for the coupling of the solar and auxiliary parts of the system. Hence, the test method forces manufacturers to think about the integral system design. In special cases, a well defined laboratory auxiliary heater can be used. However, even in these cases, the performance indicator is presented for only the specific combination of the solar combisystem and its auxiliary heater.

The applicability range of the DC test method includes solar combisystems with a collector area smaller than 15–20 m^2 and a heat store volume of 1500–2000 litres. In these cases, the prediction error in the annual system performance derived by the method remains smaller than 5%. Determination of the annual final energy used is only possible for annual conditions that correspond more or less to the test conditions. This is one of the reasons why the system performance has to be derived for the combination of one out of three climate zones, one out of three space heating loads and one domestic hot water demand, following the references in Chapters 2 and 3. This approach reduces the threshold for export, as there is no need for translation into specific national conditions with respect to climate and load.

The DC test originated in Sweden (Bales, 2002), where test sequences based on the average climate throughout the year were processed by a numerical model to reveal the annual system performance. This so-called AC/DC method was simplified into the DC test procedure.

The concept of the CCT (Concise Cycle Test) method is similar to that of the DC test method in that both are indoor test methods. With a core phase of 12 days, the CCT method uses a longer test cycle. The building is simulated on-line and the system with its controller(s) decides how heat is supplied to the building by flow temperature and flow rate, whereas the DC method predefines the space heating load according to a load file. A significant advantage of the floating load of the CCT is that all of the system functions may be assessed. The disadvantage is that there is no uniform or predictable energy use for space heating, which complicates characterization of the system's energy-related performance. Unlike the DC method, the CCT method can in principle be used to characterize solar combisystems where the system intentionally uses the building's thermal mass to optimize its heat storage strategy, e.g. when there is a heavy heating floor. Extreme examples of systems using the floor for heat storage and distribution are the French direct solar floor systems (see Sections 4.4.3 and 4.4.5). A test facility is shown in Figure 10.4.

At the time of publication, both test procedures still need validation and more practical experience. CEN/TC 312 is aware of the developments in this respect.

More information on the DC and the CCT methods can be found in Technical Reports of Task 26 of the IEA Solar Heating and Cooling Programme (Visser, 2002; Naron and Visser, 2002; Vogelsanger 2002).

Figure 10.4. Installation space of the solar combisystem test facility at SPF in Rapperswil, Switzerland

10.4 CERTIFICATION OF SOLAR HEATING SYSTEMS

The standards for collectors and factory-made systems EN 12975–1&2 and EN 12976–1&2, as described in Sections 10.2.1 and 10.3 respectively, will serve as the basis for a European certificate for solar thermal products. At the time of publication, the European Solar Industry Federation ESTIF and 13 test institutions representing 11 European countries are working together to establish the so-called Solar Keymark (see Figure 10.5). The Solar Keymark certifies conformity of solar collectors and factory-made solar domestic hot water systems with the European standards (Nielsen, 2001).

Figure 10.5. The Solar Keymark logo

The Solar Keymark is one of several Keymarks that make up the official CEN/CENELEC European Certification Mark System for demonstrating compliance of products with European standards (CEN/CENELEC, 2001). This general Keymark is a third-party certification mark demonstrating to users and consumers reliable quality and reliable performance information. The accompanying Mark Scheme includes not only the link to the standards but also a link to the requirements on factory production control according to ISO 9000, including periodic surveillance. Bodies engaged in certification, testing and inspection must fulfil the requirements of the relevant EN 45000/17000 series standard in order for them to be accredited for the scope of their activity.

Keymarks can only be issued in conjunction with national marks. These national marks may, however, contain limited additional requirements, e.g. building regulations, specific safety aspects and further processing of performance figures.

The objective of the Solar Keymark is to open up the European market and establish a common European quality mark. The Solar Keymark will be voluntary, but it is expected that it will be widely used because the European standards are implemented as national standards in all CEN member countries. More up-to-date information can be found at the Solar Keymark website: http://www.solarkeymark.org.

REFERENCES

Bales C, 2002, *Combitest – Initial Development of the AC/DC Test Method*, Technical report, IEA Solar Heating & Cooling Programme Task 26, http://www.iea-shc.org/task26

CEN/CENELEC, 2001, *Internal Regulations. Part 4: Certification*, second draft revision, July 2001, Brussels, Belgium, http://www.cenelec.org/

DIN V 4757–4: 1995, 1995, *Solarthermische Anlagen – Sonnenkollektoren – Teil 4: Bestimmung von Wirkungsgrad, Wärmekapazität und Druckabfall* (no longer valid)

Drück H, 2000, *MULTIPORT store model for TRNSYS, Type 140, Version 1.99*, Institut für Thermodynamik und Wärmetechnik (ITW), Universität Stuttgart, Stuttgart, Germany.

Drück H and Hahne E, 1997, *Thermal Testing of Stores for Solar Domestic Hot Water Systems*, Final report from IEA SH&C Programme, Task 14, Dynamic Component and System Testing Group, IEA Report no. T.14.DCST.1A. 1997 (ed. H. Visser and T. Pauschinger).

EN 45000/17000: Series of standards on conformity assessment and accreditation of laboratories

Fischer S, Perers B, Bergquist P, Hellström B, 2001, 'Collector test method under quasi-dynamic conditions according to the European Standard EN 12975–2', in, *Proceedings of ISES 2001 Solar World Congress, Adelaide, Australia*, http://www.ises.org

ISO 9806–1: 1994, 1994, *Test methods for solar collectors – Part 1: Thermal performance of glazed liquid heating collectors including pressure drop*

ISO 9806–3: 1995, 1995, *Test methods for solar collectors – Part 3: Thermal performance of unglazed liquid heating collectors (sensible heat transfer only) including pressure drop*

ISO 9459–2: 1995, 1995, *Solar heating – Domestic water heating systems – Outdoor test methods for system performance characterization and yearly performance prediction of solar-only systems*

ISO/DIS 9459–5: 1996, 1996, *Solar heating – Domestic water heating systems – Part 5: System performance characterization by means of whole-system tests and computer simulation*

ISO 9000, Series of standards on quality management and quality assurance

Naron D J and Visser H, 2002, *Development of the Direct Characterisation test procedure for Solar Combisystems*. Technical report, IEA Solar Heating & Cooling Programme Task 26, http://www.iea-shc.org/task26

Nielsen J E, 2001, 'CEN certification of solar thermal products: The Solar Keymark', in, *Proceedings of ISES 2001 Solar World Congress, Adelaide, Australia*, http://www.ises.org

Suter J-M and Brack M, 1987, *Development of a test procedure for immersed heat exchangers*, Eidgenössisches Institut für Reaktorforschung, CH – 5303 Würenlingen.

Visser H and Naron D J, 2002, *Direct Characterisation Test Procedure for Solar Combisystems*, fifth draft, December 2002. Technical report, IEA Solar Heating & Cooling Programme Task 26, http://www.iea-shc.org/task26

Visser H and van Dijk H A L, 1991, *Test Procedures for Short Term Thermal Stores*, Kluwer Academic Publishers, Dordrecht, Boston and London.

Vogelsanger P, 2002, *The Concise Cycle Test – An Indoor Test Method using a 12-day Test Cycle*. Technical report, IEA Solar Heating & Cooling Programme Task 26, http://www.iea-shc.org/task26

The European standards are available from the national standardization bodies.

Reference library

Compiled by Peter Kovács

Within IEA SH&C Task 26 a comparatively large number of experts in this field have been working together. The amount of accumulated knowledge is extensive and the essence of it has been made available in this handbook. Nevertheless, there are huge amounts of background material available to those interested, some of it surely adding information of interest concerning the outcome of Task 26. The researchers of Task 26 have accumulated a list of references that may be of interest when studying solar combisystems, and these are given below.

A1.1 CONTENTS OF THE REFERENCE LIBRARY SORTED BY AUTHOR

Author/editor name	Reference title	Year of publication	Available from
	Solare Raumheizungsanlagen	1995	AEE INTEC, Arbeitsgemeinschaft Erneuerbare Energie, Institute for Sustainable Technologies, Feldgasse 19, 8200 Gleisdorf, Austria. Fax: +43 3112 5886 – 18, e-mail: office@aee.at
	Tagung Solare Raumheizung 1996	1996	AEE INTEC
	Tagung Solare Raumheizung 1997	1997	AEE INTEC
	Tagung Solare Raumheizung 1998	1998	AEE INTEC
	Tagung Solare Raumheizung 1999	1999	AEE INTEC
	Solare Raumheizungsanlagen	2000	AEE INTEC
	Tagung Solare Raumheizung 2000	2000	AEE INTEC
	Tagung Solare Raumheizung 2001	2001	AEE INTEC
Andersen N	*Solvarmeanlæg til rumopvarmning og varmt brugsvand. Demonstrationsanlægget i Ejby*	1988	Department of Civil Engineering, Technical University of Denmark, DTU, DK-2800 Kgs. Lyngby Denmark. Tel: +45 45 25 17 00 http://www.byg.dtu.dk/
Bales C	*Evaluation of the performance of solar combistores – comparison of three test methods*	2000	http://www.eurosun2000.dk

Author/editor name	Reference title	Year of publication	Available from
Bales C	*Thermal Store Testing: Evaluation of Test Methods*	2002	Chalmers University of Technology, Dept Bldg Serv Engn, S-41296 Gothenburg, Sweden. Fax: +46 31 772 11 52, e-mail: hvac@vsect.chalmers.se
Bergmeijer P and de Geus A	*Evaluation of the Dutch second generation solar heating systems*	1988	–
Bony J, Renoult O, Pittet T, Dind Ph, Gherbi A, Prud'homme T and Gillet D	*Optimisation of combisystems*	2001	International Conference on Solar Energy in Buildings. Ecole Polytechnique Fédérale de Lausanne, Switzerland
Boye-Hansen L and Furbo S	*Solvarmeanlæg med tømning*	1995	BYG, Danish Technical University, 2800 Lyngby. http://www.byg.dtu.dk/ Report No. DTU-LV-MEDD-275
Dahm J *et al.*	*Evaluation of storage configurations with internal heat exchangers*	1998	Chalmers University, Technol Dept Bldg Serv Engn, S-41296, Gothenburg, Sweden. Fax: +46 31 772 11 52, e-mail: hvac@vsect.chalmers.se
Drück H and Hahne E	*Thermal testing of stores for solar domestic hot water systems*	1996	http://wire0.ises.org/wire/ doclibs/EuroSun96.nsf/id/ 929AD294316074A9C12565 E600373186/$File/paper.pdf
Drück, H and Hahne E	*Test and comparison of hot water stores for solar combisystems*	1998	http://kske.fgg.uni-lj.si/ eurosun98/abstracts/III_3.html
Duffie J A and Beckman W A	*Solar Engineering of Thermal Processes,* 2nd edn	1991	John Wiley and Sons, New York
Eder M *et al.*	*Heizen mit der Sonne – Handbuch zur Planung und Ausführung von solaren Heizungssystemen für Einfamilienhäuser*	1997	AEE Arbeitsgemeinschaft Erneuerbare Energie, Kärnten/Salzburg, H. v. Türlin Straße 5, Austria – 9500 Villach. Fax: +43 4242 23 2 24 1, e-mail: aee@aon.at
Ellehauge K	*Solvarmeanlaeg til kombineret brugsvands- og rumopvarmning. Udvikling af konkurrencedygtige anlaeg. Beregninger samt forsoegsanlaeg.*	1991	BYG, Danish Technical University, 2800 Lyngby. http://www.byg.dtu.dk/ Report No. DTH-LV-MEDD-223. 80 pp.
Ellehauge K	*Combined solar heating systems for domestic hot water and space heating*	1992	North Sun 1992 SINTEF, Trondheim
Ellehauge K	*Målinger på solvarmeanlæg til sommerhus i Gilleleje. Et solvarmeanlæg til kombineret opvarmning af brugsvand, gulvvarme, svømmebassin m.m*	1993	BYG, Danish Technical University, 2800 Lyngby. http://www.byg.dtu.dk/ Report No. LFV- 93–36

Author/editor name	Reference title	Year of publication	Available from
Ellehauge K	*Målinger på solvarmeanlæg til kombineret brugsvand- og rumopvarmning. 5 markedsførte solvarmeanlæg installeret hos anlægsejerne.*	1993	BYG, Danish Technical University, 2800 Lyngby. http://www.byg.dtu.dk/ Report No. LFV no. 255
Ellehauge K	*Monitoring of solar heating systems marketed in Denmark*	1993	ISES Solar World Congress 93, Budapest
Ellehauge K	*New developments on active solar heating systems, for example by using drain back in the collector loop*	1994	Northsun 94, Glasgow (UK). James & James (Science Publishers), London
Ellehauge K, Kildemoes T and Jacobsen H J	*Aktive solvarmeanlæg med større dækning af husets samlede varmebehov – udredning og skitseprojekter*	1999	Solar Energy Centre Denmark, Danish Technological Institute. http://www.solenergi.dk/center
Ellehauge K and Shah L J	*Solar combisystems in Denmark – the most common system designs*	2000	Eurosun Conference 2000 Copenhagen Denmark. http://www.eurosun2000.dk
Ellehauge K and Sæbye A	*Kombinerede solvarme og biobrændsels-anl æg – Analyser og forslag til design,*	2000	Solar Energy Centre Denmark, Danish Technological Institute. http://www.solenergi.dk/ center/
Ellehauge K, Overgaard L L and Sæbye A	*Erfaringer fra målinger på kombinerede solvarme- og biobrændselsanlæg,*	2000	Solar Energy Centre Denmark, Danish Technological Institute. http://www.solenergi.dk/ center/
Fink C, Purkarthofer P and Weiss W	*Systemkonzepte für solare Kombianlagen von Mehrfamilienwohnbauten und Ergebnisse aus Langzeitmessungen*	2001	AEE INTEC
Hausner R and Fink C	*Stagnation Behaviour of Thermal Solar Systems*	2000	http://www.eurosun2000.dk
Henden L, Rekstad J and Meir M	*Thermal performance of combined solar systems with different collector efficiencies*	2002	*Solar Energy* 72(4), 299–305, 2002
Jaboyedoff P	*Elaboration et validation dæun programme de simulation dynamique dæune installation solaire à production combinée dæeau chaude sanitaire et chauffage*	1989	ENET, Technology Transfer in the field of Energy, Egnacherstrasse 69, CH-9320 Arbon. e-mail: enet@temas.ch, http:// www. energieforschung.ch
Jaboyedoff P	*Installations solaires compactes de production combinée dæeau chaude sanitaire et chauffage – Etude paramétrique, règles pratiques de dimensionnement*	1989	ENET, Technology Transfer in the field of Energy, Egnacherstrasse 69, CH-9320 Arbon. e-mail: enet@temas.ch, http:// www.energieforschung.ch

Author/editor name	Reference title	Year of publication	Available from
Jaboyedoff P	*Installations solaires de production combinée dæeau chaude sanitaire et hauffage à injection directe – Modélisation, validation*	1990	ENET, Technology Transfer in the field of Energy, Egnacherstrasse 69, CH-9320 Arbon. e-mail: enet@temas.ch, http:// www.energieforschung.ch
Jaboyedoff P	*Installations solaires de production combinée dæeau chaude sanitaire et chauffage à injection directe – Analyse paramétrique*	1990	ENET, Technology Transfer in the field of Energy, Egnacherstrasse 69, CH-9320 Arbon. e-mail: enet@temas.ch, http:// www.energieforschung.ch
Jaboyedoff P	*Installations solaires combinées de roduction dæeau chaude sanitaire et de chauffage – Planification, synthèse*	1990	ENET, Technology Transfer in the field of Energy, Egnacherstrasse 69, CH-9320 Arbon. e-mail: enet@temas.ch, http:// www.energieforschung.ch
Jaboyedoff P	*Kombinierte Solaranlagen zur Wassererwärmung und Raumheizung – Synthese, Planungsempfehlungen*	1990	ENET, Technology Transfer in the field of Energy, Egnacherstrasse 69, CH-9320 Arbon. e-mail: enet@temas.ch, http:// www.energieforschung.ch
Johannesson K and Persson J	*Tillförlitlighetsanalys på solvärmda kombisystem*	2001	http://www.sp.se/eng/ publikationer.htm
Jordan U	*Untersuchung eines Solarspeichers zur kombinierten Trinkwassererwärmung und Heizungsunterstützung*	2002	Fortschritt-Berichte VDI, Reihe 19, Nr. 138. Dissertation. e-mail: solar@uni-kassel.de
Jordan U and Vajen K	*Influence of the DHW profile on the fractional energy savings – a case study of a solar combisystem*	2002	*Solar Energy* 73(1), 33–42, 2002. http://www.uni-kassel.de/~solar
Jordan U and Vajen K	*Einfluss verschiedener Beladeeinrichtungen auf den Ertrag eines Kombisystems*	2002	*Proceedings Gleisdorf Solar 2002, 6. Internationales Symposium für Sonnenenergienutzung. Austria.* http://www.uni-kassel.de/~solar
Kovács P and Sandberg M	*Results from testing of small heat stores for domestic hot water and space heating*	1998	http://kske.fgg.uni-lj.si/ eurosun98/abstracts/IV_2.html
Kovács P and Pettersson U	*Solvärmda kombisystem. En jämförelse mellan vakuumrör och plan solfångare genom mätning och simulering*	2002	http://www.sp.se/energy/ files/Rapporter/SP%20rapp % 202002–20.pdf
Letz T	*Evaluation et suivi des opérations liées au programme européen 1994 de promotion du plancher solaire direct à appoint intégré*	1999	Ademe (Agency for Environment and Energy Management), 500 Route des Lucioles, F-06560 Sophia-Antipolis Cedex

Author/editor name	Reference title	Year of publication	Available from
Letz T	*Projet Thermie 75 maisons PSD : bilan du programme*	1999	*CVC*, journal of AICVF, 66 rue de Rome, F-75008 Paris. http://www.aicvf.org
Lorenz K, Bales C and Broman L	*Performance comparision of combitanks using a six-day-test*	1997	http://www.northsun.org/
Lorenz K, Bales C and Börjesson K	*Provning av ackumulatorsystem för solvärmeanläggningar*	1996	http://www.du.se/ekos/serc/serc.html
Lorenz K, Bales C and Persson T	*Evaluation of solar thermal combisystems for the Swedish climate*	2000	http://www.eurosun2000.dk
Lorenz K, Persson T and Bales C	*Comparison of external DHW load side heat exchange units for the production of domestic hot water*	1997	http://www.northsun.org/
Lorenz K *et al.*	*Variation of system performance with design and climate for combisystems in Sweden*	1998	http://kske.fgg.uni-lj.si/eurosun98/abstracts/IV_2.html
Mahler B, Fisch M N and Weiss W	*Large scale solar heating systems for housing developments*	2000	http://www.eurosun2000.dk
Meir M, Rekstad J, Peter M, Henden L and Sandnes B	*Determination of the performance of solar systems with the calorimetric method*	2002	*Solar Energy* 73(3), 195–207, 2002
Mikkelsen L, Jörgensen L	*Solvarmeanlæg til rumopvarmning. En udredning baseret på to års målinger på anlæg i Greve og Gentofte.*	1981	Department of Civil Engineering, Technical University of Denmark, DTU, DK-2800 Kgs. Lyngby Denmark. Tel: +45 45 25 17 00, http://www.byg.dtu.dk/
Neumann C	*Small combined solar systems. Influence of different heating systems and building types on the thermal performance*	1996	Chalmers University, Dept of Civil Engineering, S-412 96, Göteborg, Sweden Tel: +46 31 772 11 45, Fax: +46 31 772 11 52, e-mail: hvac@vsect.chalmers.se
Oberndorfer G, Beckman W and Klein S	*Sensitivity of annual solar fraction of solar space heating and water heating systems to tank and collector heat exchanger model parameters*	1999	–
Overgaard L L and Ellehauge K	*Solar combisystems in Denmark – solar & biomass systems*	2000	*Eurosun Conference 2000* Copenhagen, Denmark. http://www.eurosun2000.dk
Pauschinger T, Drück H and Hahne E	*Comparison test of solar heating systems for domestic hot water and space heating*	1998	http://kske.fgg.uni-lj.si/eurosun98/abstracts/III_2.html
Pittet T, Bony J, Renoult O and Dind Ph	*Measurements of a solar combisystem in situ*	2002	*Eurosun 2002*, 4th ISES Europe Solar Congress, Bologna, June 2002

Author/editor name	Reference title	Year of publication	Available from
Rekstad J, Henden L, Imenes A G, Ingebretsen F, Meir M, Bjerke B and Peter M	*Effective solar energy utilisation – more dependent on system design than on solar collector efficiency*	1999	*Proceedings of the ISES Solar World Congress, Jerusalem, Israel, July 4–9, 1999*
Rekstad J, Meir M and Kristoffersen A R	*Control and energy consumption monitoring in low temperature heating systems.*	2003	*Energy and Buildings 35,* 281–291, 2003
Sandnes B, Mullane R, Rekstad J B and Meir M G	*A solar energy storage with an integrated latent heat storage system.*	2000	*Proceedings of the 3rd ISES-Europe Solar Congress, June 19–22, 2000, Copenhagen, Denmark*
Schläpfer B, Rüesch H, Bremer P, Calatayud C, Keller L and Nilsson M O	*Untersuchung von zwei Sonnenenergieanlagen zur kombinierten Wassererwärmung und Raumheizung in Mehrfamilienhäusern*	1986	ENET, Technology Transfer in the field of Energy, Egnacherstrasse 69, CH-9320 Arbon. e-mail: enet@temas.ch, http://www.energieforschung.ch
Streicher W	*Minimizing the risk of water hammer and other problems at the beginning of stagnation of solar thermal plants: a theoretical approach*	2000	http://www.eurosun2000.dk
Streicher W	*Skriptum Sonnenenergienutzung* (Lecture book)	2003	http://wt.tu-graz.ac.at (download section)
Streicher W	*Solar Combisystems – The Work of Task 26 of the Implementing Agreement on Solar Heating and Cooling of the International Energy Agency (IEA)*	2002	*World Renewable Energy Congress VII*, Cologne, 29 June – 5 July 2002, Elsevier Science, Extended Abstracts, p. 341
Streicher W *et al.*	*Vergleich von Kombisystemen, der Ansatz des IEA-SHC Task 26 Solar Combisystemsö*	2002	*12. Symposium Thermische Solarenergie*, Kloster Banz, D-96231 Staffelstein
Suter J-M, Letz T and Weiss W	*Solar combisystems – overview 2000*	2000	http://www.iea-shc.org/task26/
Vejen N	*Undersøgelse af Solvarmeanlæg til rum- og Brugsvandsopvarmning for "Sol & Træ" v. nnr*	1998	Department of Civil Engineering, Technical University of Denmark, DTU, DK-2800 Kgs. Lyngby Denmark. Tel.: +45 4525 1700
Visser H, Weiss W and Streicher W	*International attention for assessment and optimization of solar combisystems*	2001	http://www.northsun.org/
Weiss W	*Solare Raumheizungsanlagen*	2000	James & James Science Publishers, London. e-mail: jxj@jxj.com
Weiss W (ed.)	*IEA-SHC Task 26 Industry Workshop, Stuttgart, Germany*	1999	http://www.iea-shc.org/task26/

Author/editor name	Reference title	Year of publication	Available from
Weiss W (ed.)	*IEA-SHC Task 26 Industry Workshop, Borlänge, Sweden*	2000	http://www.iea-shc.org/task26/
Weiss W (ed.)	*IEA-SHC Task 26 Industry Workshop, Espoo, Finland*	2000	http://www.iea-shc.org/task26/
Weiss W (ed.)	*IEA-SHC Task 26 Industry Workshop, Delft, The Netherlands*	2001	http://www.iea-shc.org/task26/
Weiss W (ed.)	*IEA-SHC Task 26 Industry Workshop, Rapperswil, Switzerland*	2001	http://www.iea-shc.org/task26/
Weiss W (ed.)	*IEA-SHC Task 26 Industry Workshop, Oslo, Norway*	2002	http://www.iea-shc.org/task26/
Weiss W, Fink C and Thür A	*Low-energy housing estate 'Sundays'*	2000	http://www.eurosun2000.dk

Appendix 2
Vocabulary

Jean-Marc Suter, Ulrike Jordan and Dagmar Jaehnig

This vocabulary lists a number of terms used in this handbook, with their definition, symbol, physical units and comments. These terms were selected according to the following criteria:

- some of the terms are not commonly used
- other terms are common but their precise interpretation is less generally known or different from author to author, hence clarification was required
- finally, a third group of terms may be misleading for non-native English readers, because similar terms have a different meaning in foreign languages.

The first subsection of this vocabulary includes the selected terms and definitions. The second subsection gives a list of symbols and abbreviations used throughout the handbook. The third subsection is a list of terms and definitions specific to Chapters 6 and 8.

A2.1 TERMS AND DEFINITIONS

Where relevant, the source document for the definition is indicated in brackets.

auxiliary energy consumption, combined *see* combined auxiliary energy consumption

auxiliary heat source source of heat, other than solar, used to supplement the output provided by the solar heating system (ISO 9488:1999); in French, *énergie d'appoint*; in German, *Zusatzenergie*

auxiliary, long-running-time *see* long-running-time auxiliary

boiler a complete unit with burner, combustion chamber and exhaust-gas/water heat exchanger; in French, *chaudière*; in German, *Heizkessel*

burner the burner, with or without a combustion chamber, but not including the exhaust-gas/water heat exchanger

cell, photovoltaic *see* photovoltaic cell

collector, solar (thermal) *see* solar (thermal) collector

combined auxiliary energy consumption the sum of the final energy consumption of the auxiliary boiler and the primary energy consumption of the electrical heating element in a solar heating system

combined total energy consumption the sum of the combined auxiliary energy consumption and the primary parasitic energy consumption of a heating system

combisystem, solar *see* solar combisystem

contribution, solar *see* solar contribution

drainback system a solar thermal system in which, as part of the normal working cycle, the heat transfer fluid is drained from the solar collector into a storage vessel when the pump is turned off, and refills the collector when the pump is turned on again (ISO 9488:1999)

energy consumption, combined auxiliary *see* combined auxiliary energy consumption

energy consumption, combined total *see* combined total energy consumption

energy, final *see* final energy

energy, parasitic *see* parasitic energy

energy, primary *see* primary energy

energy savings, fractional *see* fractional energy savings

energy, secondary *see* secondary energy

energy, useful *see* useful energy

final energy the energy supplied available to the consumer to be converted into useful energy (*Energy Dictionary*, 1992)

flow temperature (of a heat transfer fluid) temperature of the fluid before energy is removed (*Energy Dictionary*, 1992); in French, *température de départ*; in German, *Vorlauftemperatur*

forced–circulation system a solar heating system that utilizes a pump or a fan to circulate the heat transfer fluid through the collector(s) (ISO 9488:1999)

fraction, solar *see* solar fraction

fractional energy savings reduction of purchased energy achieved by the use of a solar–plus–supplementary heating system, calculated as 1 − (auxiliary energy used by solar heating system/energy used by conventional heating system), in which both systems are assumed to use the same kind of conventional energy to supply the user with the same heat quantity giving the same thermal comfort over a specified time period (ISO 9488:1999). *Note*: the assumptions made in this handbook to calculate the fractional energy savings are given in Section 6.2

global (solar) radiation hemispherical solar radiation received by a horizontal plane. *Note 1*: approximately 99% of the global solar radiation incident at the Earth's surface is contained within the wavelength range from 0.3–3 m. *Note 2*: solar engineers commonly use the term 'global radiation' in place of 'hemispherical radiation'. This use is a source of confusion if the referenced surface is not horizontal (ISO 9488:1999)

heat source, auxiliary *see* auxiliary heat source

(heat) storage the action of storing heat in a heat store

(heat) store a device designed to maintain a balance between heat production and heat consumption by temporarily storing excess heat for later delivery

heating system system for the production of heat for any purpose; in French, *installation de production de chaleur*; in German, *Heizanlage*

heating system, solar *see* solar heating system

heating system, space *see* space heating system

hemispherical (solar) radiation the solar radiation on a plane surface received from a solid angle of 2π sr (i.e. from the hemisphere above). *Note 1*: the tilt and the azimuth angles of the surface should be specified, e.g. horizontal. *Note 2*: hemispherical solar radiation is composed of direct solar radiation and diffuse solar radiation (solar radiation scattered in the atmosphere as well as solar radiation reflected by the ground). *Note 3*: solar engineers commonly use the term 'global radiation' in place of 'hemispherical radiation'. This use is a source of confusion if the referenced surface is not horizontal (ISO 9488:1999)

irradiance power density of radiation incident on a surface, i.e. the quotient of the radiant flux incident on the surface and the area of that surface, or the rate at which radiant energy is incident on a surface, per unit area of that surface. Irradiance is normally expressed in watts per square metre (W/m^2) (ISO 9488:1999)

irradiation the incident energy per unit area of a surface, found by integration of irradiance over a specified time interval, often an hour or a day. Irradiation is normally expressed in megajoules per square metre (MJ/m^2) (ISO 9488:1999)

long-running-time auxiliary in a solar combisystem, an auxiliary boiler designed to run for a long time at more or less fixed power, for example to burn wood efficiently in the form of logs

'low-flow' technology a way of designing and operating a solar heating system in which the mass flow rate in the collector loop is significantly lower than 30 l/h $m^2_{collector\ area}$. See Section 8.1.5.2

module, solar *see* solar module

panel, solar *see* solar panel

parasitic energy electricity consumed by pumps, fans and controls in a solar heating system (ISO 9488:1999); in French, *énergie auxiliaire*; in German, *Hilfsenergie*

photovoltaic cell semiconductor device that converts radiant energy (usually solar radiation) into electrical energy by means of the photovoltaic effect

primary energy energy that has not undergone any sort of conversion (*Energy Dictionary*, 1992)

radiation, global (solar) *see* global (solar) radiation

radiation, hemispherical (solar) *see* hemispherical (solar) radiation

reference system the conventional heating system used for the calculation of the fractional energy savings; *see* fractional energy savings

return temperature (of a heat transfer fluid) temperature of the fluid after energy has been removed (*Energy Dictionary*, 1992); in French, *température de retour*; in German, *Rücklauftemperatur*

savings, fractional energy *see* fractional energy savings

secondary energy energy produced by the conversion of primary energy or of another secondary energy (*Energy Dictionary*, 1992); synonym of 'derived energy'

solar combisystem a solar-plus-supplementary heating system designed to supply heat to both a space heating system and to a domestic hot water system

solar contribution energy supplied by the solar part of a solar heating system. *Note*: the solar part of a solar heating system and any associated losses need to be specified, otherwise the solar contribution is not uniquely defined (ISO 9488:1999)

solar fraction energy supplied by the solar part of a solar heating system divided by the total system load. *Note*: the solar part of a solar heating system and any associated losses need to be specified, otherwise the solar fraction is not uniquely defined (ISO 9488:1999)

solar heating system system composed of solar collectors and other components for the delivery of thermal energy (ISO 9488:1999); synonym of 'solar thermal system'. In German, *Solaranlage*, not *solares Heizsystem*. *Note*: 'solar heating system' is used as a generic term that includes solar-only systems, solar pre-heat systems and solar-plus-supplementary systems

solar module smallest complete, environmentally protected assembly of interconnected solar cells

solar panel a group of solar modules fastened together

solar–plus–supplementary system a solar heating system that utilizes both solar and an auxiliary energy source in an integrated way and is able to provide a specified heating service independently of solar energy availability (ISO 9488:1999). *Note*: the auxiliary energy device is a part of the solar-plus-supplementary system, just as solar collectors are

solar radiation, global *see* global (solar) radiation

solar radiation, hemispherical *see* hemispherical (solar) radiation

solar (thermal) collector a device designed to absorb solar radiation and to transfer the thermal energy so produced to a fluid passing through it. *Note*: the use of the term 'panel' is deprecated to avoid potential confusion with photovoltaic panels (ISO 9488:1999)

source, auxiliary heat *see* auxiliary heat source

space heating system a heating system providing heat to maintain thermal comfort in a building; in French, *installation de chauffage des locaux* or *chauffage*; in German, *Heizungsanlage*, *Heizung* or *Raumheizungsanlage*

stagnation status of a collector or system when no heat is removed by a heat transfer fluid (ISO 9488:1999)

storage, heat *see* heat storage

store, heat *see* heat store

stratifier a device for enhancing stratification in the heat store. See Section 8.1.5.1 for details. Synonym of 'stratifying unit'

stratifying unit *see* stratifier

system, drainback *see* drainback system

system, forced-circulation *see* forced-circulation system

system, heating *see* heating system

system, reference *see* reference system

system, solar heating *see* solar heating system

system, solar-plus-supplementary *see* solar-plus-supplementary system

system, space heating *see* space heating system

system, thermosiphon *see* thermosiphon system

technology, 'low-flow' *see* low-flow technology

temperature, flow *see* flow temperature

temperature, return *see* return temperature

thermal collector, solar *see* solar (thermal) collector

thermosiphon system a solar heating system that utilizes only density changes of the heat transfer fluid to achieve circulation between collector and storage device or collector and heat exchanger (ISO 9488:1999)

total energy consumption, combined *see* combined total energy consumption

useful energy the energy drawn by consumers from their own appliances after its final conversion (i.e. in its final utilization) (*Energy Dictionary*, 1992). *Note*: light, mechanical energy and comfort heat are examples of useful energy

A2.2 SYMBOLS AND ABBREVIATIONS

Main symbols

Symbol	Unit(s)	Definition
A	m^2	collector area
a_1	W/m^2K	first-order collector heat loss coefficient
a_2	W/m^2K^2	second-order collector heat loss coefficient
$\check{C}$	W/K	heat capacity rate of DHW draw-off
c_p	kJ/kgK	specific heat
E	Wh/a	final or primary energy consumption (thermal, electrical or combined)
h	m	height
G	W/m^2	solar irradiance
H	$MJ/m^2, kWh/m^2$	solar irradiation
$\dot{m}$	kg/s	mass flow rate
P	W	power, thermal or electrical
$prob$	$-$	probability
Q	Wh/a	annual thermal energy
t	s, h	time in seconds or hours
T	$°C$	temperature
UA	W/K	heat-transfer capacity rate
V	m^3	volume
$\dot{V}$	$m^3/h, l/min$	volume flow rate
W	Wh/a	annual electrical energy
x	$-$	exponent of the penalty functions; see Section 6.2.2
Δt	s	operation time of a component; simulation time step
η	$-$	mean annual efficiency
η_0	$-$	optical collector efficiency, zero-loss collector efficiency (ISO 9488:1999)
θ	$°$	angle of incidence, between collector surface normal and incident direct radiation
λ	W/mK	thermal conductivity (in the USA the common symbol is k)
σ	$-$	standard deviation

Subscripts

amb	ambient
boiler	boiler
burner	burner
col	collector
el	electricity
el. heater	electrical heating element
est	estimated
int	solar thermal system with internal heat exchanger to charge the store
ext	(1) solar thermal system with external heat exchanger to charge the store; (2) extended

loss	heat loss
nom	nominal
on/off	device 'on' (in operation) or 'off'
par	parasitic
red	reduced penalty (difference between penalties of solar combisystem and reference system); see Section 6.2.2
ref	conventional reference system
sim	simulated
stby	stand-by
store	storage tank
therm	thermal

Abbreviations

DHW	domestic hot water
FSC	fractional solar consumption; see Section 6.3
MFH	multi-family house
SFH	single-family house
SH	space heating

A2.3 TERMS AND DEFINITIONS SPECIFIC TO CHAPTERS 6 AND 8

With the notation and symbols described in Sections A.2.1 and A.2.2, the following terms are used in Chapters 6 and 8:

Q_{SH} — space heating demand

Q_{DHW} — domestic hot water demand

$Q_{loss,ref}$ — reference-system losses

$E_{ref,month} = \dfrac{Q_{SH} + Q_{DHW} + Q_{loss,ref}}{\eta_{boiler,ref}}$ — monthly final energy demand of reference-system boiler

$E_{ref} = \dfrac{Q_{SH} + Q_{DHW} + Q_{loss,ref}}{\eta_{boiler,ref}}$ — annual final energy demand of reference-system boiler

Q_{boiler} — thermal energy load of auxiliary boiler

η_{boiler} — mean annual efficiency of auxiliary boiler

$E_{boiler} = \dfrac{Q_{boiler}}{\eta_{boiler}}$ — final energy consumption of auxiliary boiler

$W_{el.heater}$ — thermal energy load of electrical heating element

$\eta_{el.heater}$

mean annual efficiency of electrical heating element

$$E_{el.heater} = \frac{Q_{el.heater}}{\eta_{el.heater}}$$

primary energy consumption of electrical heating element

W_{par}

parasitic energy consumption of solar combisystem

η_{el}

electric power generation efficiency

$$E_{par} = \frac{W_{par}}{\eta_{el}}$$

primary parasitic energy consumption of solar combisystem

$W_{par,ref}$

parasitic energy consumption of reference system

$$E_{par,ref} = \frac{W_{par,ref}}{\eta_{el}}$$

primary parasitic energy consumption of reference system

$$E_{aux} = E_{boiler} + E_{el.heater}$$

combined auxiliary energy consumption of solar combisystem

$$E_{total} = E_{aux} + E_{par}$$

combined total energy consumption of solar combisystem (the losses from refining and transportation of the fuels were neglected)

$$E_{total,ref} = E_{ref} + E_{par,ref}$$

combined total energy consumption of reference system

REFERENCES

Energy Dictionary/Dictionnaire de l'énergie/Energiewörterbuch/Diccionario de la energia, 1992, Jouve S I (ed.), World Energy Council (WEC)/Conseil mondial de l'énergie, Paris.

ISO 9488:1999 *Solar energy – Vocabulary/Energie solaire – Vocabulaire. International standard/Norme internationale*, ISO, Geneva, 1999. This is a trilingual standard also including terms and definitions in German, which has been adopted as the European standard EN ISO 9488. Available from the national standardization institutes.

IEA Solar Heating and Cooling Programme

Werner Weiss

The International Energy Agency (IEA) was established in 1974 as an autonomous agency within the framework of the Organization for Economic Co-operation and Development (OECD) to carry out a comprehensive programme of energy co-operation among its 25 member countries and the Commission of the European Communities.

An important part of the Agency's programme involves collaboration in the research, development and demonstration of new energy technologies to reduce excessive reliance on imported oil, increase long-term energy security and reduce greenhouse gas emissions. The IEA's R&D activities are headed by the Committee on Energy Research and Technology (CERT) and supported by a small Secretariat staff, headquartered in Paris. In addition, three Working Parties are charged with monitoring the various collaborative energy agreements, identifying new areas for co-operation, and advising the CERT on policy matters.

Collaborative programmes in the various energy technology areas are conducted under Implementing Agreements, which are signed by contracting parties (government agencies or entities designated by them). There are currently 42 Implementing Agreements, covering fossil-fuel technologies, renewable energy technologies, efficient energy end-use technologies, nuclear fusion science and technology, and energy technology information centres.

The Solar Heating and Cooling Programme was one of the first IEA Implementing Agreements to be established. Since 1977, its 21 members have been collaborating to advance active solar, passive solar and photovoltaic technologies and their application in buildings. These members are:

Australia	Finland	Norway
Austria	France	Portugal
Belgium	Italy	Spain
Canada	Japan	Sweden
Denmark	Mexico	Switzerland
European Commission	Netherlands	United Kingdom
Germany	New Zealand	United States

As of October 2003, a total of 33 Tasks have been initiated, 24 of which have been completed. Each Task is managed by an Operating Agent from one of the participating countries. Overall control of the programme rests with an Executive Committee comprising of one representative from each contracting party to the Implementing Agreement. In addition, a number of special ad hoc activities – working groups, conferences and workshops have been organized.

The Tasks of the IEA Solar Heating and Cooling Programme, both completed and current, are as follows.

A3.1 COMPLETED TASKS

(Status: October 2003)

Task 1   Investigation of the Performance of Solar Heating and Cooling Systems
Task 2   Co-ordination of Solar Heating and Cooling R&D
Task 3   Performance Testing of Solar Collectors
Task 4   Development of an Insolation Handbook and Instrument Package
Task 5   Use of Existing Meteorological Information for Solar Energy Application
Task 6   Performance of Solar Systems Using Evacuated Collectors
Task 7   Central Solar Heating Plants with Seasonal Storage
Task 8   Passive and Hybrid Solar Low-Energy Buildings
Task 9   Solar Radiation and Pyranometry Studies
Task 10   Solar Materials R&D
Task 11   Passive and Hybrid Solar Commercial Buildings
Task 12   Building Energy Analysis and Design Tools for Solar Applications
Task 13   Advanced Solar Low-Energy Buildings
Task 14   Advanced Active Solar Energy Systems
Task 16   Photovoltaics in Buildings
Task 17   Measuring and Modelling Spectral Radiation
Task 18   Advanced Glazing and Associated Materials for Solar and Building Applications
Task 19   Solar Air Systems
Task 20   Solar Energy in Building Renovation
Task 21   Daylight in Buildings
Task 22   Building Energy Analysis Tools
Task 23   Optimization of Solar Energy Use in Large Buildings
Task 24   Solar Procurement
Task 26   Star Combisystems

A3.2 COMPLETED WORKING GROUPS

(Status: October 2003)

CSHPSS
ISOLDE
Materials in Solar Thermal Collectors
Evaluation of Task 13 Houses

A3.3 CURRENT TASKS

Task 25   Solar-Assisted Air Conditioning of Buildings
Task 27   Performance of Solar Façade Components
Task 28   Solar Sustainable Housing
Task 29   Solar Crop Drying
Task 31   Daylighting Buildings in the 21st Century
Task 32   Advanced Storage Concepts for Solar Thermal Systems in Low-Energy
           Buildings
Task 33   Solar Heat for Industrial Process

A3.4 CURRENT WORKING GROUP

PV/Thermal Systems

To receive a publications catalogue or learn more about the IEA Solar Heating and Cooling Programme, visit the Programme's website at http://www.iea-shc.org or contact the SHC Executive Secretary, Pamela Murphy, Morse Associates Inc., 1808 Corcoran Street, NW, Washington, DC 20009, USA, Tel: +1 202 483 2393, Fax: +1 202 265 2248, e-mail: pmurphy@MorseAssociatesInc.com.

Appendix 4
Task 26

Werner Weiss

Task 26 was one major research project of the Solar Heating and Cooling Programme. The Task involved 35 experts from nine European countries and the USA, and from 16 solar industries.

The Operating Agent for this Task was Austria, represented by Werner Weiss from AEE INTEC.

From December 1998 to December 2002, the participating experts reviewed, analysed and compared solar combisystems that were on the market at the beginning of the Task. In a second step, selected systems were optimized, tested and improved in co-operation with the industry.

Task 26 focused on solar combisystems for detached single-family houses, groups of single-family houses and multi-family buildings with their own heating installations. It did not refer to solar district heating systems or systems with seasonal storage or central solar heating plants with seasonal storage.

To accomplish the objectives of the Task, the participants carried out the research and development in the framework of the following three Subtasks:

- *Subtask A:* Solar Combisystems Survey and Dissemination of Task Results. Lead country: Switzerland, represented by Jean-Marc Suter, Suter Consulting, Berne
- *Subtask B:* Development of Performance Test Methods and Numerical Models for Combisystems and their Components. Lead country: the Netherlands, represented by Huib Visser, TNO, Delft
- *Subtask C:* Optimization of Combisystems for the Market. Lead country: Austria, represented by Wolfgang Streicher, Graz University of Technology, Graz

In addition to this design handbook, the results of Task 26 are given in several technical reports, design tools and the proceedings of six industry workshops, which can be downloaded from the website of the IEA Solar Heating and Cooling Programme, http://www.iea-shc.org/task26/.

A4.1 PARTICIPANTS

Austria

Werner Weiss, Irene Bergmann, Robert Hausner and Dagmar Jaehnig
AEE INTEC, Arbeitsgemeinschaft Erneuerbare Energie, Institute for Sustainable Technologies, Feldgasse 19, A-8200 Gleisdorf

Wolfgang Streicher and Richard Heimrath
Graz University of Technology, Institute of Thermal Engineering, Inffeldgasse 25, A-8010 Graz

Denmark

Simon Furbo, Louise Jivan Shah and Elsa Andersen
Solar Energy Center Denmark, Technical University of Denmark, Department of Buildings and Energy, Building 118, DK-2800 Lyngby

Klaus Ellehauge
Solar Energy Center Denmark, Teknologisk Institut, DK-8000 Aarhus C

Finland

Petri Konttinen
Helsinki University of Technology, Advanced Energy Systems, PO Box 2200, FIN-02015 HUT

France

Thomas Letz
ASDER, PO Box 45, 299, rue du Granier, F-73230 Saint Alban-Leysse

Philippe Papillon
Clipsol-Recherche, Zone Industrielle, F-73100 Trevignin

Rodolphe Morlot
CSTB, Energie, Environment Interieur et Automatisimes, Route des Lucioles, Boite postale 209, F-06904 Sophia Antipolis Cedex

Germany

Harald Drück and Henner Kerskes
Stuttgart University, ITW, Pfaffenwaldring 6, D-70550 Stuttgart

Klaus Vajen and Ulrike Jordan
Kassel University, Department of Mechanical Engineering, Solar and System Technology, D-34109 Kassel

Norway

Michaela Meir, Markus Peter and Bjørnar Sandnes
University of Oslo, Department of Physics, PO Box 1048, Blindern, N-0316 Oslo

Sweden	**Peter Kovács** SP – Swedish National Testing and Research Institute, PO Box 857, S-501 15 Boras
	Chris Bales and Bengt Perers Högskolan Dalarna, Solar Energy Research Center – SERC, EKOS, S-78188 Borlänge
	Stefan Larsson Vattenfall Utveckling AB, S-814 26 Älvkarleby
Switzerland	**Jean-C. Hadorn** Swiss Research Programme, CH-1035 Bournens
	Jean-Marc Suter Suter Consulting, PO Box 130, CH-3000 Berne 16
	Ueli Frei, Peter Vogelsanger and Beat Menzi SPF-HSR, PO Box 1475, CH-8640 Rapperswil
	Philippe Dind, Olivier Renoult, Jacques Bony and Thierry Pittet School of Engineering (EIVD), Route de Cheseaux 1, CH-1400 Yverdon-les-Bains
The Netherlands	**Huib Visser** TNO, Building and Construction Research, Department of Sustainable Energy and Buildings, PO Box 49, NL-2600 AA Delft Visiting address: Van Mourik Broeckmanweg 6, NL-2826 XE Delft
USA	**William A. Beckman** University of Wisconsin, Solar Energy Lab, 1500 Engineering Drive, Madison, WI 53706

A4.2 INDUSTRY PARTICIPANTS

Austria	**Christian Holter** SO.L.I.D., Herrgottwiesgasse 188, A- 8055 Graz
	Martin Bergmayr Solarteam GmbH, Jörgmayrstrasse 12, A-4111 Walding
	Peter Prasser Sonnenkraft GmbH, Industriepark, A-9300 St. Veit an der Glan
Denmark	**E. Brender** Batec A/S, Danmarksvej 8, DK 4681 Herfolge

Finland
Janne Jokinen
Fortum Power and Heat, New Technology Business,
PO Box 20, 00048 Fortum

France
Philippe Papillon
Clipsol, Zone Industrielle, F-73100 Trevignin

Germany
Thomas Krause and Dagmar Jaehnig
SOLVIS GmbH & Co KG, Grotrian-Steinweg-Strasse 12,
D-38112 Braunschweig

Andreas Siegemund
Consolar Energiespeicher- und Regelungssysteme GmbH,
Dreieichstrasse 48, D-60594 Frankfurt

Norway
John Rekstad
SolarNor AS, Erling Skjalgssons gate 19 B, N-0267 Oslo

Sweden
Bo Ronnkvist
Borö-Pannan AB, Bangardsuagen 1, S-95231 Kalix

Switzerland
M. C. Jobin
AGENA, Le Grand Pré, CH-1510 Moudon

Fritz Schuppisser
SOLTOP Schuppisser AG, St. Gallerstrasse 7,
CH-8353 ELGG

Josef Jenni
Jenni Energietechnik AG, Lochbachstrasse 22,
CH-3414 Oberburg

The Netherlands
Jos Luttikholt
ATAG Verwarming B.V., PO Box 105,
NL-7130 AC Lichtenvoorde

Erwin Janssen
Daalderop B.V., PO Box 7, NL-4000 AA Tiel

Paul Kratz
Zonne-Energie Nederland, De Run 5421,
NL-5504 DG Veldhoven

Index